THE CASINO GAMBLER'S GUIDE

THE CASINO

1817

GAMBLER'S GUIDE

Enlarged Edition

ALLAN N. WILSON

HARPER & ROW, PUBLISHERS | NEW YORK AND EVANSTON

Contents

vi | CONTENTS

Introduction

Ever since a distinguished British statistician named Pearson investigated roulette records from Monte Carlo in the 1890s, scientists have become increasingly interested in the vulnerability of gambling games. Pearson's original writings reflected a belief that he had found gross discrepancies in the behavior of the Monte Carlo wheels. Later he developed a method of mathematical analysis for roulette which showed the wheel's performance to be less spectacular than he originally believed. Pearson himself did not dally at the tables, but a number of his scientific successors found and then profited by remarkable deviations on the single numbers, as first suggested by him. Despite sixty-five years of scientific inquiry public attention has seldom been drawn to the endeavors of such analysts, either at roulette or at other gambling games.

This book's purpose is to give the reader the most scientifically reliable information available on *all* of the major casino gambling games. Thus we present here much information that has never been published before, along with an up-to-date synthesis of the gambling literature.

The organization of the book reflects the fact that, at the current writing, two games are especially susceptible to successful attack by the player. Hence greater space is devoted to roulette and to blackjack than to other games (though be assured that the information on other casino games is as thorough and complete as the circumstances warrant). Three chapters on the law of averages, on systems, and on bet-sizing give a new slant on topics of general importance to all games.

Roulette is covered first, because it is probably the game that comes to mind first when the word "casino" is mentioned. It is the gaming aristocrat of several centuries, and has been subjected to considerable analysis. At Monte Carlo, for example, private operators duly record the day's sequence of play, and at the corner bookstore there you can buy the latest issue of *Monte-Carlo Revue Scientifique,* the month's log, totaling between 5 and 10,000 trials for one of the wheels at the casino. Yet on this side of the Atlantic no one has ever before published even a short duration account of plays on a casino roulette wheel. In the appendix of this book we offer long-run records on three wheels, for samples ranging from 30,000 to 80,000 plays. These sequences were of continuous play; for unlike the casino at Monte Carlo, which is open only part of the day, Nevada casinos operate on a 24-hour basis. The playing experiences derived from clocking are recounted in Chapters 3 and 4.

Blackjack (or "21") is the second major topic. It is, of course, well-known and Ed Thorp's book, *Beat the Dealer,* recently opened the way for new betting methods (a few casinos were impressed enough to change their rules.) Chapters 5 through 9 offer a comprehensive playing strategy and Chapter 7 introduces a new and simple-to-learn point-count system for playing a winning game of blackjack. Its performance in the casinos is elaborately documented.

Chapter 9 reviews what more than half a dozen different "pros" have written on blackjack in their books on gambling, and warns the reader that in this game, above all others, he must be selective about his authority for a playing strategy. For example, two authors from the *same casino* have each written a book about gambling; they espouse *opposite* recommendations in certain identical blackjack situations! Nowhere must you guard against deceptions and misinformation more than in books and magazines that claim to reveal accurate blackjack systems.

Subsequent chapters treat other common games like keno, craps, and slot machines. Baccarat, a relative newcomer to the American scene, receives its first *full* explanation. Very little has been written in English about the proper way to compute the percentages at baccarat or chemin de fer. Nor has that old classic, faro-bank, ever received scientific analysis.

Common misconceptions about the "law of averages" are discussed in Chapter 15, and in Chapter 16 betting "systems" are fully analyzed. The new computer technique of "simulation," artificially producing random sequences, sheds new light on systems which were previously too intricate to analyze by direct methods. The reader is shown how he can test virtually any betting scheme by simulating the game at home. The outcome of a series of throws of the dice at craps, for example, can be identified with the sequence of two-digit random pairs, outlined in Appendix F. You simply use pairs containing the digits 1 through 6 only (e.g., 1–1, 1–3, 2–6, 5–3, 6–6), and reject any pair containing a 7, 8, 9, or 0. What an elegant and easy way for the reader to transport himself to a casino, and to simulate the action of his favorite game.

The problem of sizing bets in games that give the player only a slight edge is explained in Chapter 17. New data are presented for the proper bank-to-bet ratio for single-number play at roulette, and general principles are developed that are applicable both to casino games and to private gambling games. This chapter has broad implications for people involved in any speculative activity.

The book concludes with a chapter on the future of casino gambling, predicting the changes that the science of electronics will bring to the casino.

THE CASINO GAMBLER'S GUIDE

General Description
of Roulette

Roulette is the most glamorous of all the casino games. An air of elegance surrounds the roulette table, and its spinning wheel seems to be a perfect agent by which the goddess of fortune may intervene in the affairs of mortal man. How much superior is this unapproachable mechanistic device to those games like dice and cards, where human hands may tamper with fate.

But more than glamour, the game to me presents a certain irresistible challenge. The roulette is intended to be a symmetrical gambling device, the odds for which always favor the house. In the long run, it would appear that a player must inevitably lose. But due to a certain degree of asymmetry in the wheel's production, or due to its later wear, the odds may shift enough to favor a player on certain bets. The shrewd observer may spot such a case and actually be able to play a winning game. Herein lies the challenge.

THE AMERICAN DOUBLE-ZERO WHEEL

Most persons have seen a roulette game, either in a casino or in the movies. Nonetheless, a few words of description are in order. We shall first describe the more familiar American double-zero game, bearing in mind that the single-zero is very similar. The wheel is somewhat less than 2 feet in diameter, and rotates about a vertical axis. Around its circumference are 38 numbered compartments into which the whirling ivory ball may fall. The wheel sits inside a conical rim, which slopes down toward the center. At the top of the sloping rim is a circular track, essentially a groove on the inside of a cylindrical wall. At the beginning of the play, the wheel is set turning slowly by the operator, who is known on the Continent as the "croupier," but in more direct American language as the "dealer." The ivory sphere is propelled onto its track by the dealer in the opposite direction of rotation from the wheel, and at a much higher speed. It runs around in the track perhaps five to ten times before friction slows it down to the point where it no longer has sufficient momentum to stay in the track. The ball then falls inward and spirals down the rim toward the spinning wheel.

Because of its fine bearings, the wheel spins at a nearly constant rate, and only occasionally needs to be given a slight push by the dealer. The author has seen a wheel spin idly for many minutes before being brought to rest by friction. (The axle and bearings of the most widely used wheel in the United States are made as a side line by a high-precision tool company. A good roulette wheel, with the rim, track, and table, costs at least a thousand dollars, mainly because it must be built to fairly exacting tolerances.) In the downward travels along the sloping rim, the path of the ball may be deflected if it chances to hit one of a number of diamond-shaped projections imbedded in the rim. The purpose of these deflectors is to give the dealer less control over the path of the ball. At the bottom of the rim, the ball reaches the wheel, where very likely it will bounce around several times among the vertical metal partitions that separate the compartments before it finally snuggles to rest in one compartment.

THE SINGLE-NUMBER BET

The number on this lucky compartment is the winning number. If a player had wagered $1.00 on this number and the ball falls into its place, the dealer would pay him $35 and also permit him to keep his $1.00 bet. Money wagered on all of the other 37 numbers would be won by the house. If the wheel is, for all practical purposes, mechanically perfect, and if there is no skullduggery on the part of the operator, then in the long run, it is clear that the player can pick the winning number on an average of once in 38 times. This follows from the assumption that each of the 38 numbers is equally likely to win.

If the wheel serves its intended purpose of providing a random distribution of winning numbers, then there is no relation whatever between the preceding winning number and the one that wins next time. The wheel has *no memory*. Suppose that the player wagers $1.00 each time on one number. Out of each 38 trials, on the average, he wins $35 and loses $37. Thus, he has an expected loss of $2.00 for every 38 ventured. His average loss per play is 2/38 of a dollar, or 5.26¢. Accordingly, the casino has a 5.26 percent advantage in this game.

The 38 numbers are composed of the numbers from 1 to 36 and also a zero (0) and a double-zero (00). Half of the numbers 1 to 36 are red, and the other half are black. The 0 and 00 are green. In fact, from 1 to 10 and 19 to 28, the odd numbers are red and the even ones are black; from 11 to 18 and 29 to 36, just the opposite is true. On the wheel, each pair of numbers in numerical sequence is laid out in a special way. Number 1 is diametrically opposite 2, and 3 is opposite 4, etc.; 0 is opposite 00. Another feature of the pattern is that the numbers are alternately red and black as one progresses around the wheel, except for the two green numbers. There is a definite regularity in what might appear to the casual observer to be a helter-skelter arrangement. What is the purpose of this pattern? We shall see in a minute. But first it should be pointed out that as far as betting on a single number is concerned, all 38 numbers are treated alike. One may bet on green 00 with just as much chance of winning as on red 3 or black 26. The payoff is identical for all.

EVEN-MONEY PROPOSITIONS

There is a variety of other ways to bet besides on the single numbers. For example, one may bet red to win. This is one of the "even-money" propositions. If one bets $1.00 on red, and one of the 18 red numbers wins, the house pays even money, or $1.00 in this case. (As usual, the winner also keeps his original bet.) If one of the 18 black numbers or either of the green numbers comes up, the bet on red is lost. Suppose the player wagers $1.00 each time on red. Out of 38 trials, on the average, he wins $18 and loses $20. Thus, he has an expected loss of $2.00 for every 38 ventured, and the percentage against him is exactly the same as for the bet on single numbers. If the two green numbers were not on the wheel, and if the payoff were the same, roulette would be an even game. In the language of the mathematician, it would be a *fair* game. The percentage against the player makes the game, in a mathematical sense, an *unfair* game. It is evident that the two green numbers stand symbolically for the house advantage.

It was noted previously that the red numbers are spread evenly around the wheel. This is done so that if there is any preferred sector of the wheel as a result of mechanical defect, the effect will be evened out, as far as the red numbers are concerned. For example, it is conceivable that the base of the wheel could be warped in such a way that one half of the wheel would be slightly higher than the other. Gravity being what it is, the ball would presumably land more frequently in the lower half. This would improve the chance of winning for the red numbers in the lower half, but the chance for those numbers in the higher half would be correspondingly reduced. The effect of the warpage would tend to be nullified on the even-money bets.

There are two other types of even-money propositions besides the bet on red (or black). One may bet the 18 odd numbers or the 18 even numbers of the group 1 to 36. Or one may bet on the first 18 or the second 18 numbers in this group. The payoff and the house percentage are the same as for red or black. Another bet in which a large block of numbers is played is the so-called dozen. One may select the first, second, or third dozen numbers in the group 1 to 36. Here the payoff is 2:1. A player who wagers $1.00 each time on the first dozen, for example, stands to win $24 and lose $26 in each 38 plays, on the average. Clearly the edge is still 5.26 percent.

SPLIT BETS

The betting table, as shown in Fig. 1-1, is laid out in a rectangular array. The numbers 1 to 36 appear in sequence, arranged in three columns. At the head of the array are 0 and 00. Spaces for the even-money propositions and the dozens lie along one side of the array. In addition to the wagers already mentioned, there are several "combination" or "split" bets possible on the numbers. One may bet on 2

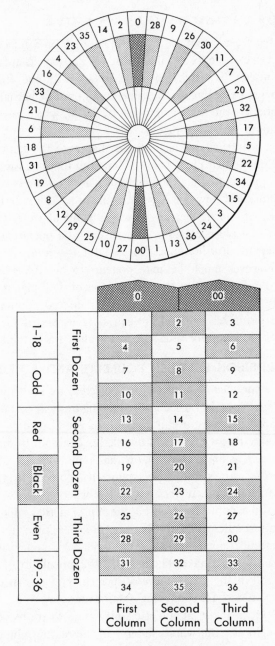

Fig. 1-1. Roulette Betting Layout

numbers that are adjacent on the betting grid, or on 3 adjacent, or on 4 or 6, or even on an entire "column" of 12. The payoffs are so chosen that the house cut is still 5.26 percent. In fact, with one single exception, the house percentage is the same on all possible bets at roulette. The exception is the five-way bet on 1-2-3-0-00, which pays 6:1 and gives the house 3/38 advantage.

There, in a nutshell, we have the mechanics of the game, and the simple arithmetic that predicts in the long run that one can expect to lose about 5 percent of the total amount placed on the betting table. One might ask just how stiff a price is this to pay for entertainment? The answer, of course, depends on one's point of view. The initial investment in a plush casino is a large sum, and operating expenses are considerable. Furthermore, the operator is not in the giveaway business, however much he may pretend to be. Accordingly, the player must accept the fact that his chances of multiplying his bankroll by any significant factor are very slim indeed. Conversely, his chances of losing his bankroll are considerable, and if he plays for any appreciable length of time, the loss is almost a certainty.

COMPARISON BETWEEN ROULETTE AND A FAIR GAME

To give some idea of what can be expected, we shall quote some figures. (The method of calculating these figures will be taken up in a later chapter.) A very useful criterion of the chance of success is the probability that a player will double his bankroll. In an even, or fair, game, such as flipping a coin, one has a 50:50 chance of winning or going broke; this is true if we assume that both participants start with the same amount. It does not matter whether the two contestants wager their entire bankroll on one flip or if they subdivide the bankroll into smaller units and bet one unit at a time. Each player has a 50 percent chance of winning his opponent's money, and hence of doubling his initial stake. The fact that the probability of doubling one's bankroll in this fair game is 50 percent provides an extremely convenient yardstick for comparing unfair games.

To illustrate, a player at roulette who wishes to try to double his bankroll might bet the whole amount in one daring plunge on an even-money proposition, such as betting on red. His chance of success is 18/38, or 47.37 percent. The player's chance of doubling in one big plunge is evidently almost as good as the 50 percent chance in a fair game. A more cautious player might think he could do better by subdividing his bank into 100 units and betting one unit at a time *on a number*. It turns out that the probability that he will win an extra 100 units is about 43 percent and the chance that he will go broke is 57 percent. Win or lose, this contest is likely to take several hours at least. If the bank were subdivided into 200 units, the probability of winning an extra 200 units would be 36 percent; and of losing, 64 percent. This contest would take even longer. Finally, if the subdivision were into 1000 individual units, the probability of doubling the bank would be only about 5 percent, with a 95 percent chance of going "bust" in the attempt. And this case would be a veritable marathon, taking *days* to decide.

ROULETTE "SYSTEMS"

The moral of the foregoing story is plain. The longer one plays, the bigger the chance of going broke. Countless "systems" and betting schemes of great complexity have been proposed to get around this simple principle. There are progressions and antiprogressions, and pyramids and antipyramids, and myriads of other betting schedules. In effect, the system maker attempts to take a series of plays, on each of which there is an expected loss, and somehow add them together to get an expected win. This is clearly impossible. It is true that the system player *can* design methods of bet selection that yield a large chance of winning a small amount, but he can do this *only* at the expense of a *more than compensating* chance of losing his entire bankroll. A typical system might work out so that a player has five chances out of six of winning 10 percent of his initial bank, and one chance out of six of losing 100 percent of his initial bank. The fallacies in the simpler systems are easy to point out. Unfortunately, the more complicated ones often involve much labor for a proper analysis.

A later chapter will be devoted to an analysis of certain systems and their fallacies. But the subject of system play should be mentioned here because roulette is a singularly attractive game for the system players. The impersonal nature of the machine causes it to rate among many players as the most reliable method of generating a random sequence of numbers. The layout of the roulette game is such as to lend itself to the taking of notes; the game is played sitting down, and there is generally more space available. Also, the tempo of play is slow enough so that there is time between plays to perform brief computations. All in all, roulette is ideal for the gambler who likes to write down the sequence of events and attempt to analyze trends and make predictions. Without question, the presence of these "systémiers," immersed in their absurd little calculations, gives the appearance that roulette is strictly for the intellectuals. If there were no system players, much of the aura of mystery and mathematics would be missing from the roulette game. Numerous casinos cater to them, furnishing pads and pencils free. Since the system gamblers play over such a long period of time, they inevitably lose one bankroll after another. The author knows of one such player who lost more than a million dollars on systems over a period of several years!

THE AMERICAN SINGLE-ZERO WHEEL

Any roulette player who has his wits about him prefers to play on a single-zero wheel. This type of wheel has long been the standard in casinos abroad, and gradually in recent years it has been introduced in some of the American clubs. The payoffs are the same as on the double-zero wheel. Accordingly the house advantage is only 1/37 instead of 2/38, which is 2.70 percent—down to almost half that of the double-zero wheel! It will forever be a mystery to this author why roulette players did not *flock* to the clubs that first introduced the more generous wheel. An even bigger mystery is how those clubs that sport *both* types of wheel can do any business on the two-zero wheel.

THE EUROPEAN WHEEL HAS BEST ODDS

In the European casinos, a further variation in the handling of the even-money bets brings the house advantage *on those propositions* down to a mere 1.35 percent. Suppose that one is betting red to win, and the green (zero) is the winning number. Instead of the croupier immediately raking in the bet, as he would do in an American casino, he momentarily sets the bet aside, to await the outcome of the next play. The bet is said to be "en prison." If red comes before black in the subsequent action, the croupier returns the bet to the player (but without the usual payoff). If black comes before red, the bet is lost for good. If green appears, no decision is effected, and another spin must be made. Apart from this rather novel feature, the even-money game is conducted in the usual way. When the "en prison" aspect is taken into account, the house margin figures out to be 1.35 percent. The popularity of roulette in foreign countries may well be attributed to a house margin only one-fourth as great as in American casinos.

POSSIBILITY OF CHEATING BY THE HOUSE

No discussion of this game would be complete without a few words about the subject of *cheating* at roulette. Any game that is as time-honored and far-flung as roulette is bound to have potentialities for crooked minds, on either side of the table. When a dealer has been spinning that wheel year after year, it is conceivable that he could develop the ability to exert *some* effect on the result of the play, however small this effect might be. With great regularity in the speed of spinning the wheel and of throwing the ball, it is possible that a dealer could influence where the ball lands. In particular, he might be able to make it less likely for the ball to land in one sector of the wheel than in another. This might be very advantageous for the house, if the bets were especially heavy in one particular sector. Suppose that a dealer could confine the ball to a specified *half* of the wheel, say, on 10 percent of his attempts, and on the other 90 percent of his attempts, he had no control at all, so that the ball arrived at random. If a player were betting a number on the half of the wheel that the dealer was able to control, this would cut his chances of winning to 90 percent of that on a fair wheel. An ordinary 1/38 number would be reduced to a 1/42 number, and the house advantage would soar from 5 to 15 percent. One cannot help but be impressed by the fact that a dealer who was successful in his manipulation only 10 percent of the time would thereby *triple* the house margin against the bettor!

One must not forget that it would be virtually impossible to *prove* that a dealer was engaging in such a manipulation! For this reason, it is perhaps fortunate that it would take considerable skill for a dealer to be able to do this. As mentioned earlier, the author watched numerous dealers to see if their spin of the ball was consistent to within a fraction of one revolution around the wheel. He did not spot anyone who seemed to be this consistent, but this certainly did not rule out the possibility.

There are many *mechanical* ways to rig a wheel, of course. One of the most popular involves electromagnets concealed around the periphery of the wheel, and a ball with a steel core; by pressing buttons under the table, the dealer can exert a profound effect on the course of the ball. Considering that the house already has a 5 percent advantage, it does seem a little greedy to employ a gimmick like this. Nonetheless, it should be suspected at most any illegal casino outside the state of Nevada. And even in Nevada, considering the blackjack cheating conditions described in Chapter 8, those casinos may not be entirely above suspicion in the operation of the roulette tables.

CHEATING BY THE PLAYERS

Presumably, there are other ways by which a larcenous operator can fleece a roulette player. But without question, there are more ways by which players attempt to chisel against the house. One of the most popular is *sugaring* the bet. After a player has won, he may reach out and pretend to count his chips so as to see how much he is going to collect, but actually he may slip another chip onto his stack. Or the player may engage in a little *nudging*. With similar pretense to examine a bet, he may adroitly nudge his bet from a losing square to a winning square. Dealers usually combat these maneuvers by insisting that the players keep hands off their chips until all losing chips have been raked in and all winning bets have been paid off. But sometimes, when the play is real hectic, a crooked player who pretends to be a newcomer at the game and seems not to understand all the rules may get away with a little of this chiseling. It is the job of the dealer, and the pit boss behind him, to hold this sort of thing to a minimum.

Sometimes crooked players steal bets from other players, too. But what really takes nerve is to "doctor up" a roulette wheel. One dealer at Harolds told us how they had apprehended a fellow who had sneaked into the wheel room and was laying thin lead sheets in the pockets of certain numbers. Evidently, this smart aleck figured that he could deaden the bounce of the ball, and make those pockets more likely to hang onto the ball.

A practice that is perhaps not illegal, but is certainly dubious, is that of waiting until the ball has all but plunked into the winning number and then suddenly laying down a bet at the last second. This, of course, is completely under the control of the dealer. A strict dealer will insist that no more bets may be made after the ball is set in motion. (In the European casinos, a small ceremony precedes the play. Just before spinning the ball, the dealer solemnly announces, "*Rien ne va plus*," a literal translation of which is "Nothing goes any more.") But many American dealers willingly flex the rule, in the interests of getting more money down on the table. Then a problem arises: At what precise second before the ball drops should the betting be called to a halt? Now, inasmuch as the ball often bounces around rather than dropping immediately into a pocket, this is a question to which it is hard to give a scientific answer. Many dealers seem to think it is pretty hard for the player to make a prediction, and accordingly, they allow betting until just the last few seconds. Others are more cautious, in varying degrees, and may go to the extreme of stopping bets when the ball is started. One thing is sure: A successful big bettor would not be permitted to indulge in very much of this last-second wagering!

SUMMARY

So much for larcenous thoughts. The brief coverage on that topic is intended only as a warning that such things can and do happen. Now let us pick up the thread of the honest game, where we left off a few pages back. We have seen that various versions of roulette have differing percentages for the house, ranging from 5.26 percent down to 1.35 percent. These values apply when the wheel serves its intended purpose of producing a random distribution of equally likely winning numbers. On any such "normal" wheel, the player can look forward in the long run only to a loss. And it matters very little whether he plays lightheartedly for fun or with a serious hope to win. The relentless, turning wheel knows nothing of the player's dreams or state of mind!

Intelligent people universally accept these facts, for some of the most brilliant mathematicians of all time have studied the game. The study of probability had its humble beginnings in the analysis of games of chance, and out of this has grown a great new field of mathematics known as statistics. The computation of roulette odds is as simple for the present-day statistician, as arithmetic is for the engineer trained in calculus. It is a significant fact that the greater a person's mathematical training, the less likely he is to be found in the halls of chance. This may be due in part to a sophisticated mathematical mind's finding casino games to be a dull pastime. But more likely it is because the mathematical mind revolts at the thought of such unprofitable odds. It is certainly not because such persons are ivory tower misfits, lacking in any sense of "practical" application. The scientists who design rocket engines and electronic computers and television transmitters and atomic power plants are an extremely practical breed. Their brothers, who build atom smashers and study the stars and invent new mathematical theorems, are slightly less "practical," but only in the sense that the fruits of their labors lie still in the future. The inescapable conclusions that all of these thousands of technically trained people have reached concerning simple games of chance should not be taken lightly by their fellow citizens who are less mathematically inclined. To possess mathematical talent is a privilege. But a true mark of intelligence among those who are not mathematically endowed is the willingness to accept the findings of those who are.

All that has been said about the likelihood of loss at roulette may be changed if there is a mechanical imperfection in the wheel, for then all numbers may not be equally likely to win. This may make the difference between roulette for fun at a loss and roulette for MORE fun at a profit. This fascinating prospect will be taken up in great detail in the next three chapters.

Biased Wheel Pioneers

2

Since a roulette wheel is a man-made device, it is obviously impossible to make a perfect one. Certainly, the manufacturer tries to make a good product, for otherwise he wouldn't sell very many. But once the wheel has left the factory and been placed in use, it is subject to wear and other influences, the effect of which is difficult to determine. Any critical observer who has watched the impact of the fast-moving ball against the oncoming wheel cannot help but wonder if some small change does not occur on every play. When there is a good solid hit in which the ball bounces back, the exchange of momentum is often sufficient to cause an abrupt and noticeable reduction in the speed of the spinning wheel. Subject to these repeated collisions, it is inevitable that the metal partitions between numbers will loosen up. Also, the paint on the numbers wears down and the wooden fibers beneath become exposed.

Of course the larger casinos usually have their wheels overhauled periodically. A shabby looking wheel, or a betting table with holes worn in the cloth, will certainly not attract the wealthier patrons. But aside from the social necessity for trim appearance, the casino operator really has no guide to tell him when repairs should be made. Even if a pocket is worn a little deeper, or one of the metal slots is noticeably loose, who can tell what actual change this produces in the frequency of occurrence of numbers near this defect? Even if one were to *measure* these changes with a micrometer, it would be almost impossible to draw any quantitative conclusions regarding the shift in probabilities. If one compartment were 5 percent bigger in area than the others, it would be by no means evident that the chance of occurrence of this number would be 5 percent higher; the effect of the motion of the ball would have to be taken into account, and this would be no easy task.

The only practical way to appraise these effects is to *clock* the wheel, that is, to record the frequency of occurrence of the numbers over a long period of time. Even then the analysis is fraught with hidden perils! With too small a sample of numbers, ordinary fluctuations could mask an underlying bias and lead the observer to erroneous conclusions. Meanwhile, as one is clocking, the wear goes on and the situation is continuously changing. The prospect is enough to send chills up and down the spine of even the best-trained scientist!

The number of players who have clocked a wheel at Monte Carlo is legion. For a nominal sum, one can even buy detailed records of the winning numbers, which are published by a private agency that collects them. Most of the players who keep track of the numbers are merely looking for "runs" or other sequences on which to try out their worthless systems. Few references tell in any detail of an actual imperfection in a Monte Carlo wheel.

BREAKING THE BANK

Toward the end of the nineteenth century, a clever British mechanic named Jaggers made the first genuinely successful assault on the coffers of Monte Carlo. A superb account is given in Charles Kingston's book, *The Romance of Monte Carlo*. Although not a man of means, Jaggers hired six clerks to clock six wheels for more than a month. When he had compiled a list of the numbers that came up most frequently because of defects in the cylinders, Jaggers and his staff gambled on them with steady and almost uninterrupted success. Despite very modest initial capital, he was a winner to the extent of £14,000 on the first day, and four successive days' play brought him a £60,000 total (about $300,000)!

The casino directors at first suspected foul play, and wasted much time on that approach. Then they switched the wheels around during the time the casino was closed for the day. Jaggers and cohorts did not catch on quickly, and lost back two-thirds of the winnings.

But Jaggers fooled them by suddenly identifying the wheels correctly and rolling his fortune up to £90,000. Then the manufacturer of the roulette wheels was summoned from Paris to help extinguish the Jaggers conflagration. He redesigned the wheel by replacing the old immovable partitions between the numbers with new movable partitions. The pockets for the little white ball could then be changed about at will by the casino, and never needed to be the same for two succeeding days. Jaggers' data fell by the wayside, and after some losses, he came to the conclusion that the casino had reasserted its supremacy.

Nonetheless, Jaggers returned victorious to England, to the tune of a personal profit of £50,000 (a quarter of a million dollars). Wisely, he made no subsequent trips to the Riviera.

Ironically, Jaggers was not the hero who inspired the song about "The Man Who Broke the Bank at Monte Carlo," much though he deserved it over anyone else. This honor was reserved for an English swindler named Charles Wells, who went to the casino in the summer of 1891 with £4000, funds obtained from numerous victims who thought he was a brilliant engineer and inventor. Blessed with fantastic luck, he won thousands without a consistent (let alone scientific) method. By the end of the summer season, he was the most famous and sought-after celebrity on the Riviera. One year later he was broke.

The term *breaking the bank* is a misnomer. Many people assume that it means winning all funds of the casino. Actually, when a player succeeds in exhausting the chips on one table, he is said to have "broken the bank" *at that table;* then play must be momentarily suspended until fresh funds can be brought from the vault. (Sometimes it has been reported that a black, funereal cloth is draped over the table, and action at the table discontinued for the remainder of the day.)

But the starting bank at each table is only a small fraction of the casino's total fortune, and nobody has ever made a sizable dent in that. There have been wealthy patrons who have won amounts in the neighborhood of a million dollars, but practically all have lost their winnings, plus considerable interest to boot! The casino's publicity men would like the world to believe that it is being fleeced by clever players with monotonous regularity. But the plain fact of the matter is that the players who have permanently retained any large casino winnings, such as the methodical Mr. Jaggers plus a few lucky splurgers who knew when to quit, could probably be counted on the fingers of one hand. It would take an adding machine to rack up the total of players who have lost great fortunes.

AMERICA'S MOST SPECTACULAR COUP

This story starts back in the fall of 1947 at the University of Chicago. Two bright, young students who had taken bachelor degrees at Cal Tech were pursuing graduate work at Chicago: Albert Hibbs in math and Roy Walford in medicine. In some silly challenge, Hibbs' ever-restless mind became focused on the notion of a bias, and presently he was taking data on a toy roulette wheel. What started as a lark became a serious endeavor. Soon, it seemed, the school was a bore, and the lure of easy money beckoned irresistibly.

Taking a holiday from classes, this eager pair rattled across the plains to Reno in an old model-A Ford. As they pulled in to the Biggest Little City in the World, the first hall of chance that loomed up before them was the Palace Club. The boys slipped in to look things over. They did not know how receptive a club would be to a continuous clocking of one of their wheels. So they stood by a wheel and memorized five or six numbers in a row, and then slipped surreptitiously over to a corner to jot them down in a little black book. It soon dawned on them that sitting at a table and writing down the data would be *less* conspicuous than repeatedly sneaking back and forth to the corner!

After more than a week of sampling, they concluded that one particular number was "hot." Drawing on their bank of little more than $100, they proceeded to bet a half-dollar on this number, straight up, on every spin of the wheel. Their success was phenomenal. Gradually increasing their bets up to several dollars, they ran their stake up to $5000 within 40 hours! During this period of time, the house attempted to break up their winning streak by numerous hostile actions. The speed of the wheel was varied from fast to slow, and a

My Own Roulette Adventures

3

My own entry into the roulette business was triggered by the flood of publicity on the coup at the Pioneer Club. Inspiring accounts of the success of Hibbs and Walford were printed in the West Coast newspapers, and I followed them with rapt attention. At the time, I was a student in physics at the University of California at Berkeley. Between classes in atomic particles and quantum statistics, I was constantly distracted by the thought of applying my knowledge of math and physics to the roulette. Then fate threw me in with Bob Bowers, another physicist who had witnessed Hibbs and Walford in action at Harolds Club.

OFF TO HAROLDS CLUB

After their sensational run in Las Vegas, my classmate and I could hardly wait for the spring semester to end. Since neither of us had a car, and Reno was 200 miles over the hills, we looked for a third man, preferably with an old flivver. We found such a person in a young math major, Henry Kaiser. Late in June we rattled eastward across California to the gambler's paradise. We checked in at the Golden Hotel carrying our rented electric adding machine. Then we breezed into Harolds to examine the roulette situation. We believed that the mechanical defects of a wheel were of a sufficiently subtle nature that one would rarely be able to find a "hot" wheel just by looking at it. Anything that would stare you in the face would obviously have been repaired by the club a long time ago. Accordingly we selected a wheel solely on the basis of comfort. We plunked down with our clipboard and counter and began to clock. On our clipboard we had a data sheet. In a vertical column at the left was a list of the numbers in their order of appearance around the wheel. Starting arbitrarily at the top with 00, it went 00-1-13-36-24-3-15, etc. This was much superior to listing them in plain numerical order.

We started with the counter set at 1. Suppose that number 22 was the first number to win on the wheel after we sat down. Then we would place a 1 in the row bearing the label 22 at the left, and then click the counter up to 2. If number 0 was the next winner, we would place a 2 in the row bearing the label 0, and then click the counter up to 3. If number 10 won next, we would put a 3 in the 10 row, and so forth. Soon we had a running chart of how the numbers were doing. On each sheet, we recorded a total of 380 trials, and then started a new sheet. If all numbers were equally likely, par for each number would be 10 wins in 380 trials. If a number was above par, its row stuck out beyond 10; for a number below par, its row fell short. Fluctuations about the average of 10 were extremely frequent. Sometimes a number would go mad and hit more than 20 times, or go cold and hit less than 5 times. Occasionally a number would even skip for more than 380 spins in a row, and it would draw a blank on the data sheet.

A typical data sheet is shown in Fig. 3-1. It is easy to see that some numbers were running ahead temporarily for a couple of hours, and some were running behind. Usually, a sheet represented 3 to 5 hours of clocking. A sheet of 380 was a very small sample. Thousands of trials were necessary to determine any significant trends.

Very shortly we lost Henry. His draft status was uncertain, so he bowed out to seek a more respectable occupation. Subsequently, we picked up another partner, who was a science major from Cal Tech. Eventually, he took off for an Alaskan vacation. Despite the fact that a round-the-clock operation is rougher for two men than three, Bob and I were not too sorry to see him go. In our opinion he was not cut out temperamentally for the job.

The reader may wonder why we decided on a continuous 24-hour play. Couldn't one play intermittently and thereby enjoy a sensible schedule? The answer is, of course, that we had to keep our eye on

Date ......Sat. 7/17.... Period Number ....(188)...

Time ......8:00 → 10:30 A.M. Data Taken By ......Wilson..

	1	2	3	4	5	6	7	8	9	10	11	12	13	14	15	16	17	18
00	43	52	75	107	130	190	202	242	263	268	361							
1	37	94	147	215	249	281	296	328										
13	183	209	217	233	276	286	299	323	372									
36	27	51	153	165	264	272	304	353	377									
24	61	90	138	142	158	194	216	228	294									
3	19	28	101	162	167	168	196	199	378									
15	21	48	49	65	66	103	134	136	161	176	204	312	322	333	345	368	369	
34	56	169	181	295	362	363												
22	1	62	109	126	171	203	301	347										
5	34	84	110	143	182	212	224	306	356	374								
17	11	111	122	145	185	223	226	234	330	332	364	365						
32	36	67	127	144	184	192	236	250	251	346	350							
20	23	68	106	163	173	186	219	290	305	320	329							
7	4	22	46	86	118	148	166	172	193	198	287	348						
11	6	13	81	83	89	141	187	188	247	271	288	335	360					
30	12	24	32	175	180	200	240	262	293	380								
26	31	45	50	155	211	246	357											
9	5	35	71	114	160	255	278	339										
28	16	33	96	99	112	121	125	128	222	230								
0	2	41	74	80	87	95	100	177	189	256	259	260	282	285	292	355		
2	9	76	82	195	229	321	376											
14	14	54	57	238	266	270	311	325	338	341	379							
35	44	55	79	104	105	139	201	279	324	334								
23	17	77	113	149	220	221	245	253	269	273	370							
4	25	42	72	137	210	267	297	302	310	317	326	354	375					
16	10	40	58	63	119	151	244	252	352	371								
33	29	116	117	159	191	239	243	314	319	349	366							
21	88	91	102	132	133	140	225	258	298									
6	78	156	206	289	343													
18	18	26	73	108	146	232	248	254	309									
31	53	93	97	120	135	152												
19	7	38	47	70	115	179	205	207	261	316	351	358	359	367				
8	59	92	123	124	178	197	235	284	303	313	337							
12	20	39	60	131	213	227	237	265	275									
29	8	98	129	174	231	257	291	307	315	327	342			More than ten :				+36
25	15	64	218	241	331	336	344							Less than ten :				−36
10	3	30	85	150	154	164	170	274	280	318	340							0
27	69	157	208	214	277	283	300	308	373								Check	

FIG. 3-1. A Typical Roulette Data Sheet

the wheel every moment of the day. Since we were hoping to detect some significant mechanical imperfection, we could not afford the risk of anything happening to the wheel in our absence.

Red 19

After several days at the table, we began to adjust to the weird routine of 4- or 6-hour shifts at the wheel. By the fifth day, red 19 was leading the field. With 13,700 trials on record, 19 had won 412 times, compared with an average of 360 for all numbers on the wheel. Those extra 55 wins had given number 19 an average of once in 33 spins. We cautiously began betting a 10¢ chip straight up on number 19. It continued to prosper, so a day later we boosted the ante to a quarter. After another 24 hours, we raised our bet to 50 cents per spin. We rocked up and down for a couple of days, and then quit betting for a while—scarcely any richer than we had started. Since our initial playing capital was around $50, this meant we had gone as high as $150 and then back down. At bets of a half-dollar, a modest losing run like 200 in a row would force us to quit playing, even on a number that was a winner in its long-term average. This was especially true when we accumulated capital on smaller bets and lost it on larger ones.

As our data rolled on up past 20,000 trials, we kept looking for other numbers that might "qualify." Several times we made runs ranging from 10¢ to 50¢ on different numbers such as red 36, black 24, and black 35. On this play we broke approximately even. Then 19 came surging along again, and after three weeks of sampling for a total of around 60,000 plays, we hopped onto the favorite again. With bets gradually rising from 50¢ to $1.25, we parlayed our $50 up to $600 in a couple of days. But no sooner did we reach this figure than we encountered a cold streak, and we were knocked down to $300. At this point we quit on 19. We were forced to conclude that the wheel was "hot," but not hot enough! After four solid weeks, we had rolled up a record of 80,000 continuous plays, which even to this day far exceeds anything this author has ever heard of. (See Appendix E for summaries of these marathon statistics.) Number 19 had maintained an over-all average of 1 in 35 for a whole month.

We shall have much more to say about that particular roulette wheel and whether or not 19 and the other "hot" numbers were just lucky and there was good scientific reason to play them. At this point, we decided to re-examine some of our basic assumptions. Perhaps a really worn-out, beat-up wheel would present much better possibilities for a biased number. With this in mind, we gave some of the other wheels in the club a once-over, and on the first floor, we found a choice-looking specimen, which looked as though it was on the verge of retirement. Paint was chipping off in numerous places, and the pockets were so badly worn that the fibered structure of the wood was readily apparent. We soon concluded it would be highly unscientific to leave town without acquiring a more balanced experience.

The Downstairs Wheel

The atmosphere at this downstairs table was noticeably different from our previous location, where there was the feeling one was engaged in a leisurely pursuit.

Not so at our new spot. The table was situated along a main aisle of traffic. On one side was the harsh call of a chuck-a-luck operator. Behind us was a keno counter. Noisy slot machines could be heard clattering nearby. On top of all this frantic action, there was the uneasy feeling of being watched by the detectives, who paraded up and down behind the one-way glass of the mirrored walls in back of the table. But we settled down with our clipboard and counter, and made a quick transition. After a couple of days, black 11 and black 29 pulled into the lead, nosing their way up to between 1/35 and 1/34. Impatient to get into action, we played one number and then the other on 25¢ and 50¢ bets. We did not fare very well, and by the end of the week had forfeited about $100 to the club. There were no indications that this second wheel was going to be any more sensational than the first one, so we gave it up. The week's work had racked up about 20,000 plays. Red 5 and red 1 had risen to the top of the roster, but we did not stay to play them. To us the biggest surprise was that black 10 was running only slightly above average. It had a tremendously worn pocket, and just by looking at the wheel, one would guess that it would catch the ball more often than the others.

After this, the great magnet of curiosity pulled us back to the original table. Red 19 was running only slightly better than 1/38, and our interest shifted to a dark horse in the form of red 18 (which was situated only two slots away from 19). In the previous four weeks of clocking, red 18 had averaged just under 1/36, but now it was getting hot. We climbed aboard, with bet size gradually rising from 10¢ to 60¢, as we piled up an excess of $175. But again a long downward oscillation set in, and we lost our profits and the playing bank as well. Ironically, ten rolls after we quit, number 18 came in again and proceeded to go into such a hot streak that if we had still been betting 60¢, we would have rocked right back up to our preceding peak! But such are the fickle ways of a gambling game. We were doomed from the start by our limited bankroll.

We stayed on to run our grand total up to 100,000 plays for that wheel. Number 18 continued to prosper for the rest of the week. *After* we had picked it as a winner, and had begun to play it ourselves on the third play, it maintained an average of better than one in 34 for the remaining four days. It seemed to rob number 19, which averaged out at one in 35.5 for the whole five weeks!

Physically exhausted, and out of playing capital, we picked up our clipboard and made our farewells. As we headed for the train depot, we realized that we had made an indelible impression on the dealers and many of the veteran gamblers. For anyone to "stay in the game" as long as we had was completely unheard of. Our original $50 bank had lasted a most remarkably long time.

CONCLUSIONS FROM 100,000 SPINS OF THE WHEEL

A critical examination of the data revealed that there were a number of amazing and unexpected features in that upstairs wheel. The most outstanding was that the best and worst numbers were *directly opposite* each other! Straight across from red 19 was black 20, averaging a miserable payoff once in 41 plays. For tabulation purposes, we grouped the first month's work into 21 successive subgroups of 3800 trials each; thus, par for a number was 100 wins per subgroup.

Number 19 ranged from 92 to 131, and 20 ranged from 75 to 113. Thus, 19 never had a really bad subgroup total; 20 never had a good one. In fact, in only one of the 21 subgroups did number 20 outdo number 19. Remarkable. Statisticians will unanimously agree that it was extremely unlikely that both 19 and 20 were actually 1/38 numbers with identity obscured by fluctuations.

Further striking consistencies in the totals for the runners-up, both for high and low honors, were also apparent. A most amazing observation was that the three best numbers (19, 36, 5) were red, and the three worst numbers (20, 11, 26) were black! Another extremely significant characteristic was the side-by-side grouping of good and bad numbers. No less than *eight* numbers in a row averaged better than 1/38, while *nine* other numbers all in a row averaged worse than 1/38. On a truly random wheel, this would be a *fantastic* coincidence. To the scientific mind, the only satisfactory explanation must lie in some defect of the wheel.

The whole collection of data on that wheel looked very peculiar. (See Appendix E.) The deviations of *many* of the numbers away from a 1/38 average were striking. We later performed what the statisticians call a *chi-square test*. This test computed the probabiilty that the collection of deviations that we had observed was due to chance alone, stemming strictly from fluctuations on a group of 38 numbers, all of whose true chance of occurrence was 1/38. Thus, we calculated the chance that 80,000 trials on a "perfect" or ideal wheel would produce the distribution which we had found. The chance turned out to be so small that it wasn't even listed in the mathematical tables commonly used for this purpose! We had to extend the tables ourselves in order to figure it out. The chance was *less* than 1 in 10 million. A mighty small chance!

EIGHT REASONS WHY A WHEEL CAN BE BIASED

1. The *color*, red or black, can apparently sometimes exert a strong influence. The effect noted before showed up on another wheel by the same manufacturer several years later. Somehow, the red and black paints produced different physical results. Perhaps the red paint had eaten into the wooden fibers. This would make the floor of the

red pocket less resilient, thus giving the ball a greater tendency to stay in the red pocket when it landed there. Or possibly the black paint made the fibers tighter, thereby tending to bounce the ball out of the black pocket more readily.

Although certain individual red numbers were quite spectacular, the red group *as a whole*, averaging 1/37.5, did not perform well enough to defeat the 5 percent house margin. Although color play sounds very tantalizing, it is perhaps best to realize that the color discrepancies are actually very small. They must be added or subtracted to all the other little factors that come into play.

2. *Warpage* of the floor of the wheel could possibly account for *blocks* of good and bad numbers. The effect would be to raise one side and lower the other. Because of the give and take of the wooden floor, warpage is much more likely to distort the wheel as a whole than it is to produce a local effect on one number only. This wheel, on which we found eight numbers in a row averaging better than 1/38 and at the same time nine in a row averaging worse, could very well have once experienced uneven exposure to heat or moisture.

3. A *crack* in the wooden floor would surely affect a numbered pocket through which it ran. You seldom get to see the underside of a wheel, where a split would be more apparent. Once the author saw a wheel in Las Vegas, removed from its cradle, and lying up-ended on the table: an immense split ran almost the full diameter of the wheel.

4. The *metal slot* between two numbers is a potent source of mechanical imperfection. The manufacturer calls the slot a *double-ring partition* because it fits between an outer and an inner circular ring. Slight variations in the height of the slots could make a tremendous difference in the wins of the numbers. A higher slot might tend to bounce the ball back, and thereby serve to trap it. On the other hand, a lower slot might permit the ball to drop down more readily, and this would also tend to trap the ball. Tightness or looseness of the slots cannot be ignored either. A very tight one would serve as a more or less rigid wall, causing more than its share of bounce-backs. In contrast, a very loose one might tend to allow the ball to roll on over to the pockets beyond.

Slight variations in the spacing of the metal slots could have a profound effect, since a number with a wider-than-average pocket would rob its neighbor with a narrower-than-average pocket.

5. The *size and weight of the ball* can be highly critical. There is a geometry factor that is all out of proportion to the mere diameter of the ball. What counts is the *difference* between this diameter and the width of the pocket (between slots). Think of a half-inch ball trying to land (1) in a pocket 1 inch wide, and (2) in a pocket 1½ inches wide. In (2) there is actually 100 percent more area available to the ball than in (1), although the pocket is only 50 percent wider! This exaggerated effect, of course, is due to the ball's being a sphere of finite size rather than a point.

Offhand, a larger ball might seem preferable, since the "difference" effect would be enhanced. But a larger ball is usually a *heavier* ball. This means greater impact and wear every time it pounds into the spinning wheel. Since we did not want the physical conditions to be changing any faster than necessary, we expressly preferred a medium-size ball. Superstitious players who were perpetually asking the dealer to switch balls were a bane to our operation. We shuddered and wished they would go away.

6. The *speed* with which the dealer spins the wheel, and the ball, can affect the outcome. When the wheel is spun very slowly, the ball may just plunk into the first pocket. A fast-spinning wheel may give the ball a big kick and bounce it all over the place before it settles into one pocket. Slow, but not *too* slow, was our preference. This gave a variety of mechanical factors a chance to come into play, since the ball often had to scoot along over several partitions before coming to a halt. When the wheel was whirled too fast, all hell broke loose. The ball flew all over the place, often getting socked into the air, and coming down almost vertically. Under those conditions, it was hard to predict just what was happening!

7. A true *rotational unbalance* is conceivable, but not likely. Gravity causes the speed to vary only if the wheel does not spin about a vertical axis. In this case, an unbalanced wheel would alternately appear to lunge and to hold back. The lighter half of the wheel would spend more time at the bottom of its path than at the top, and

the odds would be better on the lower half. Considering the quality of the bearings and other parts in the standard wheel, this condition seems rather unlikely.

8. *General wear and tear* is bound eventually to give rise to some degree of bias. The beat-up wheel on the first floor of Harolds Club was by no means the only such specimen we have seen. The plushier clubs *usually* keep their equipment in better mechanical condition, but smaller places are often forced to economize with infrequent overhauls. As long as the shabby gear does not deter the class of players to which they cater, and as long as no one is allowed to beat the defects, they have nothing to lose.

Noticeable wear generally becomes apparent after a wheel has been in operation for six months to a year. The continual play of the ivory ball upon the wheel loosens up the metal slots and erodes the paint. It is a sorry sight when the painted numbers on the bottom of the pocket are worn so badly that you can scarcely read them. Sometimes uneven wear makes the structure of the wood stand out like blood vessels on the back of a hand or the roots of a tree crawling along the ground!

What is the upshot of all this analysis? Simply this: If a number is going to beat the 1/36 average as a result of mechanical defect, then *several* of these factors must be combined in your favor. There is not much hope of a spectacular win unless a number is at least 5 percent in your favor; this means the number must be 10 percent off of average. This is a very large order, and it is not likely to exist as a consequence of only one physical defect unless it is so apparent that the house knows it too!

The many factors mentioned can just as well *hinder* a number's performance as *help* it! Therefore, we can hope for a bonanza only if a number of small defects all *add in the same direction*. But independent effects tend to cancel one another, on the average, so only infrequently can we expect to find a truly winning number.

BACK TO THE MATH BOOKS

Returning to the University, I combed furiously through its fine library. I soon discovered that games of chance had been the object of long and distinguished study. There were copies of some of the early treatises in French and German, reflecting genius of previous centuries. Best of all was a textbook written in our own language by a Russian-born math prof at Stanford University. I shall never forget the dawn of comprehension that swept over me as I thumbed through Uspensky's, *Introduction to Mathematical Probability*. His chapter on the "gambler's ruin problem" held me enthralled. (William Feller's magnificent text now gives even better coverage.)

In our case, the problem boiled down to this simple question: Assuming we have found an imperfect wheel that has a certain percentage in our favor, how should we size our bets in proportion to our total available bank? The answer to this question is inevitably a compromise between bets so large that there is a sizable chance of being knocked out by a moderate fluctuation, and bets so small that it takes forever to make any money. The player has to make the compromise himself. In fact, the decision entails factors entirely unrelated to the game itself: such as how fast the hotel bills are piling up, how long the player's physical endurance can withstand the night and day play, and how soon he must leave town to resume some other activity! But once the decision has been made, the mathematical theory predicts exactly what ratio of bank-to-bet should be used. Any realistic gambler should have a working knowledge of the results, even if he does not master the method of computation. (We cover it in Chapter 17.)

From the record of Hibbs and Walford, it is evident that they became increasingly aware of this problem. In their first play at the Palace Club, they started with only 250 betting units, but in their final triumph in Las Vegas, they adjusted their bets so that they had between 1000 and 2000 units.

The Multinomial Problem

The other crucial problem for the biased wheel player is the proper interpretation of the statistical record of wins and losses. Unfortunately, this is a much tougher mathematical nut to crack. I have seen many fine books on probability and statistics, but I have yet to find one that hits the heart of the roulette problem. The trouble is that there are too many variables.

It is easy to analyze a coin for bias. On each toss there are only two possibilities, heads or tails. The simple *bi*nomial distribution of Chapter 15 applies. But with roulette, there are 38 possibilities, giving rise to a *multi*nomial distribution. Alternatively, one can say there are 37 degrees of freedom. This means that the chance of occurrence of each of 37 numbers may be assigned independently of each other, subject only to the condition that their sum be less than 1. Then, finally, the chance for the thirty-eighth is fixed; it is necessarily 1 minus the previous sum.

Literature on the binomial problem is profuse, but the vastly more difficult multinomial question has been hardly touched. A helpful approximation is the famous Pearson chi-square test, mentioned earlier, which gives us immense confidence that severe imperfections can occur on a wheel. Unfortunately, however, no theory has shown us a clear-cut method for deciding how to qualify a particular number as a good risk. Therefore, we had to improvise. Using the chi-square tables as a point of departure, we evolved what might be described loosely as an adjusted least-squares method of fitting data. From our records made at Reno, we came up with a thumb rule for future wheels. We should accept for play any number that averaged better than 1/29 during an initial sample of 5000 plays or 1/32 for 10,000 plays. We agreed also to relax these requirements on intuition; for example, to be less demanding of red numbers than black ones.

OUR SECOND CRACK AT THE GAME

It was not until Christmas vacation in 1951 that our opportunity came again. The day after Christmas we hopped on the Southern Pacific train and rolled eastward toward Reno.

At Harolds Club, we did not see any *visible* reason for picking one wheel over another, so we settled down in the same comfortable location as before. The table was the same, but the roulette wheel clearly was not. But at least, the present wheel had been made by the same manufacturer.

We clocked for about 4½ days, rolling up some 12,000 trials. Red 3 was leading the pack, at 1/30.5; two other red contenders looked interesting (red 27 at 1/33 and red 18 at 1/34), but we decided to give our all to number 3. We began betting a quarter. With a tentative bankroll of $200, this gave us 800 units. We won steadily, and by the end of another 13,000 plays, we had almost doubled our starting bank. This called for increasing the bet to 40¢. But more important, we made an amazing discovery.

Late one night I slumped drowsily in my chair, barely alert enough to place the bet, click the counter, and record the winning number. I gazed sleepily at the wheel from a very shallow angle, half-hypnotized by its constant rotation. Suddenly I was jolted out of my reveries by the awareness of a periodic flash. It hit me like a bolt of lightning. The metal slot between 3 and 15 was reflecting light from an overhead spotlight more brightly than the other slots. What on earth could be causing that? I gave it a close look, and discovered this slot was thicker, higher, and rounder than the others. Immediately this clicked with a casual remark by one of our favorite dealers, who had said there had been loose slots on that wheel. Clearly, the mechanic had replaced a loose slot with one from a wheel of different design.

You may ask why I sat by that wheel for a week before noticing such a simple thing. Since the wheel is kept spinning every second of the day, it is hard to spot any irregularities unless you know exactly *what to look for*. Even though we had noticed a high-pitched "ping" every now and then, it had been impossible to localize because of the rapid bouncing of the ball and the continuous turning of the wheel. Now it was obvious that the substitute slot was wedged tightly in place and vibrated at a higher frequency than the others when hit by a fast-moving ball.

Our record showed clearly that, in the direction of motion of the ball, numbers just beyond 3 were being robbed of their share of wins. The extra height of the slot seemed to block the ball, but strangely, the peculiar slot was between 3 and the number just *before* it rather than just *after* it. One might think that the height of the slot would also rob 3 itself. But possibly the unusual roundness tended to nullify this effect and to roll the ball over into 3. We also noted that some numbers preceding 3 were doing better than average, perhaps due to a bounce-back effect. In short, we had a lion by the tail.

So much for the strange slot. What was happening to our bets? After rolling up more than 700 units on 25¢ bets (it would have taken 800 units to double our bank), we increased the ante to 40¢. Our bank continued to climb by another 300 units, which put us up to $300 ahead of our original starting point. But then we took a dive of 550 units, and deciding we had been a little too optimistic, lowered bets back to 25¢. We bounced back up 150 units, and then determined to quit playing for a while and take more data and think things over.

On arriving in Reno, it was our fond hope to find a Hibbs-type roulette wheel, one with a hot number running about 1/30 for a good, long time. But our little beauty, number 3, did not look as though it could do much better than 1/34 for us. Fortified with a solid physical explanation of its performance, we had full confidence that we could camp there and win money as long as the dealer would let us. We had visions of running our bankroll up to 10 or 20 thousand dollars or better. The only hitch in our scheme was the time element. We figured it would take three to six weeks to run up our money to a respectable sum. Vacation time was fast running out. Unless something "big" were to break in Reno, we would have to leave.

Gradually a plan took shape. We would persuade someone to back us on a grand scale—someone who was already a big roulette player. The obvious candidate was a man we had first noticed when we first visited Reno. He looked like a cowpoke, but was obviously a well-funded gambler. In fact, he was one of Nevada's richest men, an eccentric multimillionaire. When we came to Reno to play in the winter of 1951, we learned that during the previous three years he had been Harold's best customer, to the tune of a reputed $1 million! He had been known to lose as much as $70,000 in a single foray. He lived unobtrusively in the fashionable Mount Rose section of Reno, but in the spring of 1952, he was unexpectedly catapulted into the harsh glare of public curiosity when his home was burglarized of a safe containing more than a million dollars worth of securities, cash, and jewels. This story is bizarre and amusing, but to relate it here would be to digress from the purpose of this book. At any rate, we proposed to get this man to stake us on the roulette wheel. After arranging a meeting, we displayed our records on that glorious number 3, and gave him a strong pitch. At first he seemed reluctant to play any more roulette. He said that during the previous three years his fortune had remained intact, but he had lost the interest! Finally he said he would think it over, and contact us at the casino. Several days went by, but there was still no word from our grubstaker. After six days of nervous waiting, we were just about to quit and go home, when he showed up at the casino, and bought $10,000 worth of chips. Then he began taking a record of his own. We watched number 3 continue to roll like an express train. Shortly after our new partner sat down, number 3 hit, and then repeated, and then hit again four plays later. He was quite impressed. Then, finally, he pushed that big stack of chips over to us and gave the magic words, "Start playing, boys."

At this point, the pit boss unexpectedly sent a mechanic in to test the wheel. First he laid a carpenter's level across the rim. The bubble didn't show a true horizontal, so he cranked up the feet of the table until he was better satisfied. Actually, we didn't care a hoot about that because we didn't believe that a slight tilt could affect the success of any number very much. But then he began feeling the metal slots between the numbers. When he came to number 3, he got very excited, and went running off to tell his boss.

Our Plan Blows Up

Meanwhile, we commenced playing, at $4.00 per spin instead of the quarters we had played previously. The agreement was that winnings would be split 20:80, but our supporter had upped the ante from $5000 to $10,000 and had spelled out a smaller percentage for us. This was okay with us. We played for about an hour with the new stakes, rocking up and down, when suddenly the owner himself appeared on the scene. He stopped the action immediately. Then he picked up the ivory ball and conducted his own little test on the wheel. He held the ball against the metal slots, spun the wheel very fast, and listened to the noise that the ball made upon the slots as it went around, "Klunk-klunk-klunk-ping—klunk-klunk-klunk-ping." That was enough for him, and he growled that the mechanic who was responsible for that wheel should be fired. He ordered a new wheel!

Everybody was stunned, for this was the first time in the history of the club that the management had ever changed a wheel on any roulette player. It was supposed to be the biggest and most generous club in Nevada, always willing to give the customer a break. But here it was changing a wheel on a man who had lost $1 million there, without giving him a chance to win even $50,000 or $100,000. Everyone was astonished: the players, the spectators, the dealers, and even the pit bosses. We were utterly crushed, of course, for all our data-taking became useless.

From a business point of view, the management did the right thing. We had made the *strategic mistake* of getting to back us a man who was substantially richer than the management. The full impact of this didn't dawn upon us until the moment the wheel was changed.

How did we make out with the $4.00 bets before the game was stopped? We oscillated up and down. At one point we were ahead $270. At the moment we quit play, we were behind $250. To us, this was a momentary downward fluctuation. We had perfect confidence that number 3 would continue as a long-term winner, just as it had performed in the past. But the fact that we were slightly in the hole when we were forced to quit mildly piqued our backer. He complained to the management about this, and because he was the club's best customer, they made restitution to him. In fact, we had good reason to believe they paid him back more than he had lost on our short play.

So, our honeymoon with our millionaire friend ended in discord, and all our dreams of quick wealth vanished into thin air. We had an interesting adventure to show for all our effort, but we weren't one penny richer, considering that what we had won on our own stake hardly covered costs of the trip. Furthermore, since the management had switched wheels on us, we concluded that any other club owner would do it too, and the possibilities of beating the roulette seemed remote indeed.

Later Episodes

4

After our experience in Reno, we stopped searching for biased wheels. Nonetheless, we actually did have occasion to play another one several years later. It was quite unplanned. In the summer of 1955, we rendezvoused in Reno to explore the possibilities of winning at blackjack. One evening, having played some blackjack here and there, we sauntered into the Nevada Club. Our attention was immediately attracted to the roulette layout, which contained no less than three single-zero wheels in a row. To our utter amazement, over one of these wheels was a gigantic scoreboard. It had 37 mechanical registers, displaying the number of wins for each number on the wheel.

ACTION ON A SINGLE-ZERO WHEEL

The record showed more than 26,000 trials. Number 33 was way out in front with 866 wins versus a normal 705. It was averaging 1/30, a veritable Hibbs-type number! Also, numbers 0 and 2 were rated at 1/32. Considering the size of the sample, *all* these numbers were hotter than any we had ever seen before. We stared at each other in numb disbelief, and then asked what we were waiting for!

My partner Bob took the night shift, and bet 75 cents each on 33 and 0 each time. All night long our two numbers came roaring in, and we rolled up more than $300. When Bob's wife came to relieve him for breakfast, however, the nonchalant attitude of the operators changed. They realized a "syndicate" was in operation, and promptly reversed the usual directions of rotation of ball and wheel. Then, later in the day when I took over, the boss ordered *alternate* rotations of ball and wheel, a la Monte Carlo. My bank rocked up and down on $1.00 bets, but the downs took over, and by 6 P.M. I had lost back all but $125 of our previous night's winnings. We quit, reasonably convinced that the management would not allow a big win on scientific play.

A COOLER CLIMATE FOR BIAS PLAYERS?

Subsequently I struck up a conversation with one of the habitués of the club, whose gambling activity was dictated by the signs of the zodiac. He realized the point of bias play and said that many people had been playing dominant numbers on single-zero wheels in this club over a period of several years. Some, in fact, had been successful, but the club had installed the registers for its own protection and generally discouraged such players—first by alternate rotation, then by changing wheels. One man was held to a $2.00 bet on any number, whereas the usual limit was $25.

Our informant knew of three times that the club had switched wheels, and of two occasions when others had done so (*since* our own misadventure). All this tended to confirm the conclusion we had reached three years earlier: Even though it might land them some juicy publicity, most club owners were in no mood to lose big hunks of money on imperfect roulette wheels. Nonetheless, reports of "college boys" winning large amounts with "systems" on the roulette appear periodically in the news media. Not all are fiction, as witnessed by the following remarkable action.

In the summer of 1957, two University of Nevada students, called the "Jones Boys," allegedly won a large sum on a biased wheel at a Reno club. Eventually the wheel was changed. Then in the summer of 1958, the same pair turned up in Las Vegas and engaged in two remarkable coups. Both operations were witnessed, so there is no doubt that they occurred.

At the time of their arrival in Las Vegas, the students had attained the same entrepreneurial status as Al Hibbs, hiring others to do preliminary clocking. Their agents sampled round the clock for eight days at a downtown club, placing 5¢ bets to hold their place at the table. Then the masters marched in, and immediately wagered $10.00 per spin on each of eight adjacent numbers. Thus, they played a "sector" of the wheel. It was the busy Fourth of July week end, and the Jones Boys were then unknown in Las Vegas. Consequently, their play attracted little attention at first, especially since they had an initial downward fluctuation of $3000. Playing in 6-hour shifts around the clock, however, they soon recovered the loss and forged ahead at the end of 24 hours. As time progressed, the management became increasingly concerned, and gradually introduced countermeasures in the form of varying the speed of wheel and ball. When this proved to be of no avail, they finally changed the wheel at the end of 40 hours of play. Thereupon the players cashed in their chips, some $12,000 ahead, and departed.

This might have been considered a satisfactory end to their Las Vegas operations, but there was a bigger coup to come. Although the students temporarily left town, their "casers" did not. To the sharp observer, the casers could be seen busily circulating from club to club in search of another suitably biased wheel. These precursors, incidentally, never appeared to write anything down; nor, for that matter, neither did their mentors. Unquestionably, this modus operandi tended to conceal their objectives. The hired hands evidently found a wheel that met their specifications at another casino, and they played it for six days with 5¢ chips. During the first week of August, the students showed up and commenced a play on this wheel. Again they selected a sector, but this time with some gaps between the numbers played; they bet on five numbers altogether. Instead of staking a fixed $10.00 wager, as they had at the other club, they played a silly little cycle of $5.00, $10.00, and $15.00. This was clearly intended as camouflage, but it is doubtful that any such purpose was accomplished.

Amazingly, they were allowed to play for 72 consecutive hours, during which they won $20,000. It appeared that the pit bosses and other management personnel firmly believed that it was all due to luck and that the standard roulette wheel simply *could not* possess enough bias for a player to win consistently. Nonetheless, somebody's patience finally wore thin. At the end of the three cycles of 24-hour night-and-day play, the players were approached by the management and told to leave.

It is easy to make a rough estimate of the advantage that appeared to be working for the players during the second visit to Las Vegas. They played for 72 hours, at a rate of somewhere around 100 decisions per hour, for a total of around 7000 decisions. They won $20,000, or about $3.00 per decision. They bet an average of $10.00 per spin, on each of five numbers, or $50 per decision. The profit was thus $3.00 per $50 investment, or 6 percent, on the average. Allowing for fluctuations, the percentage on the numbers that they were playing was between 4 and 8 percent. Certainly this is not inconsistent with what we have already recounted earlier in this chapter and in the previous two chapters. The element of sector play is a fascinating angle. The reader will recall from earlier discussion that one of the wheels at Harolds Club showed distinct sectional tendencies. But the Jones Boys manifestly uncovered something much more spectacular. I should be most interested to see their data.

These doings of the Jones Boys in Las Vegas rounds out my picture of spectacular bias play on American wheels, but no account would be complete without coverage of a sensational occurrence that reputedly took place in Argentina in 1951. It cannot be classified as a truly "recent" event, but since reports from abroad are rather rare, this is as good a place as any to bring it up. My source of information is *Time* magazine for February 12, 1951, and this is the only reference to this episode that I have ever seen.

South of the Border

It all began in 1947 in the little coast town of Necochea. In the small casino there, a certain small-time gambler took to studying the whims and behavior of the roulette wheels. After recording several thousand consecutive turns, he found that eight or nine numbers seemed to turn up more frequently than the others. By playing a pattern of the high-frequency numbers and rechecking his computations, he began to win modestly but consistently. Despite all the normal casino precautions, he kept on winning.

By 1948 he had developed great confidence in his method. So he proceeded to train four assistants and shifted operations to the huge, government-owned casino at fashionable Mar del Plata, a resort city some 200 miles south of Buenos Aires. There the pupils soon shoved the master into the background and formed syndicates of their own. The worried management alerted the croupiers to keep records on the growing number of consistent winners. By 1950, the losses to the new syndicates were so high that the casino director was fired.

But that did not cure the trouble. As the turn of the year rolled around, the hottest syndicate at Mar del Plata had 20 members and raked in profits estimated as high as six million pesos. (At 14 pesos per dollar in 1951, that amounted to around a quarter of a million dollars!) The syndicate was headed by a one-time sailor. Among the other big money-makers were fruit hucksters, waiters, and farmers, who were soon buying Cadillacs, Buicks, and beach-front property. Known only by nicknames such as El Crespo (Curly), El Vasquito (Little Basque), or Juancito (Johnny), each gang member had his own assigned wheel, which he had studied thoroughly. The management routine of shuffling wheels apparently failed because the gamblers knew the wheels so well that they could identify them by the tiniest mar or scratch, the faintest offshade of color in the varnish.

Finally, in desperation, Mar del Plata yelled for help. Early in 1951, all known syndicate members were arrested, although they had broken no law. They were classified as professional gamblers with bad records, and permanently barred from the Argentine casinos! Thus ended a four-year siege at the Monte Carlo of Argentina. This surely must represent the culmination in biased wheel play!

A CHALLENGE TO THE MATHEMATICIANS

Despite the many assaults recorded in these chapters, there exists no widely accepted doctrine for identifying an imperfect wheel. Our crude, semiquantitative approach described in the preceding chapter leaves much to be desired from the rigorous mathematical point of view. We wholeheartedly invite any interested professional mathematician to attack the problem, namely, on what statistical basis should you decide whether to play a given roulette number? The mathematician might first confine himself to the "simple" case, in which the true probabilities of occurrence of the numbers are assumed constant (not changing in time). If any genius then wishes to become sophisticated, let him consider the possibility that the changing physical situation causes the probabilities to change with time! Results should be published in some appropriate statistics journal, where they can be evaluated and commented on by scholars whose professional specialty is statistics. Only in the journals can the problem receive the treatment that it merits.

The challenge also remains for all the young adventurers, the minimum requirement being lots of time for the search. As long as man makes roulette wheels, there will be imperfections, as the reader may see from the records in Appendix E. But let these researchers do their homework well, and gird strongly for the battle. The whirling ladies respect only those who come well armed with knowledge!

Basic Blackjack— An Even Game

5

Blackjack (or "21") is the only casino game in which an amateur can learn to win consistently over the long run. In fact, it is surprisingly easy to learn, but in order to discourage you from trying to learn, the blackjack dealers and casino operators will undoubtedly tell you that you have to be an Einstein or a Boston lawyer to succeed. Don't you believe what they say. Go ahead and read this and the subsequent four chapters, and you'll be amazed at what you can win!

THE FIVE LESSONS ON BLACKJACK

To give you a picture of what the five chapters cover, we summarize their content very briefly. (1) This chapter describes the *basic* game and shows the proper strategy whereby you can completely eliminate any house advantage even when you restrict yourself to a constant bet size. (2) Chapter 6 develops the scientific basis for the statements of the present chapter. It covers my own vast playing experience in the casinos, and furthermore provides overwhelming evidence obtained by calculations on electronic computers, directed both by myself and by a number of other scientists. (3) Chapter 7 shows how to win by keeping track of the cards and by making appropriate variations in your bet size. (4) Chapter 8 debates the measures that the casino can take against the successful player, and what factors will affect the future of this intriguing game. (5) Chapter 9 gives a critical assessment of other books that cover the game.

All in all, you will find these five chapters a most exciting and thorough coverage of this popular casino game.

BACKGROUND INFORMATION

The first thing to understand about blackjack is that the game was not set up originally with specified odds against the player. In this important sense, it is vastly different from craps, roulette, and the other games in which the basic odds are easy to figure. Blackjack evolved from other card games. To be sure, the casinos have regularly made plenty of money with it. But this is because the general gambling public has played a very poor game of blackjack, and not because the game cannot be beaten. Until recently, there has never been a detailed scientific analysis of the proper strategy for playing this game. Instead, there has been a bewildering miasma of misinformation and confusing notions. Veteran blackjack dealers have given all sorts of conflicting advice.

This state of affairs existed until only a few years ago. Gradually there was an awakening of interest among persons with scientific training, who possessed the ability to analyze this game correctly. This movement was beginning to roll by the mid-1950s, and it has snowballed ever since. I was one of the pioneers in this work, and I am well informed on what has been done by practically all other scientific investigators. We have reached the point where the game of blackjack is now well understood. Even if you are a novice, you can learn to play a much better than average game of blackjack, just by adopting a few rules laid down by an expert.

REVIEW OF THE CASINO RULES FOR BLACKJACK*

Before presenting casino rules, we must make sure the reader is acquainted with the basic elements of play. We are talking about the casino game, played with a 52-card deck, in which the player's first two cards are dealt to him face down, and in which the first of the dealer's two cards is dealt face up. The object of the game, the payoffs, and the various common options will be discussed here briefly.

* These rules prevail as of the writing of this book. See also page 159.

As the alternate name of "21" implies, the object of the game is to obtain a total of 21 in your hand, or as close to that as possible, without exceeding 21. If you are not satisfied with the total on your first two cards, you may draw additional cards until you are satisfied, but if you go over 21, you automatically lose. When you and the other players are either satisfied with the first two cards or have drawn to satisfactory totals, then the dealer completes his hand. In the casinos, the dealer must draw to 16 or less, and must stand on 17 or more. If you have not gone over 21, and if the dealer proceeds to go over, then you win automatically. Otherwise, the two hands are compared, and the higher hand wins. If the two totals are the same, it is a draw, and no money is exchanged. (Note that the dealer does *not* collect on a tie.)

If you receive an ace and a 10-value card in the first two cards dealt, that is just dandy. This special combination is called a *blackjack* or *natural,* and you are immediately paid off at a 3:2 ratio (except in the infrequent case that the dealer also has one, in which case it is a tie). You get this pleasant little bonus on the average of about once in 21½ hands. It is interesting to note that you do not have to have a *black* jack or even any jack at all, in order to win this bonus. All picture cards (king, queen, and jack) count 10, as well as a card with 10 pips on it; so, any of these cards coupled with an ace yields the bonus.

Ordinarily, you have the option of counting the ace as 1 or 11, whichever you please. But when accompanied by a 10-count card, the ace should obviously be counted as 11. Incidentally, when the dealer gets a blackjack and you do not, you lose automatically, but only at even money. So, when your blackjacks are compared with the dealer's, the extra payoff adds a noticeable factor to your side of the ledger.

There are several options of play, which can be utilized to great advantage. Under certain conditions, for example, it is expedient to *double-down* on the first two cards. Here you elect to draw one and only one additional card, and because of this limitation, you are allowed to double your bet. Since 16 of the 52 cards in the deck are 10-value cards, one of the best times to consider doubling-down is when you have a two-card total of 11 or 10. There is a good chance of drawing a 10, and hence obtaining a total of 21 or 20. The strategy for doubling-down will be given presently.

It should be noted here, however, that there is some variation in the conditions under which you are permitted to double-down. In the major casinos on the "strip" in Las Vegas, you may double-down on *any* first two cards (except a blackjack); this includes a total of 9 or 8, as well as so-called *soft* hands, in which an ace is coupled with a non-10-value card (for example, an ace and a six). Many people who double-down on 11 and 10 regularly would not consider doubling-down under other circumstances. Actually, the situations just mentioned are also sometimes advantageous. In Reno, the casinos allow you to double *only* on 11 and 10, but this is liberalized by letting you do it on any number of cards if they total 11 or 10. In addition to original two-card hands, there frequently occur three-card combinations (and even occasionally four-card combinations) in which the Reno double-down is very advantageous. Whether you are playing under Las Vegas or Reno rules, proper doubling-down can add a definite increment to your game. It is well worth the small effort in learning when you should do it!

Another optional play is the *splitting* of a pair. If you are dealt two cards of identical value, you may double your bet and treat each of these cards as if it were the first card in a new hand. Your original bet goes on one of these hands, and the extra bet goes on the other. On each of these hands, you now draw until you are satisfied, or else you have "gone bust," in exactly the same way as an ordinary hand (the sole exception is in splitting a pair of aces, wherein you are allowed to draw only one card to each ace; if you draw a 10, it counts as an ordinary 21, not as a blackjack). The proper splitting of pairs is an important part of good blackjack strategy, just like doubling-down. For example, a pair of 8s should always be split. The two-card total of 16 is the worst possible total you can have; if you draw, you will go bust on any card bigger than a 5. On the other hand, an individual 8 is a good starting point, since there is a considerable chance of drawing a 10 or otherwise improving the total to between 17 and 21.

As with doubling-down, the decision of whether or not to split in any given situation may well depend on the dealer's up-card. We shall say more about this later. Again, there are minor variations in the other options that casinos may permit on the split. Some places invite you to split again if the third card is the same; or if you draw to 10 or 11 on the new hands, you may have the chance to double-down.

Significantly, in casino play, the dealer is never allowed to exercise any of the options on his own hand. In fact, as far as the play of the cards is concerned, the dealer could just as well be replaced by a robot, which always draws to 16 and stands on 17. However, a robot would not be able to amuse you with conversation.

Having briefly reviewed the rules, we may well ask whether the game of blackjack favors the player or the house, for it is plain that the game contains several advantages and one large disadvantage for the player. These are presented in Table 5-1.

TABLE 5-1. PRELIMINARY EVALUATION OF BLACKJACK

Advantages for Player	Disadvantage to Player
1. Player is paid 3:2 on a *blackjack* (or natural).	1. Player must draw before dealer draws.
2. Player may double-down in favorable circumstances.	No other disadvantages!
3. Player may split a pair in favorable circumstances.	
4. Player sees one of dealer's cards and may use this information in deciding how to play his hand.	

Please notice that the table is labeled a "preliminary" evaluation of blackjack. This means that to begin with, we are confining our discussion to the basic game, subject to two very definite restrictions. (1) Our decisions are based strictly on the knowledge of the dealer's up-card and the cards in our own hand. (2) Our bet size is fixed, that is, we are making a flat bet. Later on we shall explore the effect of taking into account the other cards that have been played previously, and the effect of varying our bet size. To put our knowledge of the game of blackjack on a sound foundation, it is imperative for us first to understand thoroughly the basic game.

Although our table indicates there is only one disadvantage against the player in this game, it turns out to be a substantial handicap, and we shall see shortly that we must keep our wits about us in order to overcome it. The fact that the player always makes the first draw means that if the player's hand "breaks" (goes over 21), he loses immediately, and the dealer need not complete his own hand. Therefore, there are times when the dealer has a poor initial two-card start, but is not obliged to try to improve it, and thereby does not take the risk of going over himself.

If the player did not have the compensating advantages shown in our chart, the requirement that he draw first would give the casino just under a 7 percent edge in this game. Fortunately for the player, the use of a proper strategy for the various options described previously can essentially cancel out this one big advantage of the dealer's.

It is rather easy to demonstrate the figure of just under 7 percent, quoted above. Imagine that the four advantages listed for the player are momentarily suspended and that the player decides to mimick the dealer in his play. This means that the player would always draw to 16 or less, and stand on 17 or more, just as the dealer does. It can be readily verified that if you play this way, you will obtain a total from 17 through 21 about three-quarters of the time, and will break about one-quarter of the time. (All you have to do is deal several hundred hands to yourself, and this approximate ratio will be quite evident.)

Now the hands on which both player and dealer get 17 through 21 will tend to balance out each other. There will be a certain number of actual draws, and the remaining wins and losses will cancel one another. Also, there will be some hands when the player has 17 through 21, and the dealer draws and goes bust. On the other hand, when the player goes over 21, he loses. On three-quarters of these breaking hands, however, he would lose anyway, since the dealer is obliged to draw until he has 17 or more. So, the only time the player has any justified complaint is when he goes bust, and the dealer would *also* have gone bust. To be fair, this situation should be a tie, but instead the player loses. The fraction of hands on which this occurs is 1/4 of 1/4, or 1/16. Percentagewise, this is a disadvantage of 6¼ percent. (More precisely, this figure is closer to 7 percent because busts occur slightly more than one-quarter of the time. The important thing to grasp is the order of magnitude of the advantage that the dealer possesses as a result of the player's having to draw first.)

The Extra Payoff on a Blackjack

Now that we know the dealer advantage that the player must seek to overcome, we consider the several advantages that the player has and which he can use to counteract the dealer's edge. The first on our list is the fact that blackjacks are paid at 1½:1 (same ratio as 3:2) rather than at 1:1. The probability of an untied blackjack is simply

$$\left(\frac{2 \times 4 \times 16}{52 \times 51}\right)\left(1 - \frac{2 \times 3 \times 15}{50 \times 49}\right) = 0.04649$$

It will be seen that this figure bears out the previous statement that the chance of getting an untied blackjack is about 1/21.5; the quantity in the first parentheses is the chance that you will have a blackjack; the quantity in the second parentheses is the chance that the dealer simultaneously will *not* (the latter, of course, being just 1 minus the chance that the dealer will have one). The calculation proceeds in a very straightforward manner. The number 4 implies the number of aces in the 52-card deck, and 16 is the number of 10-value cards (king, queen, jack, 10). The factor 2 is introduced to take account of the fact that you may draw the ace first and the 10-value card second, or vice versa. In the second parentheses, the number 3 reflects the number of remaining aces, and 15 is the number of remaining 10-value cards.

The conclusion is that on a one-unit bet you will collect, on the average, an additional $0.5 \times 0.04649 = 0.02325$ unit. Hence, the bonus payoff on the blackjack is worth 2.325 percent to the player. If this advantage is subtracted from the previously cited figure of slightly under 7 percent disadvantage due to the player having to hit first, there remains only about 4½ percent disadvantage. Since the blackjack bonus is automatic, this figure of 4½ percent represents the real edge that the player must nullify by the application of good play.

Other Player Advantages at Blackjack

The evaluation of the remaining three advantages listed for the player in the Table 5-1 is a quite complicated matter. Myriads of possible card combinations enter the picture. In any case, the maximum benefit is attainable only if the player follows the right strategy, to be described shortly. Assuming such intelligent play, it may be shown by computation, and verified by dealing cards, that the various contributions are as follows:

1. Slightly more than 1½ percent for proper doubling-down.
2. Slightly less than ½ percent for proper splitting of pairs.
3. About 2½ percent for proper standing on certain situations where the dealer would draw with the same total, and for proper hitting on a few "soft" hands where the dealer would stand.

These figures apply, we stress again, *only* when the player uses the right strategy all the way down the line. A mediocre strategy might recoup only 2½ percent out of this 4½ percent, leaving the dealer with a net 2 percent advantage. A poor strategy might recover only ½ percent, resulting in a 4 percent margin for the dealer. In fact, it is even possible to do worse than the apparent limit of 4½ percent, for the preceding illustrations represent various "sins of omission," so to speak, wherein the player fails to do the proper different thing from what the dealer would do with the same hand. But "sins of commission" are possible, too, when the player should do the same thing as the dealer would do but does otherwise. For example, in basic blackjack, it does not pay to split 10s, since 10-10 is such an excellent two-card hand to begin with. If you make the mistake of splitting, you add still more to the dealer's margin. Thus, it is possible to play the game with an edge of 5 or even 6 percent against you (and there are undoubtedly many incompetent players who support the casinos with such witless play). To do worse than this, however, would probably require some sort of unfortunate genius for doing all the wrong things!

Normal Hit or Stand Strategy

The proper strategy for basic blackjack is shown in chart form in Fig. 5-1. It is easy to commit to memory because many of the de-

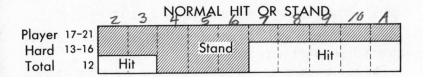

NORMAL HIT OR STAND

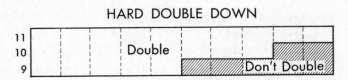

HARD DOUBLE DOWN

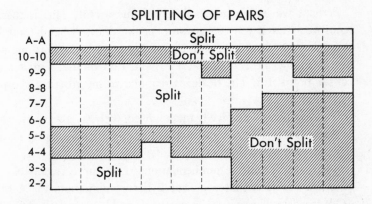

SPLITTING OF PAIRS

SOFT HANDS

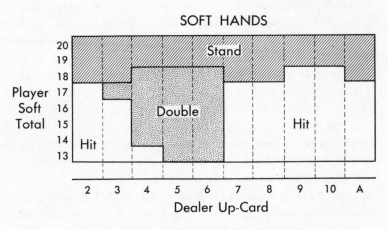

Fig. 5-1. Proper Strategy for Basic Blackjack

cisions fall logically into little groups. To help the reader learn it, the strategy is presented in sections.

The first section is the most important one. It covers the *normal hit or stand* strategy. The rule is ultrasimple. When the dealer shows a "good" card (that is, 7, 8, 9, 10, or ace), hit a stiff (defined in the next paragraph). When the dealer shows a "poor" card (that is, 2, 3, 4, 5, or 6), stand on a stiff. (There is one small exception to this rule, namely, to hit 12 once if the dealer shows a 2 or 3.) This knowledge of what to do with a stiff is the most important single part of correct strategy. If you play this right, you are already well on the road to a good game of blackjack.

Perhaps we had better explicitly define a *stiff*. This is merely a hand with which you can go bust on the draw. A hand totaling 12 through 16 is therefore a stiff, the presumption being that one would not ordinarily hit 17 or higher. A hand that totals 11 or less is, of course, not a stiff. The dealer is required to hit all stiffs; the player can do as he likes.

Those persons who give blanket advice, such as "always hit a stiff," or "never hit a stiff," are distinctly in error. The proper play on a stiff depends very much on what the dealer's up-card is.

Qualitatively, our recommendations seem quite reasonable. Suppose, for example, that you have a 10-6 combination, for a total of 16. If the dealer has a 7 showing, you should hit your stiff. The reason is that the dealer is so likely to have you beaten on his two cards, or so likely to beat you if he has to draw, that you cannot afford to stand on your 16. It is true that you are very likely to bust if you do this, but nonetheless you must take that risk. A total of 16 is the worst possible total to draw to, but it turns out that you will lose 10¢ less on the dollar if you hit it than if you stand. The expectation is a 48.3¢ loss if you stand, but a loss of only 37.7¢ if you hit.

In the preceding paragraph, we have given a "plausibility argument" for the proper course of action, but in the final analysis, the only truly convincing argument is the mathematical comparison of outcomes of the different courses of action. This is why actual values are cited to back it up. In closer cases, you cannot depend on intuition. Such an instance is 10-6 versus 10, where you lose 3.6¢ less on the dollar if you hit rather than stand. On the other hand, consider 10-4-2 versus 10 (you have hit 10-4 and drawn a 2). Although the player total is also 16 here, it turns out that you should stand on this hand. Surprise, surprise! You win 0.7¢ more on the dollar. (This may seem weird, but stop and think about the effect of trading that 6 in your hand for a 4 and a 2. You are putting back into the deck a card that will bust you and removing two cards that would help you.)

All this goes to show that the case of 16 versus 10 is a rather close one. At this point, the mind of any sharp reader will be racing ahead to similar situations. What about 5-5-6 versus 10, you may ask, or 5-4-4-3 versus 10? Or to look at another marginal situation, just how much does 8-4 versus 3 differ from 10-2 versus 3? Obviously, we are now discussing some pretty fine points. It is one thing to remember the major rules and another to know the minor variations in the borderline cases. My advice to the beginner is to stick to the basic strategy. It hurts you only slightly to err in the borderline cases. (See footnote on page 119 for additional information.)

In this chapter, we are dealing with the basic strategy. This strategy for the basic game is correct *on the average*. It applies specifically to the first deal out of a fresh 52-card deck, or in general, to the play on *any* round where previous cards have not been tallied. In the latter case, you may just as well be dealing out of a fresh deck, for it averages out that way. This is an important concept to grasp because it simplifies analysis of the game.

Hard Double-down Strategy

The second section of the strategy is the *hard double-down* strategy. Here we are talking about hands that do not contain any aces. Figure 5-1 shows that you should (a) always double on a total of 11, (b) double on a total of 10 unless the dealer's up-card is an ace or 10, and (c) double on a total of 9 unless the dealer shows 7 or higher. Needless to say, 11 is the best total on which to double, and therefore it is recommended unreservedly. The edge in favor of doubling gets successively smaller for 10 and for 9, so there are more exceptions for these. A double on 8 versus 5 or 6 generally gives a slight advantage, but there is no normal situation calling for a double on 7 or lower.

The reason it is so advantageous to be allowed to double bet size in these indicated situations is quite elementary. You stand a good chance of drawing to a high total with the one card you are allowed, and therefore you would not ordinarily want any more cards anyway. In a majority of cases, you will beat the dealer, and hence you will win more money when you double the bet. Of course you must balance against this the chance that you will draw a low card and lose on such a draw except when the dealer goes bust.

An excellent double-down setup is 11 versus 6. Since the dealer shows a poor card, you would not draw more than once in any event. The probabilities are roughly 0.61 to win, 0.08 to tie, and 0.31 to lose. The expectation is roughly $0.61 - 0.31 = +0.30$, or a net profit of 30¢ per $1.00 bet. When you double the bet size to $2.00, the profit is simply twice as great. Therefore, anyone who fails to double-down in this situation sacrifices about 30¢ in extra profit margin!

Splitting of Pairs Strategy

The third section of Fig. 5-1 shows the *splitting of pairs* strategy. Favorable pair-splitting situations arise about 2 percent of the time. This is about one-fourth as frequently as the double-downs. It also turns out that the additional profit margin for all correct splits is about one-fourth the additional total for all proper double-downs. On the average, then, the individual split situations offer an improvement comparable to that of the double-downs. So, to be consistent, you should pay as much attention to proper splitting as to proper doubling-down.

In splitting, the essential idea is that you are trading a poor starting situation for two better ones, and increasing your bet at the same time. A case in point is 8-8 versus 7. If the player hand is regarded as a straight 16, the dealer has the player over a barrel. You have to hit, but you come off badly. The probabilities are roughly 0.27 to win, 0.06 to tie, and 0.67 to lose, for a net loss of $67 - 27$ or 40¢ on the dollar. (The case is similar to 10-6 versus 7, mentioned on page 50.) However, it is a far different story if you split the pair and try two new hands, each with a starting value of 8. You now actually stand to beat the dealer, with an expected net win of 10¢ on each hand, or 20¢ over-all. By splitting, you have converted a 40¢ loss to a 20¢ win, for a net improvement of 60¢ on the original dollar bet! What more need be said?

(We have assumed that if you draw 2 or 3 to your 8, you may then double-down on this new total of 10 or 11. But even if this is not allowed, there is still a very wide margin in favor of splitting.)

The example just cited is one of the most dramatic splits available. A big loss is converted to a significant win. More generally, you succeed only in reducing the extent of a loss. This is illustrated with 8-8 versus 10. Here you have an expected net loss of around 50¢ if you simply hit the 16. If you split, you get an expected net loss of about 20¢ per hand, or 40¢ total. Thus, you have reduced the expected loss by 10¢. This is a much smaller change, but still it is very worth while.

The chart shows that you should split a pair of 8s under all circumstances. The opportunity to trade the total of 16 for two hands starting from 8 is definitely favorable for all values of the dealer up-card. The 8-8 split is a good deal for the player.

Another attractive split is the ace pair. Here you exchange an initial 2 (or 12) for two hands of 11 each (since only one card may be drawn to each ace in this split, you would always count this starting value as 11 rather than 1). It is almost as though you have two chances to double-down on 11. The difference lies in the choice of alternative if you elect not to split. Here you would be starting from 2 (or 12). With a hard two-card total of 11, if you elected not to double-down, you would be starting from 11, but with no restriction to draw only one card.

On each split ace there is around 30 percent chance of drawing a 10 and thereby holding an unbeatable total of 21. This lure makes the splitting of ace pairs very popular, and rightly so. This split is favorable for all values of the dealer up-card and should be taken without hesitation.

Other pairs should be split only against certain values of the dealer up-card, or else not at all. Be guided by the table.

Soft-Hands Strategy

The final section in Fig. 5-1 is the *soft-hands* strategy. In principle, this could be included as part of previous strategies, but for convenience, it is treated separately because of the dual-valued nature of the ace. The main question is when to hit and when to stand pat on a soft hand. Also, for players in Las Vegas, where you are allowed to double-down on any two cards, there is the question of when to exercise that option.

Basically, you should never settle for a soft total lower than 18. You should hit a soft hand until you have at least soft 18, or until you have attained a hard total of at least 12 (whereupon you would revert to normal hitting strategy). For example, suppose you have ace-2 versus 8. Your hand is a soft 13, since it may be counted as either 13 or 3. If you draw ace through 4, you get soft 14 through soft 17, respectively. According to our rule, you must keep on hitting. If you draw 5 through 8, you have cards that total 18 through 21, respectively. Any of these totals is acceptable. If you draw 9 or 10, your combination is a hard 12 or 13. You should then revert to normal strategy for handling a stiff, which in this case would call for continuing to hit against 8 until your hand totaled 17 or better.

If the dealer shows a real high card (namely 9, 10, or ace), you must be one step more aggressive. You must shoot for soft 19. If you overshoot on the draw, so that it becomes necessary to count your ace as 1 rather than 11, then again you must go back to standard hitting strategy for your stiff.

In Las Vegas, the option of doubling-down on any first two cards gives rise to certain favorable soft double-downs. Consider for example ace-4 versus 6. The merit of doubling-down in this case rests on a combination of two factors. First, there is a respectable chance of drawing a card like 6, 5, or 4, which would produce a total difficult for the dealer to compete against. Secondly, even if the draw card does not improve matters at all, there is still a good likelihood that the dealer will break. Between these two factors, the odds work out in favor of the double-down.

From the chart, you can see that soft double-downs are taken only when the dealer shows a rather poor card and when your own hand is not already a likely winner. Specifically, you do not double-down on soft 19 or 20.

Summary on Strategy

Soft hands come up about 10 percent of the time, so it is good to have a general idea what to do with them. But it must be admitted that memorizing all the little details of handling soft hands can be somewhat tedious, because each individual combination of player-dealer cards may arise only once in several hundred hands. (In all candor, I must admit that sometimes I have to look them up on my flash cards!) But do not be discouraged if you cannot remember every one of the soft-hand rules. Many of them do not involve large margins. Your game will not be a failure if you slip up on a couple of these. The important thing is to concentrate on other aspects of the basic strategy. The normal hitting strategy is a cinch, so you should focus your attention mainly on the hard double-downs and the pair splits. After these have been mastered, you can round out the picture with the soft-hand strategy.

Previously, we asserted that by following our basic strategy, you can gain back 4½ percent, thereby canceling the −4½ percent you can expect when copying the dealer's rules for drawing. This is a fantastically handsome return for the small effort required to learn the preceding chart. It may be too much to memorize all in one sitting, but with a little practice, it falls easily into line.

The Assumed Conditions of Play

We should state explicitly the assumed conditions of play under which the basic strategy applies. (1) The dealer must draw until he has a total of 17 or better. The dealer is assumed to stand on soft 17, or any higher soft hand. (2) After splitting any pair (except aces), you may double-down on two-card combinations formed in the new separate hands. (3) You may not split again if you draw a third card of the same value as the pair cards. (4) "Insurance" betting is not taken into consideration. However, it will be discussed later in the chapter. (5) The number of players may be any number from one to six (full table). It is assumed that the player looks only at his own cards and the dealer's up-card. He does not look at his neighbor's cards, nor does he remember cards from any previous round of play. (These restrictions will be lifted in subsequent chapters. But here we are concerned with the "basic" game, wherein each hand may as well be considered as dealt out of a fresh deck.)

The above five points, plus the review of rules at the beginning of the chapter, should serve to define the game completely. Since Las Vegas does more business than Reno, we are assuming Las Vegas rules on the double-down. But, on such minor variations as these, we should emphasize that it does not make a great deal of difference (one or two tenths of a percent). Restrictions on one account may be compensated by liberality on another. For details about this, the reader is referred to Baldwin's book or to Thorp's book, discussed in Chapters 6 and 9.

BASIC BLACKJACK IS AN EVEN GAME

The basic strategy enables you to break even at blackjack on a flat bet. To the best of my knowledge, taking all work that I know of into account, the player's effective probability to win is 0.5005 ± 0.0005, the $(\pm)$ uncertainty indicating that it is extremely difficult to pin the figure down exactly. There are millions of possible card combinations at blackjack, and only an electronic computer can cope with the chore. Even at that, there is a limit to the practicality of what can be done on a computer, although I do not doubt that some future perfectionist will do an exact computation. For our purposes, that is not necessary. To know the value of the basic game within 0.1 percent is close enough to perfect, for three very good reasons. (1) It is extremely unlikely that anyone will play enough hands *in his entire life* for it to make one iota of difference. Fluctuations would mask such a small increment until millions of hands had been played. (2) Variations in the rules from one casino to another produce differences of this order. (3) By the methods of Chapter 7, you can add another 0.5 or 1 percent, or more, to the value of your game; therefore, it is sufficient to know that the value of the basic game is within 0.1 percent of an even game, for this insures that the additional techniques do actually make it possible to play the game with a positive edge.

INSURANCE IS USUALLY A BAD BET

This chapter has now covered practically all essential points of the basic game. There remain a few odds and ends, with which we shall wind up the chapter. One of these is the matter of the *insurance* bet, which on page 55 we promised would be handled later in the chapter. At many casinos, especially in Las Vegas, the dealer will invite you to take an additional bet when his up-card is an ace. You may place an additional wager, equal to half the amount already bet, which will pay you 2:1 if the dealer's down-card is a 10-value card, and which you will lose if it is not. In this optional bet, you are thus "insuring" your hand against the possibility of loss to a dealer black-jack. Most of the time, this innocent-sounding proposition is just a "sucker" bet. In order for insurance to be a profitable bet, more than one-third of the unseen cards must be 10-value cards. This is not very often the case, so let's take a look at the odds that usually apply.

Suppose you do not look at your own cards, nor do you see any of the other players' cards, prior to deciding whether to accept the insurance bet. Then the dealer's down-card may be considered as drawn at random from the 51 cards that remain unseen. Clearly, 16 of these cards are 10s, and the other 35 are non-10s. The odds are 35:16 against the dealer having a 10 in the hole. The payoff is only 32:16 (same as 2:1). Obviously, this is a bad proposition. Per unit insurance bet, the expectation is $(+2)(16/51) + (-1)(35/51) = -3/51$. As a percent, this is approximately -6 percent. A pretty high premium to pay for insurance!

Even if you look at your two cards before deciding whether to bet, and find that they are both non-10s, the expectation is still $(+2)(16/49) + (-1)(33/49) = -1/49$, or about -2 percent. Considering how simple it is to figure that the odds are usually higher than 32:16 against winning the insurance bet, it is amazing that so many people blindly take it.

Unfortunately, the decisions of many players to insure are made on a very emotional, unscientific basis. Some players insure a strong hand on the grounds that they want to be sure of a win. Others say that insuring a weak hand is analogous to placing health insurance on a sickly person. Countless unfounded notions are heard when the dealer invites insurance. Confusion reigns supreme when the player himself has a blackjack. Actually, *all* insurance decisions can and should be based on the simple cold logic of whether more than one-third of the unseen cards are 10-value cards.

Don't Insure a Blackjack

If you hold a blackjack yourself, and have knowledge of no other cards, insurance is a *very bad* bet. Do not take it. The odds are 34:15 against you for a payoff of only 30:15 (same as 2:1). Your expectation is figured easily as $-4/49$, or about -8 percent. You are giving the house a big, fat 8 percent when you insure a blackjack!

Some dealers persistently taunt you into insuring your blackjack, with the deceptive argument that, "This is the one situation in the game where you *must* win." This statement should be amended to say, "You must win *less*, on the average, if you take insurance." The crux of the matter is that the insurance bet is *completely independent* of the bet you made originally. It is a separate side bet. Whether or not you take insurance has *absolutely no effect* on the way you will be paid on your blackjack. If the dealer does not have a blackjack, you will be paid 1½:1; if he does have a blackjack, you will draw.

Let's examine that statement, "you must win." Assume the basic bet is 1 unit; then the insurance is ½ unit. There are two alternatives: (1) You take insurance; (2) you do not take insurance. Consider (1) first. If the dealer has blackjack, you draw on your own blackjack, and win 1 unit on the insurance bet. If the dealer does not have blackjack, you win 1½ unit on your blackjack, but lose your ½ unit of insurance. In either case, your profit is 1 unit.

Consider (2) next. It is plain to see that 15/49 of the time (less than ⅓), the dealer has blackjack and you draw; your gain is zero. But 34/49 of the time (more than ⅔), the dealer does not have it, and your gain is 1½. If more than ⅔ of the time you gain 1½ unit, and for the balance of the time you draw, then your average gain is *more than 1 unit.* It is in fact $1\frac{2}{49}$ unit. Clearly, it is better not to accept insurance.

If any dealer tries to pooh-pooh this correct reason why you should not insure a blackjack, just ask him how it makes sense to accept 15:34 odds on a proposition that pays only 30:15.

Occasionally Insurance Is a Good Bet

As pointed out previously, there *can* occur situations where the insurance *is* a favorable bet. More than one-third of the remaining unseen cards must be 10-value cards. Suppose, for example, that you inspect your own hand, and you can also see the hand of a friend sitting next to you. If neither of you holds any 10s, then your expectation is $(+2)(16/47) + (-1)(31/47) = +1/47$, or approximately +2 percent. Clearly, you should take insurance here. Unfortunately, this situation does not set up very frequently. Only about 20 percent of the time will there be no 10s among the four cards contained in your hand and your neighbor's, and thus sixteen 10s among the remaining 47 cards.

If you keep track of *all* the 10s and non-10s as the deck is dealt, you can occasionally catch situations in which the percentage is much better than the +2 percent just illustrated. Indeed, near the end of the deck, if all the unseen cards were known to be 10s, insurance would be a positive gift, a sure thing. You would inevitably win, thereby collecting 200 percent on your insurance investment. Regrettably, the occurrence of such an opportunity is extremely rare.

Since insurance is an optional bet, since it is offered only at certain casinos in Nevada, and since it is usually a bad bet, it really deserves only passing mention in this present chapter on the basic game. But we shall have much more to say about it, beginning on page 126 in Chapter 7, which treats in more detail the advantages of tracking the cards as they are dealt out.

MULTIDECK BLACKJACK

All remarks so far in this chapter have been directed to the game played with a single deck of cards. Some casinos offer interesting variations of this theme, in which two or more decks are used. No discussion of the basic game would be complete without a coverage of these occasional variations.

In the double-deck (or two-deck) game, it is common for all cards to be dealt face up, except for the dealer's hole card. This game has two very strong appeals. (1) The player has the advantage of seeing a lot of cards in making his decision to stand or to draw. (2) It would appear to be much harder for the dealer to cheat.

When more than two decks are employed, the cards are generally dealt face down from a *shoe*, or box. The reason for using such a container is simply that two decks are about the limit of what a dealer can conveniently hold in his hand. The number of decks varies, but may be as many as four or six. In principle, there is no reason why the cards could not be dealt face up in the multideck game, but to my knowledge, they are usually dealt face down. One reason for this perhaps is that the top card at the sloping front of the shoe is face down, and as the card is slid out of the shoe on the deal, it is more natural to keep it face down.

The patent reason for the house to use more than one deck is to smooth out the fluctuations that occur in the fall of the cards and to decrease the proportion of *end deck* situations; by suppressing these effects, the advantages of "counting the cards" may be reduced. This statement will be more meaningful after you have read Chapters 7 and 8, but the general idea is obvious. There is no doubt but that much of the purpose is achieved. It is my belief that a good player is better off in a single-deck game with cards dealt face down than he is in a double-deck game with cards dealt face up, when all practical considerations are taken into account.

But we are getting a little ahead of ourselves to be talking about the effects of keeping track of the cards, and should confine our attention at this point to the basic game as played with some multiple of 52 cards rather than with a single pack of 52 cards. Again let us emphasize a concept. When you do not keep track of the cards, then each hand may as well be regarded as dealt out of a fresh deck, for it averages out that way. Therefore, the all-important question in this section on the multideck game is this: How does your expectation for the deal from a 104-card deck (or a 156-card deck, etc.) compare with the deal from a 52-card deck?

It turns out that the greater the number of decks, the worse off you are. In the single-deck game, we have seen that you just break even. But in the double- and multideck games, there is a perceptible edge against you, ranging up to several tenths of a percent. This may be inferred from the comparison between the correct result for the single-deck game and the Baldwin result (see page 92). Baldwin's approximation of "sampling with replacement" can be interpreted as tending to make the 52-card deck appear to contain more low cards than it actually does. Expressed in other words, sampling with replacement implies that cards are drawn from an "infinite" deck in which non-10-value cards truly have a fixed 1/13 chance of occurrence, and 10-value cards have 4/13 chance. By contrast, in the "finite" deck analysis with a single deck of cards, these probabilities change markedly as cards are drawn. The first card of a given non-10 denomination does have $4/52 = 1/13$ chance of being drawn. But the next card of this same denomination is reduced to $3/51 = 1/17$, then $2/50 = 1/25$, and finally, $1/49$ for the fourth card.

Clearly, the chance of the appearance of four cards of one denomination in a hand from a single deck is significantly less than the appearance of four such cards from a whole stack of decks, where the probability is essentially 1/13 for the subsequent cards as well as the first one. In fact, we can go even further in stressing the difference between the single deck and the "infinite" deck. With a single deck, it is impossible to draw more than four cards of a given non-10 value. With an infinite deck, any number may in principle be drawn.

When the single-deck game is analyzed by infinite deck reasoning, an error definitely creeps in. Suffice to say here that the error is almost ½ percent. Alternatively, one can say that Baldwin's value of −0.3 percent more nearly applies to the infinite deck game than to the single deck.

The somewhat abstract line of reasoning just presented may be backed up with various obvious qualitative examples. (1) Double-downs are usually very favorable bets, especially with a two-card 11, in either the single- or multideck game. But the advantage is ever so slightly lower in the latter case because the proportion of remaining cards which are 10s is slightly lower. (2) The chance of getting a blackjack is slightly lower in the multideck games. On page 47 we showed that in the single-deck case, the chance of an untied black-jack is 4.65 percent. A similar type of calculation for the double deck yields only 4.58 percent, and the limiting case of an infinite deck works out to 4.51 percent. Other similar arguments may be found. While there may also be a few on the credit side, the balance sheet will show a deficit for the multi-deck as compared to the single-deck game.

Attention should also be drawn to the fact that opportunities to make intelligent insurance bets occur less frequently in the multi-deck games. This is simply because the proportion of remaining unseen cards does not so often exceed one-third. The dealing of the current round of cards face up in the double-deck game is of some assistance in this respect, but not as much as one might guess. Maximum benefits for intelligent insurance betting are reaped only if you also remember excesses in the 10 to non-10 ratio for the preceding hands. This being the case, you are better off acquiring this information in single-deck play. The skeptical reader is advised to look ahead to the section on insurance in Chapter 7 and make comparable estimates for the double-deck or other multideck games.

REASONS WHY THE SINGLE DECK IS PREFERRED

At the present writing, the double- and multidecks are relatively infrequent in the Nevada casinos. The great majority of players prefer the single-deck game. At least three reasons are apparent. (1) When the cards are dealt face down, there is a greater element of surprise. (2) When the cards are dealt face up, the player is often not even allowed to touch his cards. This reduces the player participation and makes the game much duller. (3) Some players do not want the dealer to see the player's cards, on the grounds that there is a greater risk of dirty work. To my mind, if the player is *that* suspicious, he had better stop playing the game for his own peace of mind.

Whatever the reasons for the lesser popularity of the double- and multideck games, I cannot say that I am sorry. The odds are better on the single-deck game, and we should all do our best to encourage the casinos to keep plenty of single-deck tables open.

Confirming the Odds— with Casino Play and with Electronic Computers

6

The purpose of this chapter is to show that basic blackjack is essentially an even game. The evidence is overwhelming. I describe my own researches first, and then the work of others. My own work is divided into three areas.

Since the results of 25,000 hands of actual card play would probably be more convincing to the average reader than ten or even a hundred times that number played on a computer, I shall first show my experimental results for 25,000 hands. Then I shall show some of the sample computations that led to my knowledge of how to play those 25,000 hands properly. Finally, I shall describe how I simulated the play of hundreds of thousands of hands on an electronic digital computer. With this three-pronged attack, a complete understanding of the basic game is guaranteed!

25,000 HANDS OF BLACKJACK

The intriguing chart in Fig. 6-1 shows the outcome of my 25,000 hands at flat bets. This record spans a period of time from 1954 to 1957 (after which I considered myself to have mastered the basic game, and shifted my emphasis to variable-bet play). The solid lines indicate around 10,000 hands of actual casino play, and the dotted lines show tests totaling 15,000 hands conducted at home. Fluctuations are definitely in evidence. Note that most of the positive surges occurred in the casino, while the downward swings happened at home. Nobody can accuse me of having my good luck at home and my bad luck in the casino!

At the end of the 25,000 trials, I was 110 units to the good. This is about $1/250 = 0.004$, or $+0.4$ percent. Another way to look at it is to say that I effectively averaged 0.502 win versus 0.498 loss.

The experimental value of 0.502 effective probability of winning, for this sample of 25,000 hands, was most encouraging. However, it was not taken at full face value because of the possible effect of fluctuations. Instead, a standard statistical technique was used to bracket reasonable bounds for the true expectation.

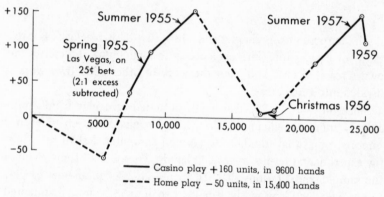

FIG. 6-1. Record of 25,000 Hands of Blackjack at Flat Bets

For a game in which p and q are close to 0.5, as in blackjack, the *relative* standard deviation in N trials is $\sqrt{N}/2$ divided by N, or $1/(2\sqrt{N})$ (see page 227). For $N = 25,000$, this comes to about $1/320$, or 0.003. Looking at Fig. 15-2 on page 226, we see that there is 68 percent chance that the true probability lies between $0.502 + 0.003$ and $0.502 - 0.003$, that is, between 0.505 and 0.499. The same graph indicates that there is a 95 percent chance that it lies between 0.508 and 0.496.

At the end of 5000 hands, I was down 70 units, and extremely discouraged about the possibilities of beating the game of blackjack at all. To emphasize how hopeless the situation seemed, observe that the excess of losses over wins at this point corresponded exactly to the accepted edge of the pass-line bet at craps, namely, -1.4 percent.

Thus, at the end of 5000 hands (no small sample), it appeared that blackjack was no better than the dice game in which the house is known to hold a decisive edge.

Fortunately the 70-unit loss was on paper. My drooping hopes were buoyed by the fact that my former roulette partner had had a few successful short trips to Reno. Eventually that initial surge into the red was more than compensated by swings into the black, and my persistence bore fruit. Besides, there were other theoretical considerations that tended to corroborate a value around 0.500, and on the grounds of which I was willing to reject as pessimistically low the numbers in the neighborhood of 0.496.

UPS-AND-DOWNS

The beginning blackjack player would do well to try to learn from Fig. 6-1 what ghastly ups-and-downs may be in store for him. The record is a telling illustration of the extent of fluctuations to be expected when you play for a long time. Of my total sample, 5000 hands was just a fraction; yet, playing 10 hours per day at a nominally busy blackjack table, one hand at a time, it would take you five days to gather such a total! It takes great faith in the long run to accept the possibility of a five-day losing streak and to keep on playing. But this sort of streak can and does happen!

It is most important to describe how and under what conditions this huge sample of 25,000 hands was played. My first stint of actual casino play was in downtown Las Vegas in the spring of 1955. (I had just completed writing my doctoral thesis and had mailed it off to my research advisor in Berkeley, so my wife and I decided to take a short spree in Las Vegas!) In those days, they used to pay 2:1 on a blackjack on a 25¢ bet. This was the table minimum, and if you bet more, you were paid at the usual 3:2 on blackjack. I played 1700 hands at the minimum 25¢ bet, and it seemed just like shooting fish in a barrel. I won more than $20. The solid line on the chart in Fig. 6-1 shows the number of "units" I would have won if my bet size had been larger, with the standard 3:2 payoff; thus the excess 2.3 percent by which the 2:1 game is better than the 3:2 game has been subtracted out.

The next play was in the summer of the same year while driving across the country and back. Going east, we hit Reno, Winnemucca, Elko, and Wells. On the westbound leg, we had a rendezvous in Reno. The point is that the 3500 hands played during that summer were dealt at a lot of different clubs, and hence were subject to some of the variations in casino rules then prevalent in northern Nevada. All bets were a dollar or more, at the usual 3:2 payoff on blackjack. Although the bet level was increased toward the end of the trip, owing to rising optimism, bets at any one sitting were at one fixed level. Hence all records were kept in terms of a one-unit bet. Any profits from the $5.00 bonus on ace-jack of spades were ignored in the record.

The next major casino play was two summers later in Las Vegas. There I won $70, using a flat $1.00 bet for 3500 hands. These games were racked up at numerous casinos up and down the "strip," plus occasional forays to the downtown places.

Most of my casino data for flat-bet play were obtained during the foregoing three episodes. In the home play, which finally tallied up to around 15,000 hands, I dealt to myself. The outcome of each individual hand was entered on a running graph, similar to that in Fig. 6-1, but with much more detail recorded. The result of each hand—win, push, or loss—was recorded as a separate point. All blackjacks, splits, and double-downs were indicated, so that they stood out from ordinary hands. The home record was therefore much more precise than the casino record. (It is doubtful that casino blackjack dealers would look favorably on data-taking at the table.) In the home sampling, I usually dealt through the complete deck, thereby getting around eight to ten hands per deck.

The reader must not think it is mere vanity that impels me to spend so long discussing my own experiences. Many, many weeks of effort went into this sample, and it is helpful to describe how the experiment was performed, and tell what conclusions should be drawn. In reading this book, you can learn from my experience what you do not have the time or opportunity to investigate for yourself. Many readers will have a sufficient background in statistical methods and in playing experience to ask incisive questions; it is only reasonable to make this presentation as explicit as possible. To announce pontifically in one sentence that the result of 25,000 hands shows such-and-such, without further explanations, would not be very scientific, nor would it be very convincing to a discriminating reader.

HOW I LEARNED THE RIGHT BASIC STRATEGY

Our next topic calls for some backtracking, for how did I know the right strategy to use in playing those 25,000 hands? The answer, of course, is that considerable analysis had been done before I put my first dollar down on blackjack. As a scientist, I did not intend to risk much in this game without at least being sure I could break even. And, incidentally, to give credit where credit is due, I should say that much of the original interest in attacking blackjack was inspired by my former roulette partner. However, with his return to the Venezuelan oil fields, plus the realization that a team effort was not needed, I was soon completely on my own by the mid-1950s.

The Simple Empirical Way to Determine Correct Strategy

In the early days, we depended very much on empirical methods for figuring out the proper strategy in a given situation. We simply dealt cards to ourselves, according to the various available alternatives, and observed which came out better after a modest sample. For example, one of the first cases investigated was that of 10-6 versus 7. We simply removed a 10, 6, and 7 from a deck of cards. Then a card was drawn at random and assigned the role of dealer's down-card.

The first alternative to test was that of standing on the 10-6. In this instance, we merely completed the dealer's hand by additional random draw (except when the down-card was ace or 10, in which case the dealer already had a satisfactory total). If the dealer went bust, it was recorded as a player win. If the dealer obtained a total from 17 to 21, it was listed as a player loss. Upon completion of the hand, all cards that had been drawn at random, including the down-card, were returned to the deck. It was then shuffled, and the process was repeated.

In the testing of the second alternative, namely, hitting 10-6 against 7, the procedure was altered as follows: The down-card was drawn the same as before. Then a player hit card was drawn. If the player went bust, the hand was immediately recorded as a player loss. If he did not bust, then the dealer's hand was completed, and a comparison between the two hands was made (unless the dealer went bust, in which case it was an outright player win). The final outcome was thus appropriately recorded as a win, tie, or loss. Then all the randomly drawn cards were returned to the deck for a shuffle and another deal. In one test, with 196 hands, the score was 53 wins and 143 losses on standing, and 59 wins, 16 ties, and 121 losses on hitting. The win minus loss value is clearly much less negative in the latter case, and hence proper strategy is to hit.

Any such empirical testing method is subject to fluctuations. The closer the decision, the more hands you should play before drawing conclusions. An appropriate number of hands for each alternative may range from 100 to 500. (If much more than 500 seem to be necessary to resolve the issue, it is probably such a close case that it really is not essential to know which is the better course of action.) There are around 50 different situations in blackjack which have to be checked out, when all the double-downs and splits are added in with the ordinary hit or stand affairs. With two alternatives in each case, and 100 to 500 hands to be played, the grand product winds up to between 10,000 and 50,000 hands. It is small wonder that information on the proper strategy at blackjack has been so slow to appear. A systematic attack requires a tremendous effort, even with all the best short cuts you can devise.

There is one type of short cut that is dear to my heart. I call it *normalization*. The purpose is to smooth out the effect of fluctuations when conducting empirical tests, and hence to reduce the number of hands that have to be played. In effect, true probabilities are assigned to the draw of some of the cards, and the remaining cards are drawn at random. It may also be appropriately referred to as a *semistatistical* method.

To illustrate, suppose you are planning to test 10-6 versus 7 by playing around 200 hands. Then the thing to do is to pick the nearest multiple of 49, which is 196. This enables you to cycle the dealer's down-card through each of the possible 49 values it might have (three cards have already been removed from the original deck, so the down-card is, in principle, drawn from the remaining 49). This removes the effect of random fluctuations in the assignment of the down-card. Even though the remaining cards are drawn at random, it will be found that results from sample to sample are more consistent this way. Alternatively, for the same percentage of error in the result, fewer hands need be played when the fourth card is cycled this way, as compared to its being drawn strictly at random.

Of course the next logical step would be to cycle the fifth card through its 48 possible values. However, each of these would have to be associated with each of the 49 values for the fourth card, giving $49 \times 48 = 2352$ possible combinations. This would be a prohibitive number unless you could simulate it on an electronic computer, and even then, you would still have to allow further for the draw of the sixth, seventh, etc., card, when necessary.

This normalization technique was used frequently to reduce the number of hands that had to be played to test various strategy decisions. But occasionally it was found desirable to check the empirical results with an exact probability calculation. All such calculations are straightforward in method, but actual detail of the work can be quite time consuming. It depends on the number of cards that may need to be drawn in order to fill out the hand. The various levels of complexity are nicely illustrated in a few examples.

SAMPLE COMPUTATIONS

The tabulations in Table 6-1 show the odds in the cases where the player holding 10-6 stands when the dealer has 7-9, 7-8, and 7-7, respectively, and also where the player hits his 10-6 when the dealer has 7-8. The dealer's up-card is taken to be 7, but the player is assumed to have no knowledge of the other card in advance.

The basic scheme is to lay out all the possibilities that can arise in drawing cards to complete the hand. Since 4 of the 52 cards are already assigned, the first card is drawn from the remaining 48. If additional cards are needed, the second is taken from the remaining 47, the next from 46, etc. For each case, the possible sequences of

TABLE 6-1. FIGURING THE ODDS IN VARIOUS PLAYER-DEALER SITUATIONS

1. Player stands on 10-6 versus 7-9 : only one card must be drawn:

	Card Drawn	Number of Combinations	Probabilities
Win	6,7,8,9,10	$3 + 3 + 4 + 3 + 15 = 28$	0.583
Lose	A,2,3,4,5	$4 + 4 + 4 + 4 + 4 = 20$	0.417
	Total possible combinations	$= 48$	1.000

2. Player stands on 10-6 versus 7-8 : at most two cards must be drawn:

Win

Cards Drawn	Number of Combinations
7-10	$(3 + 3 + 4 + 15)47 = 25 \cdot 47 = 1175$
A ; 6-10	$4(3 + 3 + 3 + 4 + 15) = 4 \cdot 28 = 112$
	1287 total wins

Lose

Cards Drawn	Number of Combinations
2-6	$(4 + 4 + 4 + 4 + 3)47 = 19 \cdot 47 = 893$
A ; A-5	$4(3 + 4 + 4 + 4 + 4) = 4 \cdot 19 = 76$
	969 total losses

	Combinations	Probabilities
Win	1287	0.570
Lose	969	0.430
$48 \times 47 = $	2256	1.000
(Possible combinations)		

3. Player stands on 10-6 versus 7-7 : at most three cards must be drawn:

Win

Cards Drawn	Number of Combinations
8-10	$(4 + 4 + 15)(47)(46) = 23 \cdot 2162 = 49,726$
A ; 7-10	$4(\quad 2 + 4 + 4 + 15)(46) = 100 \cdot 46$
2 ; 6-10	$4(3 + 2 + 4 + 4 + 15)(46) = 112 \cdot 46$
	$212 \cdot 46 = 9,752$
A ; A ; 6-10	$4(3)(3 + 2 + 4 + 4 + 15) = 12 \cdot 28 = 336$
Total wins	59,814

TABLE 6-1. FIGURING THE ODDS IN VARIOUS PLAYER-DEALER
SITUATIONS (*Cont.*)

Lose

3-7	$(4 + 4 + 4 + 3 + 2)(47)(46) =$	$17 \cdot 2162 = 36,754$	
A : 2-6	$4(4 + 4 + 4 + 4 + 3)(46) =$	$76 \cdot 46$	
2 : A-5	$4(4 + 3 + 4 + 4 + 4)(46) =$	$76 \cdot 46$	
		$152 \cdot 46 \quad = \quad 6,992$	
A : A : A-5	$4(3)(2 + 4 + 4 + 4 + 4) =$	$12 \cdot 18 \quad = \quad 216$	
Total losses		$43,962$	

	Combinations	Probabilities
Win	59,814	0.577
Lose	43,962	0.423
$48 \times 47 \times 46 = 103,776$ (Possible combinations)		1.000

---

4. Player draws on 10-6 versus 7-8 : at most three cards must be drawn:

	Cards Drawn	Number of Combinations	
Win			
	A : 7-10	$4(\qquad 25)(46) =$	$100 \cdot 46$
	2 : 2, 7-10	$4(3 + 25)$	112
	3 : 2,3, 7-10	$4(7 + 25)$	128
	4 : 2-4, 7-10	$4(11 + 25)$	144
	5 : 2-5, 7-10	$4(15 + 25)$	160
			$644 \cdot 46 = 29,624$
	A : A ; 6-10	$4(3)(28)$	$= 336$
	2 : A ; A, 6-10	$4(4)(31)$	496
	3 : A ; A,2, 6-10	$4(4)(35)$	560
	4 : A ; A-3, 6-10	$4(4)(39)$	624
	5 : A ; A-4, 6-10	$4(4)(43)$	688
			$2,704$

2,704

32,328 Total wins

Tie

A : 2 2 : 3 3 : 4 4 : 5 5 : 6 $(16 + 16 + 16 + 16 + 12)(46)$

A : A ; A 2 : A ; 2 3 : A ; 3 4 : A ; 4 5 : A ; 5 $4(6 + 12 + 12 + 12 + 12)$

$$= 3,496$$
$$216$$

3,712 Total ties

TABLE 6-1. FIGURING THE ODDS IN VARIOUS PLAYER-DEALER
SITUATIONS (Cont.)

Lose

6-10	$28(47)\,(46) =$	$28 \cdot 2{,}162 = 60{,}536$
A : 3-6	$4(15)\,(46) =$	$60 \cdot 46$
2 : 4-6	$4(11)$	44
3 : 5,6	$4(\ 7)$	28
4 : 6	$4(\ 3)$	12

$60{,}536$

$144 \cdot 46 \quad = \quad 6{,}624 \longrightarrow 6{,}624$

A : A ; 2-5	$4(3)\,(16) =$	192
2 : A ; 3-5	$4(4)\,(12)$	192
3 : A ; 4,5	$4(4)\,(\ 8)$	128
4 : A ; 5	$4(4)\,(\ 4)$	64

576

576

$67{,}736$ Total losses

	Combinations	Probabilities
Win	32,328	0.312
Tie	3,712	0.036
Lose	67,736	0.652
$48 \times 47 \times 46 =$	103,776	1.000

(Possible combinations)

cards drawn are shown, with the draw progressing to the right. Each round of draw for the dealer is separated by a semicolon (;), and in the last case (10-6 versus 7-8), where both player and dealer may draw, the player draw is separated from dealer draw by a colon (:). For each card drawn, the number of such cards available is clearly delineated in the calculation.

The procedure can be illustrated by the case of player standing on 10-6 versus 7-7. Here it is very likely that the draw of one card will suffice, but allowance must be made for up to three cards. There are $48 \times 47 \times 46 = 103{,}776$ possible orders for these cards; hence, this number serves as common denominator for the probability computations. Now, if the dealer draws an 8 through 10-value card on the first round, he goes bust, and neither a second nor a third card need be drawn. However, there is no harm in imagining that those cards are right there ready to be drawn. Thus, the probability of drawing 8 through 10 may be written either as (23) (47) (46)/(48) (47) (46), or as 23/48. Here the former is preferred because, for certain combinations of the top three cards in the deck, all three would *have to be drawn* for a decision. An example is ace-ace-ace, the probability of which is (4) (3) (2)/(48) (47) (46). To avoid mistakes and to check totals more readily, the same denominator is used throughout; the temptation to make premature cancellations is resisted.

As the dealer's down-card gets lower and lower, the computation gets more and more involved because more cards may have to be drawn. Details need not be given here. In frequent cases, as for example, 10-6 versus 7-2, I resorted to approximations in at least part of the computation; but in all cases, three decimal-place accuracy was assured. The results for all cases of 10-6 versus 7 are tabulated in Table 6-2. Clearly, in some instances, the player is better off hitting (for example, 10-6 versus 7-10), and in others, he is better off standing (for example, 10-6 versus 7-9).

Proof that 10-6 versus 7 Should Be Hit

Now suppose we do not know what the down-card is (which, of course, is the usual case). Should we hit or stand? The answer to this question is now readily obtained. We merely weight the various numerical outcomes according to their relative chance of occurrence. For the 49 possible down-cards, there are 15 cards of value 10, three cards each of value 6 and 7, and four each of value 2, 3, 4, 5, 8, 9, and ace. The relative weights are 15, 3, and 4. These are the appropriate multipliers, as shown in Table 6-2. (Actually, each one should be divided by 49, to give the probability of getting the down-card; to simplify arithmetic, we divide by 49 at the end of the computation.)

The final tally shows that if you hit, your expectation is a net loss of 0.377 unit per unit bet, but if you stand, it is 0.483 unit. In terms of a $1.00 bet, knowledge of correct strategy means a reduction of 10.6¢ on the dollar in your losses on this particular unfavorable hand. Since reducing a loss is just as important as increasing a gain, this illustration exemplifies why it is *essential* to know the correct basic strategy if you hope to win at blackjack!

TABLE 6-2. WHY YOU SHOULD HIT RATHER THAN STAND
WITH 10-6 VERSUS 7

Player	Dealer	Player Hits			Player Stands	
		Win	Tie	Lose	Win	Lose
10-6	7-2	0.227	0.062	0.711	0.224	0.776
10-6	7-3	.187	.063	.750	.212	.788
10-6	7-4	.167	.062	.771	.226	.774
10-6	7-5	.270	.038	.692	.508	.492
10-6	7-8	.312	.036	.652	.570	.430
10-6	7-9	.319	.027	.654	.583	.417
10-6	7-A	.250	.083	.667	0.	1.
		1.732	0.371	4.897	2.323	4.677
Relative weight		×4	×4	×4	×4	×4
		6.928	1.484	19.588	9.292	18.708
10-6	7-6	0.305	0.038	0.657	0.544	0.456
10-6	7-7	.319	.035	.646	.577	.423
		0.624	0.073	1.303	1.121	0.879
Relative weight		×3	×3	×3	×3	×3
		1.872	0.219	3.909	3.363	2.637
10-6	7-10	0.333	0.084	0.583	0.	1.
Relative weight		×15	×15	×15		×15
		5.000	1.250	8.750		15.
		6.928	1.484	19.588	9.292	18.708
		1.872	.219	3.909	3.363	2.637
		5.000	1.250	8.750	0.	15.
Totals		13.800	2.953	32.247	12.655	36.345
		×1	×0	×−1	×1	×−1

Net loss −32.247   −36.345
per unit +13.800   +12.655
wagered   −18.447 / 49 = −0.377   −23.690 / 49 = −0.483

The preceding discussion summarizes how I learned the proper strategy for basic blackjack: reams of computations and hundreds of hands dealt to myself at home. But determining the proper basic strategy at blackjack is only half the battle. The other half is to figure out what your expectation is when you do play according to that strategy. Now the 25,000 hands of play described earlier served to pin down the expectation within a few tenths of a percent, and was concurrently corroborated by a unique method combining computed probabilities and statistical trials for selected card combinations. Later, I gained access to an electronic computer, and generated a much more accurate figure.

INSTRUCTIVE PLAY ON A COMPUTER

I was not the first to use an electronic computer to analyze blackjack, but what I did was conceived entirely by myself, and in this respect may be considered as an original investigation. I work in the exciting aerospace field, where computers are used to do weird and wonderful things. My company had an IBM 7090 and an IBM 650, used for scientific calculations. At the time, the faster 7090 was not available to me, and I had to settle for the less powerful 650. Nonetheless, although it was a slower computer, the 650 was just as capable of performing correctly the calculations at hand.

The blackjack computations were done only at times when the machine would otherwise have been idle. Runs were usually made toward the end of the evening shift. The project had the very lowest possible priority. Indeed, there was night after night when there was no opportunity to play blackjack on the computer because space exploration came first. It took weeks to sandwich in enough time on the computer to complete the computations.

Some readers may wonder if it isn't highly irregular to be "playing games" on a computer. Actually, this sort of thing goes on to some degree at virtually every computer facility in the country. Anything that presents a challenge to the computer scientist is likely to be attempted. As a consequence, computers have been programmed to play chess and checkers, to work puzzles, to analyze the stock market, and to solve a host of other curious problems. Very often the knowledge gained in figuring out how to solve them has a direct carry-over to more practical matters. The same sort of logic that goes into playing poker applies in the very serious pursuits of business competition and war strategy. An organization that lets its computer personnel stretch their imaginations occasionally on seemingly frivolous applications stands to gain in the long run. The pressure of normal business is usually sufficient to guarantee that such larking around does not get out of hand.

The medium-size digital computer, of which the IBM 650 is an example, is not a machine that can think in the usual sense. But it can do simple arithmetic at an incredible rate, such as adding and multiplying. It can also make simple logical tests, such as determining whether one number is bigger than another. In addition, it possesses a huge "memory," in which thousands of numbers may be stored and held standing by, to be called out in a fraction of a second. These characteristics make such a computer ideal for simulating the play of simple card games. Basic blackjack is, after all, a rather simple game to play, once you assume a set of rules for all the various options. For each combination of the player's two cards and the dealer's up-card, according to the strategy given previously, there is one and only one proper course of action for the player. Also, the dealer follows a fixed course of action specified by the casino rules. In principle, it is possible to direct a digital computer to follow these same courses of action, and this is exactly what I did.

Each combination of the player's first cards and the dealer's up-card is a distinct and separate case. In order to evaluate one's expectation at blackjack, then, a very natural approach is to go through each of these combinations in the correct relative proportion of occurrence. In the following paragraphs, the manner in which this was done is described and justified.

Altogether there are 550 such *distinct* combinations. These vary in relative frequency, from cases like 10-10 versus 10, and 10-9 versus 8, down to cases like 9-9 versus 9. The fewer the 10s involved, the less frequent the case (as usual, we are assuming that all 10-value cards are lumped together). The first case has the highest probability of occurrence, namely, $16 \times 15 \times 14/52 \times 51 \times 50$. The second has a somewhat lower chance, $16 \times 4 \times 4/52 \times 51 \times 50$. The last case, containing no 10s and all cards of the same denomination, has chance $4 \times 3 \times 2/52 \times 51 \times 50$. The numerators stand in the ratio 3360:256:24, or more simply, 420:32:3. The common factor that divides out is 8. This implies that in order to deal all possible cases in proper relative proportion, you would have to deal $52 \times 51 \times 50/8 = 16,575$ hands, or some multiple of this.

For a computer, this is no strain. So, immediately the question arises whether it would be feasible to deal out the fourth card (that is, the dealer's down-card) in proper proportion. This would, in principle, require $16,575 \times 49 = 812,175$ hands because, as it turns out, there is no common factor that divides out of the 49. Now this is in the neighborhood of a million hands, which even for a computer is a quite sizable number. So I employed a trick to cut it down while still effectively retaining the advantage of being able to deal out the first four cards, all in proper proportion.

Most of the card combination probabilities do have numerical factors from which an 8 can be factored out. In some, only a 4 can be factored; in a few, it is 2. Then, finally, there are the cases like 9-9 versus 9-9, where the numerator is $4 \times 3 \times 2 \times 1$, and the 1 cannot be factored at all. My trick was to divide out the 8 where possible, and for the remainder of the cases to run more than their share but to divide their results by the appropriate factor 2, 4, or 8. By this device, the proper relative proportion was preserved, and yet only about 115,000 hands had to be played. This method was considered as giving at least the equivalent of $812,175/8 = 101,500$ hands, approximately. In round numbers, then, one pass on the computer simulated about 100,000 hands of blackjack!

The Value of "Smoothing" or "Normalizing"

Many hands, of course, require the draw of an additional card or cards beyond the fourth card. It was not feasible to assign these cards in exact proper proportion. Instead, a technique was devised for simulating random draw from the deck. With the first four cards assigned with probabilistic exactness, the fifth card was drawn at random from among the remaining 48 cards; then the sixth card was drawn from among the remaining 47 cards, etc. But with the first four cards assigned in correct proportion, and only those thereafter drawn at random, there resulted a considerable smoothing in the fluctuations that would ordinarily take place. One hundred thousand hands played by this method yield just as accurate an estimate of the true odds as a quarter of a million hands played with all cards drawn at random! This, of course, represents more than a twofold saving in computer time.

To illustrate the "smoothing" that resulted, consider the draw of blackjacks. In assigning the first four cards in proper measure, I guaranteed automatically that the player and dealer got exactly the same number of blackjacks, which is as it should be. Since one or the other, or both, get a blackjack about 9 percent of the time, it is clear that an important fluctuation possibility has been *completely removed* from the computation.

Telling the Computer How to Play Blackjack

We shall now describe the exact procedure by which my computer simulation was done. Two "programs" were written for the computer (the *word program*, as applied to a digital computer, means a set of instructions). One was the main blackjack play program and the other was an auxiliary program for preparation of the input IBM cards for the main program. Such an IBM card was needed for each of the 550 combinations of the player's two cards and the dealer's up-card, as already discussed. This card contained the values of the three cards, a relative weight number for this particular situation, and a code number indicating the type of situation (that is, normal hit or stand, split, double-down, etc.). Since I did not want to keypunch all 550 cards myself, I prepared the auxiliary program, which in effect enabled the computer to figure out the necessary information and punch out these cards for itself.

After the main program was read into the computer for a run, the input cards were read in one at a time. For each input card containing a three-card combination, the computer cycled through each of the 49 possible down-card values. A cycle consisted therefore of 49 four-card situations, the four cards composing two player cards and two dealer cards. Each of these four-card situations was played through to completion by a method to be described in the next paragraph. The number of cycles for each combination was controlled by the relative weight number mentioned above. For example, the relative weight on the card for 10-6 versus 7 was 8. Since this card doubled for 6-10 versus 7, the actual weight for 10-6 versus 7 alone was 4. This implies that the situation 10-6 versus 7 occurs $4 \times 49 = 196$ times out of 101,500 (approximately). This ratio is about 1/500, which agrees completely with the readily computed probability of $16 \times 4 \times 4/52 \times 51 \times 50$. This particular combination is therefore played in the computer simulation in its *proper relative proportion* of the total. The same is true of all other combinations.

In most cases, additional cards in excess of the first four were necessary to complete a hand. This was done by simulating random draw *without replacement* from the remaining 48-card deck. (The importance of the phrase *without replacement* is emphasized on pages 61 and 92.) The draw was accomplished by using what in computer circles is called a *random number generator*.

Initially the 52 cards in the deck were assigned numbers from 1 through 52. In each three-card situation, the appropriate three numbers were removed, and numbers 50, 51, and 52 reassigned to the lower three vacant slots. Accordingly, numbers 1 through 49 were then in use. As each cycled value of the fourth card was assigned, it was temporarily removed from among the 49. This left 48 cards, from among which the fifth card could be drawn. When a fifth card was required, a random two-digit number from 00 to 99 was generated by an appropriate sequence of instructions in the program. If the number was from 50 to 99, then 50 was subtracted from it. Also, 00 and 49 were ignored. In effect, then, a random two-digit number from 01 to 48 was obtained, which was just what was needed.

Naturally, the sixth and any other necessary subsequent cards could be chosen by the same device. The computer was instructed to "remember" each card that was taken from among the 48, so that if the same random number were generated more than once on the same round, it would be rejected as already in use. Accordingly, the sampling from the deck was performed *without replacement*. When the hand was completed, the outcome was tallied, and then the randomly drawn cards were all returned to the deck. The fourth card was also returned to the deck. At this point, all operations for the current hand were complete, so the computer moved on to the next hand. The next value in line for the fourth card was assigned, and the process repeated.

A very natural question at this point is just how did the computer tell whether to draw additional cards, that is, how did it "play out" each hand to completion? The answer to this is, in principle, quite simple. A set of instructions written for the computer duplicated the thought processes of a human player carrying the hand to completion. Or perhaps it would be better to say that *one possible set* of thought processes was duplicated, for there is no assurance that two players go through the same chain of thoughts in playing identical hands, nor even that any player goes through the same chain at different times.

To be even more precise, what was used was one possible set of thought processes by which a human could play blackjack if his logic were limited to the simple logic used by the computer. The point is that the experienced player may take in a given situation in one all-absorbing glance, and immediately render a decision on the appropriate action, without any conscious awareness of his mind going through any process of logical analysis. The memory of what to do in any given situation may be so well implanted in his brain that his reaction hardly bears any resemblance to the step-by-step processes that would be found in someone who is just beginning to learn the game.

In a sense, the computer is like a beginner, and must be taught a consistent set of tests for determining what to do at each point in the game. But once you have given it a proper set of instructions, it has a fantastic memory. Just start it going, and it will sit there grinding out thousands of hands of blackjack without one bit of advice from you—except that you must tell it when to stop!

The computer is capable of adding, subtracting, multiplying, dividing, and sensing whether the difference between two numbers is positive or negative (if the difference is zero, this particular computer classifies it as negative). If you want to have some fun some time, try setting up a sequence of instructions, limited to the preceding logic, for playing out a pair-splitting situation with any arbitrary dealer up-card; for example, 3-3 versus 4. Be sure to allow for the double-valued ace; that always lends a little frustration to the proceedings.

I worked out the proper "flow" of logic to accommodate all the different types of situations, i.e., (1) normal hit or stand (including soft hands), (2) hard double-downs, (3) soft double-downs, and (4) splits. I do not contend that I necessarily developed the best or most efficient logic in terms of minimum number of steps, but it satisfied my aesthetic needs, and it seemed to work just fine.

Computer Flow Chart for Normal Hit or Stand

A typical flow chart is shown in Fig. 6-2. The first part presents the logic necessary for the player's handling of a normal hit or stand situation, and the second part continues with the logic for the play of the dealer's hand; the latter also contains the final comparison of player and dealer hands, and the resulting tally of a win, tie, or loss for the player.

The flow chart is intended to be self-explanatory, with the aid of the key to symbols given with it. Accordingly, no additional discussion will be devoted to the flow chart except to note how simple it all looks once you get a correct one worked out. However, the simplicity is deceiving, and often it can be a challenge to dream up a completely consistent scheme of logic that works without fail for all the intended cases.

The actual coded instructions that made up the computer program are too specialized to show here. The complete program contained about 550 such instructions. About 300 of these had to do with the various logical flow paths for playing the hands, and the remaining 250 pertained to input-output operations and setting up the hands prior to play. In the input phase, the information on the input cards had to be read into the computer and stored away in properly assigned memory cells. In the output phase, all the various cumulative totals had to be appropriately transferred, for punching onto output cards (or for printing on an electric typewriter). The outcome of each individual three-card combination was carefully documented for later examination and checking. Grand totals were also accumulated as each combination spelled out its contribution, for there is no better adding machine than a high-speed electronic computer. Information pertaining to the random numbers that had been generated was also carefully preserved. All these processes, and a few others too, were essential to the performance of a valid scientific analysis.

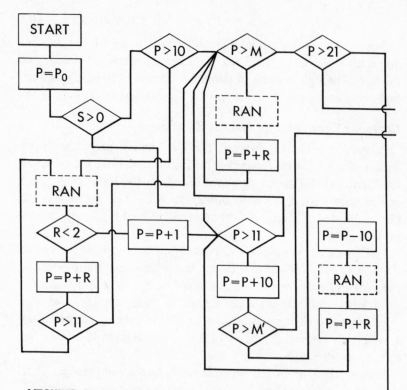

MEANING OF SYMBOLS:

P_0 = Player's initial 2-card total (ace initially counted as 1).

P = Player's total on all cards drawn up to this point in the hand.

S = Soft player hand identification code ($S = 0$ soft, $S = 1$ not soft).

D = Dealer's total on all cards drawn up to this point in the hand.

U = Up-card (dealer).

H = Hole-card (dealer).

M = Highest hard total on which player is willing to draw against U.
($M = 16$ if $U > 6$, $M = 11$ if $U < 7$ except $M = 12$ if $U = 2$ or 3.)

M' = Highest soft total on which player is willing to draw against U.

W = Cumulative player win total.

T = Cumulative player tie total.

L = Cumulative player loss total.

$A > B$ means A "is greater than" B.

$A < B$ means A "is less than" B.

RAN means random draw "sub-routine," a separate set of instructions
for simulating the random draw from the remaining deck.

R = Random draw card value.

(Note: $U + H \neq$ natural 21, by a previous test, wherein all
dealer naturals are handled separately).

FIG. 6-2.   Computer Flow Chart for Normal Hit or Stand

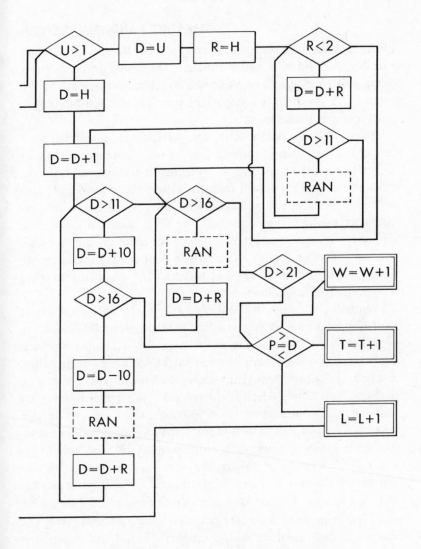

MEANINGS OF THE VARIOUS SHAPED BOXES:

Logical Test Box

Record Outcome Box
e.g., Add 1 to previous
cumulative WIN total

Algebraic Statement Box
e.g., Replace previous X
by X plus Y

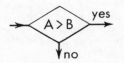

MAKING RANDOM NUMBERS

Doubtless there are readers who wonder about the random-number generator, and just how well it simulates the random draw of cards from a deck. The technique used is known to mathematicians as the *power residue method*. It is one of the most popular and thoroughly tested methods available.

An arbitrary ten-digit number, say, 8642097531, is selected as a starting number. This is multiplied by a prime number, say, 101. In the resulting product, the excess digits over 10 are removed from the left-hand end and subtracted from the extreme right-hand end. This procedure produces a new ten-digit number, which bears little resemblance to the original number. The same manipulation is then applied to this new number, to produce yet again another ten-digit number, and so on. That's all there is to it. It is a marvelous way to make a sequence of numbers that passes all the commonly accepted statistical tests for randomness.

Eventually, of course, the sequence must cycle, since there are at most 10 billion ways to form ten-digit numbers (from 0000000000 to 9999999999). As soon as the procedure yields a number that was used before (not necessarily the first in the sequence, incidentally), it simply cycles over from that number. But usually this presents no problem. You simply select a scheme that has a much longer cycle than the number of random values you need. This cycle may be computed beforehand by a branch of mathematics called *number theory*. For the sequence just described with multiplier 101, the cycle length is 206,205.* I employed this random-number generator in the first run of 100,000 hands, which required some 197,000 random pairs. When it became evident that there would be opportunity for further runs, I switched over to another generator having a longer cycle. This used eight-digit numbers, with multiplier 23, and had a period in excess of 5 million numbers. Actually, I could probably have continued to use the first generator with complete success, starting the second run where the first one left off. Although the generator would

* I am indebted to Donald Wall of the IBM Corporation for showing how to calculate this cycle value. Pertinent information may be found in the IBM reference manual, *Random Number Generation and Testing*. Also credit should be given to Dr. Mario Juncosa of the Rand Corporation for assisting in this matter.

have cycled over 9000 numbers later, this would have occurred at a different point in the sequence of the 550 different types of hands, as compared with the first run. Adequate scrambling would thus have occurred, and the second run would have been effectively independent of the first, and so on, for many, many runs. However, I decided to play it safe with the 5 million-cycle generator!

Several rounds of the process are illustrated in Table 6-3. The sequence of random two-digit numbers goes 36, 28, 30, 17, 44, 11, etc. Let us imagine that the suits are laid out in order so that the ace through king of one suit corresponds to 1 through 13, then ace through king of next suit is 14 through 26, etc. The random card sequence is 10, 2, 4, 4, 5, jack, etc. Of course the suits are immaterial in blackjack, but it helps in visualizing the process to identify a suit with each group of 13 numbers.

The short sequence quoted above looks very reasonable as a random selection. Indeed, a detailed study was made of the tabulation of thousands of numbers obtained by this process, and no irregularities were detected. All 100 two-digit numbers occurred about the same number of times, to within small anticipated statistical deviations. No bias in favor of any particular two-digit number was observed. A table of these numbers is given in Appendix F.

Could the Computer Make a Mistake?

To sum up, the simulation of random draw has been done by a method widely employed in the computer field. The possibility of imperfection in the method has been given very serious attention, and no cause for suspicion has been found.

In addition to the validity of the random-number generation, there are two other points on which we should put the reader's mind at rest. (1) How do we know that correct logic was used in all the various flow paths for playing out the hand? (2) How do we know the computer did not make any mistakes?

In answer to the first, I set up a number of test cases and played each of them through by hand in exactly the same sequence that the computer was instructed to do. All the different types of player situations were covered for at least one full cycle of the 49 possible values

TABLE 6-3. SIMULATION OF RANDOM DRAW OF CARDS USING
A RANDOM-NUMBER GENERATOR

1.   8642097531   86 (—50) = 36 (—26) = 10 of Hearts
   8642097531
   872851850631
      —87

2.   2851850544   28 (—26) = 2 of Hearts
   2851850544
   288036904944
      —28

3.   8036904916   80 (—50) = 30 (—26) = 4 of Hearts
   8036904916
   811727396516
      —81

4.   1727396435   17 (—13) = 4 of Diamonds
   1727396435
   174467039935
      —17

5.   4467039918   44 (—39) = 5 of Spades
   4467039918
   451171031718
      —45

6.   1171031673   11 (—0) = Jack of Clubs
     etc.

of the dealer's down-card. Of all the different types of situations, only one discrepancy was noted between the results of the hand sequencing and the computer sequencing. Investigation quickly revealed this was due to an incorrect instruction in my program, which caused a minor logic path to be bypassed. When it was corrected, this case also gave perfect results. At this point, I had full confidence in the validity of all the various possible logical flow paths.

As for the computer making a mistake, that is analogous to a bank making a mistake in your bank balance or to the government making a mistake in your income tax. More than 99 percent of the time, you are wrong. The modern digital computer usually does exactly what *you* tell it to do. If there is an error, it is because *you* told it to do the wrong thing, in your program of instructions. (Programers have a colorful way of expressing this: There was a "bug" in the program! A case in point was given in the preceding paragraph.) While it is true that occasionally there may occur an electrical malfunction that could cause a computing mistake, the chance that such a malfunction would pass undetected is very small. Computer design engineers are acutely aware of possible equipment failures, and elaborate checks have been devised for eliminating or otherwise minimizing them. Frequently, the operator "checks out" a computer, prior to the running of a problem, in much the same sense that a pilot checks out the controls and communication systems of an airplane before take-off. And while the computer is in operation, it frequently makes tests on itself to see that all is well. In short, a good computer, kept in a proper state of maintenance, is a very dependable device. It is far less likely to make a mistake in adding a *million* numbers electronically than are most humans in adding a *hundred* numbers by hand.

Having described how the blackjack simulation was set up on the computer, and having established the reliability of such an approach, we come now to the results. Wins, ties, and losses were tabulated for all 550 of the distinct cases that arise. The grand totals are the items of greatest interest. These are given in Table 6-4. But attention should first be drawn to two of the individual case totals, in particular those for which the true probabilities can be computed exactly. These cases afford a very good indication that the computer results are reliable.

One of the computable cases is 10-6 versus 7, which was covered in detail earlier. Just as readily computed are 10-6 versus 8 and 10-6 versus 9. Since all three cases occur with equal frequency, they can be lumped together to afford a bigger sample than one alone. In a complete computer run of about 100,000 hands, the dealer's downcard was cycled through eight times for a case like 10-6 versus 7. This gave $8 \times 49 = 392$ hands. Three such complete runs yielded 1176 hands. Finally, when all three cases were lumped together (that is, 10-6 versus 7, 8, and 9), it amounted to 3528 hands, which is no small sample.

A comparison between the outcome of these cases on the computer and exact theory is shown below. Also presented is the case of

10-8 versus 10. Here the dealer's down-card was cycled 30 times, for $30 \times 49 = 1470$ hands per run. In three runs, this gave 4410 hands. The agreement between the computer simulation and theory is excellent.

	Win	Tie	Lose
Case of 10-6 versus 7, 8, and 9:			
Computed experiment (given in number of hands)	886	213	2429
Computer experiment (given as a decimal)	0.251	0.060	0.689
Theoretical probability	0.255	0.062	0.683
Case of 10-8 versus 10:			
Computer experiment (given in number of hands)	1508	420	2482
Computer experiment (given as a decimal)	0.342	0.095	0.563
Theoretical probability	0.338	0.099	0.563

Evidently the fluctuation effect in the computer simulation of the random draw of the fifth and succeeding cards was not at all severe for such large samples of hands. Other cases gave similar confirmation. Not all were so close, but none were far enough out of line to excite alarm. Excess wins in some cases were counterbalanced by excess losses in others, and altogether the fluctuational pattern appeared reasonable. In all cases where the computer simulation could be compared with exact theory, the simulation appeared to be above reproach.

GRAND TOTALS FOR 300,000 NORMALIZED HANDS

The grand totals for three runs of 101,522 hands each are shown in Table 6-4. Since some of these hands were splits and double-downs, the total *units wagered* per run was higher, namely, 115,901. Each row will be found to add up to this number. The tallies for units won and units lost were extremely close, showing that basic blackjack is indeed a virtually even game. In about 350,000 units wagered, the difference between units won and lost was only 180. The experimental expectation was computed for each run by taking the difference between wins and losses, and dividing by 115,901. "Effective" probabilities to win and lose were also computed by using the condition that their difference be equal to the expectation value, along with the condition that their sum be exactly 1.

Because of the statistical fluctuations, the three expectation values were not identical, but they were all very close to zero. It was purely coincidental that the three runs gave successively more favorable results for the player. No significance should be attached to this. Nor should it be thought that runs were conducted until a positive result was obtained. Actually, the first two runs were made in fairly close

TABLE 6-4. RESULTS OF THREE RUNS OF BASIC BLACKJACK
ON AN IBM 650 COMPUTER

Run No.	Units Won	Units Tied	Units Lost
1	53,242	9,229	53,430
2	53,437	9,169	53,295
3	53,385	9,357	53,159

	Effective Probability		
	To Win	To Lose	Expectation
1	0.4992	0.5008	−0.0016
2	0.5006	0.4994	+0.0012
3	0.5010	0.4990	+0.0020
		3)	+0.0016
			+0.0005
			or +0.05 %

succession, and the third was made months later when a holiday presented a good opportunity.

The simulation contained a mixture of situations, ranging from exact determinism (when only four cards were required) to essentially random draw (when the first four cards assigned were all low and numerous additional cards were drawn at random to complete the hand). A somewhat sophisticated statistical argument leads to the conclusion that 300,000 hands dealt in this manner are equivalent to about 750,000 hands all dealt at random.* The standard deviation (see page 227) in the expectation value $p - q$ can be shown to be approximately

$$\frac{2\sqrt{Npq}}{N} = \frac{1}{\sqrt{N}} = \frac{1}{\sqrt{750,000}} = 0.0012 \text{ or } 0.12\%$$

This value of uncertainty is so low that there can be no question that my simulation has pinned down basic blackjack to virtually an even game. The player expectation is so close to zero that for the three reasons given on page 56, it is virtually pointless to pursue the computation any further! But how remarkable it is that the casinos should be banking a game in which it has no advantage whatever against a flat-bet player who takes the trouble to memorize a few simple rules.

* Dr. Edward Thorp gave me a hint which clarified this matter.

OTHER SCIENTISTS AND THEIR WORK ON BLACKJACK

A number of other scientifically trained persons have made their own contributions to the attack on blackjack. In fact, high-speed digital computers were used as far back as ten years ago, a fact that may come as a surprise to many readers. Since powerful computers have been available since the early 1950s, it is provocative to ask why the recent surge, and why the original slow progress. To a certain extent, the initial slowness was due to the fact that most investigations were, if not actually regarded as secret, at least rather isolated and not well-publicized. But equally important was the fact that early models of the game were sufficiently inaccurate that pessimistic results were obtained, and the researchers were discouraged from further pursuit.

The graph in Fig. 6-3 shows the history of attempts to compute the player's expectation for the so-called basic game, with fixed bet size and no card memory. On the vertical is plotted the expectation value, and on the horizontal is given the approximate year. Data points are labeled in terms of the laboratories where the work was done; this emphasizes that scientists at the large, aerospace companies and their computer suppliers have dominated the scene. It is interesting to observe how the results tend to converge toward a value of +0.1 percent, assuming the most favorable combination of variations in the casino rules of play.

Pioneering Efforts at Los Alamos

The first major effort was made at the Atomic Energy Commission's laboratory at Los Alamos, New Mexico. That facility has always been in the forefront of computing capacity, and its nuclear scientists en route to the atomic proving grounds north of Las Vegas, Nevada, have long been subjected to the temptation of the tables. Their simulation was modeled on a complete random-draw basis, the cards being shuffled by a random-number generation technique and then in effect "dealt" to a table full of players and the dealer. Despite a run of several million hands on an IBM 701, a disappointingly low value of −0.7 percent was achieved. Apparently the explanation lies in the fact that all correct strategy decisions had not been worked

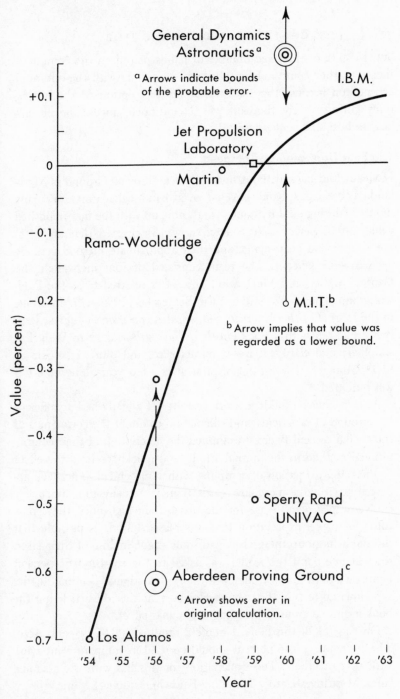

FIG. 6-3. Graph Showing Progress in Calculation of Optimum Player Expectation for Basic Game

out. In spite of the huge number of hands played on the computer, therefore, they could not be expected to come up with the optimum expectation because they had not completely optimized the hitting rules. Unfortunately, the work was discontinued, since it did not appear to bear sufficient promise.

The Four Horsemen of Aberdeen

Meanwhile, back at the Army's Aberdeen Proving Ground in Maryland, a tenacious band hovered over hand calculators for many months (during off-duty hours), and came up with the first published value, −0.62 percent. Years later, it was discovered that an arithmetic error had been made, and their approximate method actually yielded −0.3 percent. The team consisted of four men—Baldwin, Cantey, Maisel, and McDermott—hereafter referred to as the Baldwin group. They broke into print in September, 1956, with an article in the *Journal of the American Statistical Association*. The next year, they came out with a book entitled, *Playing Blackjack to Win*. For simplicity and clarity, it was a masterpiece, and quite a bargain at $1.75. Strangely, it went out of print after a few years, long before it was outdated.

At the time the Baldwin work appeared, I already had a sufficient background of experience and calculation to doubt the correctness of their −0.6 percent figure. I examined the description of their computational method in the journal article, and quickly realized the effect of their approximation of sampling with replacement. The deck appeared to contain more low cards than it actually did. Since low cards are in general worse for the player than high ones, they got a value for player expectation that was biased low. It is possible that the Baldwin group themselves had some vague inkling of their error, since at one point the reader was asked to "accept the 0.62 percent figure on a faith in the accuracy of their calculations," pending further experimental tests in the casinos. However, neither the article nor the book indicated an understanding of the bias effect.

On page 89 of this book, I quote a result of +0.05 percent. Actually the figure +0.16 percent should be used in comparing my work with that of others. The explanation for this lies with the assumed rules. Most investigators, including Baldwin, assume the "most favorable" variations. However, in my own computer simulation, I did not allow for doubling-down after splitting. This was principally because I did not want to be bothered with another logic loop in my computer program, but also because I have played at a number of clubs where such doubling-down is not permitted. This option is worth 0.11 percent to the player. Accordingly, this increment has been added to my simulation result for purposes of comparison with the results found by other people.

Epstein at Ramo-Wooldridge

At about the same time the Baldwin crew embarked on its labors in Maryland, another eager beaver was hard at work in Los Angeles. This was Richard Epstein, who was then an electronics engineer for the Ramo-Wooldridge Corporation, the overseer of the Atlas missile development. I met him in 1956, when he spoke at a technical meeting in San Diego on the subject of probability and game theory. I sat there agog as he flashed a slide of his "decision matrix" on the screen, wherein he displayed the net percentage difference in the expectation for hitting versus standing for *all* possible stiffs. Along with similar tables for splits and double-downs, he claimed to have worked out an effective probability for the player of 0.4993, which corresponded to an expectation of −0.0014, or −0.14 percent. He went on to claim that with appropriate card memory and sizable bet variation, the effective probability could be raised to 0.53, giving the player a net 6 percent advantage.

My reaction to the latter statement was that, from a practical standpoint, it was somewhat exaggerated. Nonetheless, I lost no time in cultivating this new "comrade-at-arms," the first person I had met who was working independently on blackjack. It turned out that he had access to a Remington Rand 1103 computer at Ramo. Using direct probability calculations, still limited, but not quite so much in error by approximation as was Baldwin, he obtained the −0.14 percent.

Blackjack at Martin, Denver

In 1959 there appeared in a Las Vegas newspaper a delightful advertisement inviting the reader to become a better blackjack player, "better than the experts," in fact. All you had to do was send $2.00 to the Statistical Specialties Company in Littleton, Colorado. My $2.00 yielded a plastic card giving a complete hitting strategy, similar to that in Baldwin's book, and a one-page letter of advice. An expectation of 0.0 percent was cited, along with some general comments that were clearly written by someone of intelligence and integrity; no extravagant claims were made.

Subsequent correspondence revealed that the man behind this operation was Robert H. Lea, who signed himself as "president" of the company. He had done direct probability calculations, using an IBM 650 computer, and actually had obtained −0.01 percent (but note that he employed the 650 in a manner different from the way I had used it). Presumably he was using a better model than those used by Baldwin or Epstein, or had been lucky enough to have compensating errors.

Univac Gets into the Act

Up to this point, IBM seemed to have dominated the blackjack scene, but this was changed by another development in 1959. A promoter for the Sperry Rand Corporation, maker of Univac computers, installed one at the Showboat Hotel. It had dual duty: a publicity gimmick to attract curious gamblers and a genuine aid in hotel accounting tasks. The Showboat does a lot of business with the tourists and has its own special attractions, including a gigantic bingo hall. Big signs sprang up along the highways leading into Las Vegas, proclaiming that Univac would improve your chance to win at the Showboat: "Correct odds for all the games." "How to manage your bets." Etc., etc. These signs really had pulling power, and they pulled me in, too, as I sauntered up to the Univac desk on a hot summer afternoon in 1959. Waiting my turn in the queue, I asked for the works on blackjack. The girl smiled sweetly, and said that Univac could answer one question for me. So I asked if you should hit 16 versus 10, since this was a marginal situation for which I knew the right answer.

The girl went to the key-punch machine and prepared a coded card with my question on it. Then she took a special stack of cards from a drawer, and fed all the cards into a hopper. Lights started flashing on and off as the cards were processed. Then, suddenly, the sequence stopped, and a new card was ejected from the machine with the answer on it: Hit 16 against 10. This was very impressive, except that I was *not* impressed, mainly because I could see that Univac was not really computing. The answers had all been precalculated and were already punched onto the cards of the master deck. The card reader was simply comparing my question card with each successive card in the master deck until it found the one for 16 versus 10. The appropriate action was also coded on that master card, so the answer was merely copied from it.

Anyone who has worked around computers could spot that immediately. It was not completely phony, but certainly it was deceptive. The tip-off was the vintage of the computer. It was an old Univac 120, and did not appear to have the capacity for the complex blackjack problem. But to the uninformed, it was putting up a good front.

My purpose was to see if the Univac strategy coincided with the already published Baldwin strategy. Since a dozen or more points had to be checked, the prospect of my cycling through that queue so many times was unthinkable. Presently I circumvented the problem by coming in one morning before opening time. The place was completely deserted. Looking around, I discovered the master deck on top of a file. Taking a quick peek, I confirmed that their recommendations were almost identical with Baldwin's. While I was doing this, none of the casino personnel paid any attention to me; evidently they thought I was one of the computer crew. A janitor did come by and turn up the lights so I could see what I was doing. When he casually inquired about my connection with the setup, I told him I was a spy for IBM, and he went away!

The need for the cloak-and-dagger approach dissolved a few months later. The Showboat began passing out cards the size of a regular IBM card, with the strategy all laid out. With a big stamp "Proved by Univac," one card contained normal hit-or-stand strategy and the other contained double-down and splitting strategies. This move clearly helped expedite the line of gawkers at the Univac counter. On my next trip to Los Angeles, I went to the local Univac office and tracked down the man behind the calculations. His name was Georges Picot, a former French diplomat. This talented gentle- man claimed to have programed a blackjack simulation in one after- noon and to have run it off in 2½ hours on the latest Univac model, which was much faster and larger than the one at the Showboat Hotel in Las Vegas. His objective was to check out the Baldwin strategy, but he ignored soft double-downs. He tested numerous situations statistically, playing them both pro and con, and whichever strategy worked out better, he took that to be the correct one. How- ever, his sample size was too small to give the right answer in all cases, and consequently some of the Univac recommendations dif- fered from those of Baldwin. I believe he reported about 50,000 total trials, with a net expectation for the player of about −0.5 percent. As we have seen, this is low.

Eventually the Univac disappeared from the Showboat, and the supply of blackjack strategy cards dried up. Either the publicity value wore off, or astute players began eating into their profits. Only the fading billboards on Highway 91 remain as mute reminders of this clever pitch.

Bamford's Black Box

Perhaps the Univac episode served to put Las Vegas on its guard, for in 1960, an incident occurred in which the casinos revealed their attitude toward a mechanized attack on blackjack. A clever young engineer named Robert Bamford, who worked at the celebrated Jet Propulsion Lab in Pasadena, built an electrical "black box" which could automatically figure shifts in strategy.

The heart of the device was an array of electrical resistors in which current and voltage ratios changed in accordance with card situations dialed in by switches. There were approximations, for sure, but still it was an extremely ingenious affair. The whole works was contained within two metal boxes of an over-all size no larger than a loaf of bread. One box bristled with ten knobs by which the operator dialed in the number of remaining cards of each value. The other box had knobs, too, for setting the player total, dealer up-card, and strategy under test (that is, hit, stand, double-down, split). Right in the middle of this box was a meter. The deflection of the pointer to right or left from center showed whether the strategy under test gave a positive or negative result. Thus, the operator could tell whether to take another card or to stand pat. Furthermore, the *amount* of deflection of the pointer was a direct measure of the numerical advantage or disadvantage.

Bamford took his black box to Las Vegas in December, 1960, and challenged the casinos on the "strip." He and a helper marched into the Flamingo Hotel and prepared to roll into action. For 10 minutes they played unmolested with very modest bets and picked up about $30 and a crowd of curious onlookers. Then the dealer began to shuffle after every hand. A hassle ensued over this matter, and after a while they moved down the "strip" to another casino. Similar difficulties arose. The upshot was that none of the clubs would let them play unimpeded. The best deal they could get was permission to play at a fixed-bet size, which removed most of their advantage, but certainly not all. After winning a couple of hundred dollars, they returned to Pasadena, sadder but wiser. Evidently mechanical (or electrical) aids were taboo in Vegas!

Although I did not witness this episode in person, I read about it in the *Pasadena Star-News*. Shortly thereafter I met Bamford, and with characteristic enthusiasm, he put on a colorful demonstration of his brainchild. He quickly agreed that the basic game, without card memory or bet variation, is just about even. Then he claimed that by using his black box when the cards were dealt to the bottom of the deck, he could swing about a 2 percent advantage on flat bets. With modest bet variation, moreover, he asserted the effective advantage could be boosted to about 4 percent. The casino operators must have believed something of the same sort, or more!

Dr. Thorp and "Beat the Dealer"

A new star burst in the firmament of the blackjack "greats" in 1961, a veritable supernova at that. Appearing at the January meeting of the American Mathematical Society in Washington, D.C., Dr.

Edward Thorp, then on the staff of MIT, offered "a favorable strategy for twenty-one." His was the most popular session at the conference and was packed with mathematicians and reporters. In his paper, he told how he had used an IBM 704 at MIT for new and startling revelations on the theory of how to play blackjack. Enterprising young Thorp had first contacted the Baldwin group and borrowed a boxful of calculations from them. Using their work as a point of departure, he applied their method, but with greater computational accuracy, by use of an IBM 704 computer. He obtained a player expectation of −0.21 percent, which he regarded as a *lower bound* on the correct value because he was aware of the error due to sampling with replacement.

Up to this point, Thorp was just "one of the boys," as far as blackjack calculations go. Then he made an ingenious leap forward. He utilized the computer to figure also how one's playing strategy should be altered as the composition of the deck changed, that is, as the cards are dealt out. Taking as a criterion the ratio of non-10-value cards to 10-value cards (remaining to be dealt), he also established the player's expectation for different values of this crucial ratio. This and similar approaches had been *thought* of by many people before, and indeed a number of persons including myself had made various actual attempts to get useful results by hand play and rough estimations. But it was for Thorp to first *implement* this exceedingly arduous computation by using an electronic computer.

This all formed the principal basis for his exciting and authoritative book, *Beat the Dealer*. More about his methods and conclusions will be mentioned in coming chapters. Suffice to say here that Thorp, who at this writing is a math professor at the New Mexico State University, has made a handsome profit on his researches!

Julian Braun and the Chicago Datacenter

Most recently there has emerged a new giant on the scene, Julian Braun of the IBM Corporation. Using the latest available computers, he has simulated tens of millions of hands of blackjack under various conditions, and has come up with about +0.1 percent for the basic game. His work is undoubtedly the most valid of all because he has directly simulated the play of hands through the deck as actually conducted in the casinos.

By virtue of his position as programing specialist at the IBM Data-center in Chicago, Braun had very free access to the excellent 7044 computer. He not only ran through-the-deck simulations with both fixed and varying strategies, but also refined the Thorp calculations as to strategy alteration. He is a most meticulous person, with a burning passion to get the blackjack figures right! His work, too, will receive additional discussion in subsequent chapters here.

Although he has not formally published, Braun did speak on his work at the Fall Joint Computer Conference, held (of all places) in Las Vegas in November, 1963. The occasion was an evening panel discussion devoted to the use of computers to study games of chance and skill. Thorp presided as master of ceremonies, and this author was the lead-off speaker, surveying the history and current status of blackjack analysis. We drew an audience of several hundred, which was remarkable, considering that we were competing with dinner shows like the Lido de Paris!

Who Is Next?

It is provocative to ask who will carry the art still further, but I pose that question almost tongue in cheek. Braun has done fantastically detailed work. Since he has very generously made his results available to me, I personally would be hard pressed to find much more to do on a computer even if I had "carte blanche" with one. Eventually, someone will invent a miniaturized device for tracking the cards and indicating correct strategy, but the basic analysis appears essentially complete. So, we must conclude now by paying tribute to the dogged scientists whose toils have been recounted here for the first time, and whose collective efforts have proved indeed that basic blackjack is an even game!

Card-Counting Methods for Playing a Winning Game

7

Blackjack can be beaten in the long run! This may be stated as a positive fact, assuming conditions of play that commonly prevail as of the date of writing this manuscript. This is not to say that it is easy to beat, for it requires intelligent effort and great patience. Nor is it to say that the casino operators will necessarily allow you to win from them over any extended time, for they may modify the operating conditions or even bar you from play. Nonetheless, the fact remains that the capability is there. I have proved it myself after some 10,000 hands of variable bet-size play in the Las Vegas casinos.

We have seen in the preceding two chapters that the "basic" blackjack is virtually a dead-even game. Properly played, it is so close to an even proposition that at flat bets, you would have to play an extremely long time before the slight deviation from an even game would emerge as a definite trend unobscured by fluctuations in luck. Therefore, it is entirely reasonable that when you keep track of the cards, vary your bet size according to the changing probabilities, and make alterations in your strategy to draw or stand, you can certainly play the game with the advantage on your side rather than on the side of the house. A further slight benefit is possible by selecting the optimum seat among a table of players. And where the "insurance" bet is offered, as in Las Vegas, you can enjoy a nominal additional boost by making judicious insurance bets when the situation is favorable.

Depending on the degree of bet-size variation, all these possibilities add up to an advantage of the order of 1 to 3 percent in favor of the player. This is a most remarkable fact, for in no other casino game does the potentiality of a player advantage normally exist. On the other hand, it is a small edge indeed, and you must play for a long time to have any reasonable assurance of coming out well ahead. Fluctuations may well be your pitfall if you do not operate with a very healthy bank-to-bet ratio, as explained in Chapter 17 on "How to Size Your Bets." Even to show a long-term profit that will cover your expenses calls for a considerable bankroll. But even though the chance for a player of limited means to parlay a fortune is very remote, still it is well worth learning to play this game right. Why play the other games where you quickly lose? At blackjack, you have (at worst) an even game, and with a little application, the chance to do better than that. Even in a short-term play, you have a reasonable chance to enjoy a winning fluctuation if you are not too greedy. This game is the *best* that the casino offers you!

CARD COUNTING

The basis of playing a long-term winning game, as opposed to a mere even game as described in the two previous chapters, lies in counting the cards as they are dealt out. There is a variety of methods for doing this. In general, the more effective a method is, the more detail the player must keep track of, and the more decisions he must make during the course of play. However, it is not necessary to have a "photographic memory" or otherwise to be extremely skilled in order to play a reasonably good game. Of course every little bit helps, and each player should strive to play the best game that he can. But the important thing to understand is that every player can find a method that suits his temperament and ability.

This chapter discusses most of the known practical methods of card counting. About the simplest of these is the "Wilson point count method" (apart from trivial methods in which all you keep track of is the number of cards of one denomination which have showed up, say, aces; such methods are usually very ineffectual because the information tallied is so limited). Despite its simplicity, I have had good results with my method, and recommend it to the beginner.

Also to be discussed are the more demanding, but also more effective methods such as 10-count ratio, hi-lo, and Thorp's "ultimate" strategy.

Before getting into the mechanics of counting, however, we begin with some general remarks to lay the groundwork. Also, we show the results of a count system in action, to show the reader that it is worth the effort. Perhaps the best place to start is with the first account that I ever heard about anyone who won consistently at blackjack. This was told by a woman dealer at Harolds Club in Reno. She described a man called "Greasy John," who evidently possessed some personal attributes that discouraged other people from playing with him, thus assuring him head-to-head action, with as many simultaneous hands as he so chose. He possessed a remarkable memory for cards. His style was to go along at minimum bets until a high-potential situation arose. Then he hauled out his wallet and hit it with all he could, often to the tune of a $500 house limit. For example, suppose that he was playing alone against the dealer, and suppose that the deal had progressed to the point where only four cards remained in the deck. If he knew that these four cards happened to consist of an ace and three 10-value cards, this was a very juicy situation. There was a 50:50 chance that he would get a blackjack. If he got it, he would get paid at 1½:1, while if the dealer got it, he would lose at only even money. With a $500 bet, every two times that this situation set up, on the average, he would clear $250! Needless to say, he could afford to bounce along at 50¢ or $1.00, even going down quite a bit on these small bets, when there was occasionally such a handsome compensation.

Such an extreme situation as this occurred only once in several hundred deals through the deck. But he had lots of patience. Besides, there were enough other situations with a smaller but still definite advantage that would arise and which had sufficient frequency to warrant covering them with substantial bets. This player is reputed to have won tens of thousands with this mode of play. Any house that would accept his play was just asking to lose. The dealer at Harolds Club told me that she had never been able to beat him.

In the past few years, I have also learned of the modus operandi of other famous count players, such as System Smitty and Joe Bernstein. (Harold Smith's autobiography *I Want to Quit Winners* recounts an intriguing episode in which Bernstein won $14,000 in 24 hours at Harolds Club, by "counting aces," until Harold put a stop to it.) A couple of other such luminaries are mentioned in Basil Woon's book entitled, *Gambling in Nevada*, published in 1953. But, by and large, the names and techniques of winning blackjack players are among the least publicized items in the Nevada gambling picture. In general, these players have no wish to divulge their activities, nor do the casinos.

Motivated by the fragmentary evidence that a few others before me had indeed been able to beat the game, I conducted home experiments to set up my own criteria for the so-called rich situations. By patient, tedious calculation and empirical analysis, I shaped my own style for a winning game. The summer of 1959 saw it put to the test.

MY OWN CASINO WIN RECORD

The chart in Fig. 7-1 shows the outcome of my variable bet-size play in the Las Vegas casinos. Considering the modest resources at my disposal, and the consequent modest bets, a profit in the thousands was remarkable. Unit-wise, the record was amazing. It could only be the product of a superior method of play!

This method for winning has embodied the elements cited in the second paragraph of this chapter, with principal emphasis on the "Wilson point-count method" for determining when to change bet size. The latter might be described as analogous to the Goren point-count method for bidding in bridge; the latter is known by millions of card players, and is currently the most widely used aid in that game. The mechanics of my point-count method for blackjack are even simpler than Goren's for bridge. It will be described shortly.

The graph displays dollars of profit versus number of hands played. It is divided into two sections. In the first, I was playing with silver dollars, and in the second, with $5.00 chips. The dotted line at −400 indicates that my original stake was $400.

This adventure was conducted mainly during a 2½ week stay in Las Vegas during the summer of 1959. Some 7400 hands were racked

up at that time. The balance of hands were obtained during subsequent week-end trips in later years. I started with a basic bet of five
silver dollars. This bet level was ranged up to as many as 15 silver
dollars during favorable situations, and down to the minimum of one
silver dollar in unfavorable situations. The two extremes did not
actually occur very often, and most of the time the bet level was in
the vicinity of $5.00.

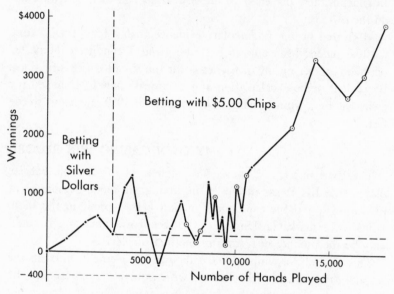

FIG. 7-1.   The Wilson Point-Count Method in Action

The first week was highly successful. At one point I was ahead
$600. By week's end, after 3500 hands, the profit had slipped back to
$300. Nonetheless, I was sufficiently encouraged to boost the ante to
a basic $10.00 bet. Furthermore, I was tired of manipulating 15 differ-
ent bet levels with the silver dollars, and had a strong urge to graduate to $5.00 chips. Accordingly, I set the basic bet at two chips,
swinging it up to a maximum of six, and down to a minimum of 1.
No sooner did I switch over to the higher level than my winnings
soared up another $800 within the next 600 hands. It was exhilarating!

This state of affairs fulfilled a primary objective of attaining a total playing bank of $1500 (my original $400 plus $1100 captured on the tables).

I was feeling pretty cocky at this point, and decided to graduate to a 1-3-8-chip betting scheme, mainly so that my minimum bet would be a smaller fraction of the basic bet. (Thus, the new minimum was one-third instead of the previous one-half of the basic bet.) After a momentary $200 upswing, I went into a terrifying nosedive, which within 1000 plays drove my capital down by $1500. It practically wiped me out. But I fought on, and finally the pendulum swung back in the other direction.

By now the dealers were finding my face familiar. Many of them realized that I was not playing like the average gambler who gives them anywhere between 2 and 5 percent the best of it, and who often gets cleaned out in one sitting. So gradually I began to be subjected to countermeasures from some of the dealers. This made it harder to win. Despite this, I swung it back up to +$900 at one point, but then retreated to +$500. Here I decided to quit, after 7400 hands, and more than two weeks of fairly regular play. I had placed close to $75,000 in bets on the tables and had $500 profit to show for it at this point, less than 1 percent, but definitely a positive gain.

Later on, I managed to slip up to Las Vegas and Reno on various week ends to continue the test. My objective was simply to get further into the "long run," not to win any specified amount. The available margin at this game is such that only after many, many plays can you expect to be very much ahead of the game.

THE WILSON POINT-COUNT SYSTEM

The Wilson point-count system for blackjack is extremely simple. It is based on the fact that the most favorable cards for the player are the aces and 10s. If the deck from which hands remain yet to be dealt contains an excess of aces and 10s, then in general you have a positive expectation; if it contains a deficiency of aces and 10s, in general you have a negative expectation.

This principle is obvious in the extreme cases. For example, one of the ultrarich end-deck situations that Greasy John liked so much was recounted on page 102. That was the case of one ace and three 10s remaining. Another similar case is that of two aces and four 10s. Here the chance of an untied player blackjack is not quite so high, but this is offset by the fact that if the player draws both aces, he may split and surely draw 10s to win. On the other hand, if the dealer gets both aces, he must lump them together and then go bust as he draws two 10s. The reader can easily dream up other such juicy situations. Many of them are loaded with a bonus in the form of a very favorable insurance bet. (The ultimate in insurance would be the Greasy John situation, with the ace falling as the dealer's up-card. With the dealer's down-card *known* to be a 10, the insurance bet would be a sure thing!)

Extreme situations, of either type, occur very infrequently. On the other hand, the proportion of cards remaining to be dealt is very seldom exactly that of a 52-card deck. The deck is either "rich" or "poor," in some varying degree, practically all of the time. To take advantage of this fact, the Wilson point-count system assigns the following point values to the cards that still remain:

Ace	+4 points
Ten-value card	+1 point
All others	−1 point

Since there are four aces, sixteen 10-value cards, and 32 other cards, we see that there are the same number of plus points as there are minus points in the complete deck. This coincidence is a very happy feature of this counting system. When all the cards in the deck have been dealt out, the point count should be back at zero. This gives a very convenient way to check accuracy in counting.

Since the cards are usually handled very rapidly in blackjack, it is my opinion that the best way to carry out the counting method is in two phases: (1) As the cards are dealt out for the current hand, simply add mentally a 1 for each card dealt, regardless of denomination. (2) As the cards are turned over for the settlement of each hand, subtract off five points for each ace you see, and two points for each 10-value card.

This procedure accomplishes the same result as deducting four points for each ace that has been removed from the deck, and deducting one point for each 10, and adding one for each non-10, non-ace card. But it is easier to conduct the count by the two-phase method because the player seldom sees the faces of the cards dealt to the other players until after all the cards have been turned over for the settlement. Using the two-phase method, the player can do most of his mental arithmetic during the relatively calm phase (1), as the first two cards are being dealt around, and as subsequent cards are drawn. Then, just a small number of mental operations remain for the hectic phase (2), where the cards are being turned over, bets paid off, and cards scooped up by the dealer. Anyone who has attempted to keep track of the cards at blackjack will readily understand the practical aspects of this recommendation.

The mechanics of the technique are illustrated in the two examples laid out in Table 7-1. Arbitrarily, three players are assumed in the examples, but the method applies for any number of players, from one up to a full table of six. Consider the first round in example 1. With the dealer starting from a freshly shuffled full deck, the "prior" count is zero. Two cards are dealt to each of the three players and to the dealer. Hence, the momentary count is now +8. Since the dealer's up-card is an 8, all players should follow the previously discussed strategy of Chapter 5 and draw until they have a total of at least 17. When the first player draws his card, the point count goes up automatically to +9. Since the first player is now satisfied with his hand A-5-3, for a total of 19, the second player now draws a card. Here the point count rises to +10. Unfortunately, he pulls a queen, thereby going over 21. So, he has to turn his cards over and show that he has gone bust. Accordingly, there is a "settlement" at this point, and it is time to subtract four points for the two queens that are exposed to view and then scooped up by the dealer. The count is now +6. The third player draws a card and is quite pleased with his total of 21! The point count is raised to +7. The dealer now shows all his cards. With less than 17 on the first two cards, he draws another. The count is then +8. Since the dealer now has a total on which he must stop, the cards of players one and three are turned over for their settlement. Among all the cards that are face up on the table, only the ace in the

TABLE 7-1. APPLICATION OF THE WILSON POINT-COUNT
SYSTEM FOR BLACKJACK

Arbitrary case of three players versus dealer. First hand is assumed
dealt from a fresh deck; thus, initial point-count is zero.

Example 1

	8 (up)	7 (up)	9 (up)	10 (up)	Leftover cards
Dealer					
2 cards:	4	Q	6	J	6
Draw cards:	7		K		
Player	A Q 8	2 3 4	A 5 7	5 J A	A
2 cards:	5 6 6	9 10 K	10 J 4	3 9 K	9
Draw cards:	3 Q 7	5 K 2	10 Q	8	2
		2	4	J	8
					3
Prior count + cards dealt on this hand	+12	+16	+19	+14	+5
High-card subtraction	−9	−8	−15	−15	−5
Total count	+3	+8	+4	−1	0 (Check)

Example 2

	7 (up)	5 (up)	9 (up)	4 (up)	Leftover cards
Dealer					
2 cards:	3	5	10	3	Q
Draw cards:	Q	3		8	7
		K		4	9
Player	4 7 8	4 A 10	2 8 5	3 A 7	6
2 cards:	6 A 6	2 5 K	Q J 10	6 2 Q	J
Draw cards:	J 9	A 10	8 9	K J	2
		K			
Prior count + cards dealt on this hand	+11	+15	+5	+9	+4
High-card subtraction	−9	−20	−8	−11	−4
Total count	+2	−5	−3	−2	0 (Check)

first player's hand is of interest. Five points are subtracted for that, and the net count at the end of the first round is +3.

The remaining deck is slightly rich, and as we go into the second round, the situation is a little more favorable than average for the player. The new "prior" count for this round is +3, that is, the total count at the end of round one. Again eight cards are dealt around, and the count becomes +11. The first player draws two cards this time, and the count is +13. The second player's draw brings it to +14. Again he is unlucky and goes bust. As his cards are turned over, we subtract 4 for the two 10-value cards, for a count of +10. The third player now takes two cards, for +12. The dealer now exposes his down-card, indicating that his total is satisfactory. So, he turns over the cards of players one and three, compares totals, and makes payoffs. Here our attention is drawn to the queen in the dealer's hand and the king in the third player's hand. For these we subtract four points, reaching a net count at the end of the second round of +8.

The remaining deck is now considerably richer than usual. With essentially half the deck left (actually 27 cards), there is an extra ace and two extra 10-value cards, and a corresponding deficiency in other cards. Such a situation with a count of +8 is not too frequent, and the player would do well to take advantage of it and boost his bet size. As it turns out here, in round three, he would not regret it. (However, in round four, which is also entered with a positive point count, the dealer obtains some compensation.) In this illustration, the players as a group have been luckier than they would usually be. The dealer could just as well have gotten one of the blackjacks. Nonetheless, when the point count is plus, the player has a better expectation than average, and he should act accordingly.

The detailed tally of points which we traced through for rounds one and two ought to be sufficient to demonstrate how it goes. Therefore we shall not go through the actual tally for rounds three and four. We should point out, however, that there will usually be cards left over after the last round. If these cards are seen, the final count after 52 cards should check out to zero, as shown in Table 7-1.

In example 2, the counting procedure is illustrated again. Here it turns out that after two rounds, a slight excess of high cards has been bled off. The player is less likely to fare well in this circumstance. Again, the hands that are chosen are quite arbitrary, and are intended primarily to show, as in example 1, how the point count fluctuates up and down in the course of the deal.

If the reader finds it easier to count the points in some other order, he should, of course, feel free to do so. For example, any high card can, in principle, be deducted at the first instant it is seen. To illustrate, in the first round of example 1, the first player can deduct for the ace that he holds as soon as he picks up his cards and sees it. Some people may prefer to do this. However, in my opinion, it is less confusing to wait until the dealer is about to pick up the cards that have been turned face up, and to tally all the high cards then.

Whenever the cards are shuffled, the counting must start over. Thus, the net count must always reflect the status of the deck from which cards will be drawn on the next round. The precise effect of this requirement depends on what the dealer does when a round ends with insufficient cards left in the deck to play another full round. Custom varies from one casino to another, sometimes from one dealer to another in the same casino, and even from one time to another with the same dealer. In some casinos it is an invariant rule that the cards are dealt right down to the card with which the deck was sealed after the previous shuffle. Where this rule is not in effect, the procedure seems to be up to the dealer's discretion. Some dealers insist on enough cards for a full deal around. Others reshuffle if less than about a half-dozen cards are left.

Some very dramatic shifts in point count can occur when cards are dealt right down to the bottom of the deck. Suppose that when going into the last round, there is a high plus count, and there are not enough cards to complete the round. When the last card is reached, the dealer then shuffles all the previously collected cards, but the cards for the current round must remain on the table. As the deal continues, if just a few cards are dealt to complete the round, it is quite likely that the point count going into the next round will be a low count.

As an illustration, suppose there remain to be dealt to three players and the dealer, on the last round, the following assortment of cards: 4-A-10-5-2-5-K-5-A-K-10. The point count going into this situation is +7. Suppose also that when the previously collected cards are shuffled, the next two cards to come out are 3-K. (This combination of cards actually is the same as that shown for round two of example 2, but it must be borne in mind that it is now assumed to occur at the end of the deck rather than on round two.) This round is now complete, a settlement is made, and the cards are collected. Making the count on the above 13 cards, as if they had just been dealt out of a fresh deck, we see that we now go into the next round with a count of −7. There has been a marked "flip-over" in point count at the end of the deck!

Fast changes in point count are one of the exciting features of this game, and they force the player to keep on his toes. Nonetheless, the basic idea of the point counting is a rather elementary thing, and with a little bit of practice, the average blackjack player should catch on quickly. Hence, assuming that the mechanics of counting is understood, we shall now talk about the fluctuations in count and what they mean in terms of winning odds.

Relation Between Point Count and Probability of Winning

We said to begin with that the idea is to obtain some measure of the excess or deficiency of aces and 10s. The point count is such a measure. In theory, the count could be as high as +32 or as low as −32. But, in practice, it rarely ranges in value beyond +10 or −10. My experience as regards the approximate relative frequency with which various point-count values occur is shown in the graph in Table 7-3. We see that zero is the most common count and that the distribution tapers off on either side for deviations away from zero. Deviations up to +5 or −5 are seen to occur with reasonable frequency, and even values up to +10 or −10 do happen occasionally. Values beyond that point are very infrequent, however.

Having specified how often a given point count occurs, we now ask how to interpret this count, in terms of the probability of winning with this count. By dealing hands from decks that had been depleted of high or low cards in various numbers, and by correlating the results, I came up with a neat rule of thumb. The player's expected *profit*, expressed as a percent, is just about half the Wilson point-count value. (When the count is negative, he then has an expected *loss* of this amount.) This simple prediction is tabulated in Table 7-2 where it has been assumed as a point of departure that in the

TABLE 7-2. SHIFT IN PLAYER'S ODDS FOR WINNING AS THE
WILSON POINT COUNT VARIES

Wilson Point Count	Probability of Winning p	Expectation (decimal) p − q = 2p − 1	Expectation (percentage) (100 × decimal)	
.				
.				
.				
+10	0.525	+0.050	+5.0	profit
.				
.				
+5	0.5125	+0.025	+2.5	profit
+4	0.510	+0.020	+2.0	profit
+3	0.5075	+0.015	+1.5	profit
+2	0.505	+0.010	+1.0	profit
+1	0.5025	+0.005	+0.5	profit
0	0.500	0	0	even game
−1	0.4975	−0.005	−0.5	loss
−2	0.495	−0.010	−1.0	loss
−3	0.4925	−0.015	−1.5	loss
−4	0.490	−0.020	−2.0	loss
−5	0.4875	−0.025	−2.5	loss
.				
.				
.				
−10	0.475	−0.050	−5.0	loss
.				
.				
.				

NOTE: The figures for probability and for expectation should not be construed as exact but only as rough values. Furthermore, they represent average values, for each given point count.

basic game (with zero point count), the player has exactly 0.500 *effective* chance to win (see pages 56 and 88).

Figuring the Net Profit Advantage with Wilson Point Count

Knowing the relative distribution of favorable and unfavorable point count situations, we can now readily figure the net effective advantage for any arbitrary betting scheme. Take for example the 1(3)7 scale of bets I used during a portion of my summer escapade in 1959. We seek a sum of weighted contributions from each possible situation. Each weighted contribution is merely the product of a bet value times a relative frequency of occurrence times the advantage for that particular situation.

This straightforward computation is shown in Table 7-3. The

TABLE 7-3. POINT COUNT PLUS BET-VARIATION METHOD
FOR PRODUCING A PROFIT

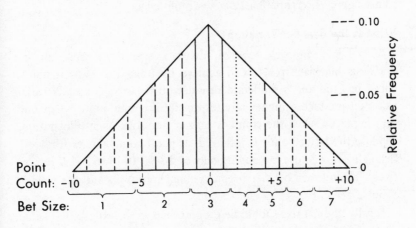

I	II	III	IV	V	VI
Point Count	Bet Size	Relative Frequency	Product (II × III)	Expected Profit	Product (IV × V)
+9	7	0.01	0.07	+0.045	+0.00315
+8	7	0.02	0.14	+0.040	+0.00560
+7	6	0.03	0.18	+0.035	+0.00630
+6	6	0.04	0.24	+0.030	+0.00720
+5	5	0.05	0.25	+0.025	+0.00625
+4	5	0.06	0.30	+0.020	+0.00600
+3	4	0.07	0.28	+0.015	+0.00420
+2	4	0.08	0.32	+0.010	+0.00320
+1	3	0.09	0.27	+0.005	+0.00135
0	3	0.10	0.30	0	+0.04325
−1	3	0.09	0.27	−0.005	−0.00135
−2	2	0.08	0.16	−0.010	−0.00160
−3	2	0.07	0.14	−0.015	−0.00210
−4	2	0.06	0.12	−0.020	−0.00240
−5	2	0.05	0.10	−0.025	−0.00250
−6	1	0.04	0.04	−0.030	−0.00120
−7	1	0.03	0.03	−0.035	−0.00105
−8	1	0.02	0.02	−0.040	−0.00080
−9	1	0.01	0.01	−0.045	−0.00045
			3.24		−0.01345

$$\frac{+0.04325 - 0.01345}{3.24} = \frac{+0.0298}{3.24}$$
$$= +0.0092;$$

thus, 0.92 percent, or approximately 1 percent effective net profit.

entries in the last column are totaled and divided by the average bet size of 3.24 units, giving +0.0092, or 0.92 percent. Expressed as a round figure, this is about a 1 *percent* profit edge!

What Is the Best Bet Variation?*

The 1 percent yield quoted above is typical of what an industrious blackjack player can achieve by using the Wilson point-count method and a moderate variation in bet size. A steeper variation will produce a higher rate, especially if a minimum bet of one unit is placed when the count is zero or negative. As an illustration, suppose the latter policy is followed; as point count ranges from +1 through +9, one uses ascending bets of 2-3-5-7-10-13-16-20-25, respectively. The average bet size becomes about four units and the yield is about 2 percent.

Ideally, the bet size should be *proportional to* the expectation value on that hand. This is consistent with the development of Chapter 17 on how to size your bets. Figure 17-1 shows that for any given assigned chance of success (in the face of inevitable fluctuations), a doubling of the player's edge reduces the number of betting units required by half. For a given bankroll, of course this implies that twice as big a bet is permitted.

Whatever the theory predicts for optimum bet variation, what matters in practice is how big a swing the dealer will tolerate. In general, it has been my policy to try to avoid aggravating the dealer, and I have seldom employed a steeper bet variation than that shown in Table 7-3. When the all-important factor of dealer psychology is taken into account, I believe that a compromise of gradual variation gets better results than the "go-for-broke" jolt of abrupt bet changes.

Limitations of the Wilson Point-Count System

It is important to understand that the shift in player's odds as a function of point count, as given in Table 7-2, represents an average. A given point count can, in general, be made up in a number of different ways. Each of these different combinations of cards, which total the same point value, may have a different expectation. So, each

* See also Appendix G, "Optimal Betting."

value indicated in the table is an *average* over different expectations, all for the same point value.

For example, take the case where the last four cards consist of an ace and three 10s. The player has an 0.5 chance to win, with a 1.5 payoff, and the same chance of losing, at only 1.0 unit. His expectation is $0.5 \times 1.5 - 0.5 \times 1.0 = 0.25$, for a whopping 25 percent average profit in this situation (it would be even juicier if insurance were available, for the latter would be a sure thing). Yet, the point count going into this case is $+7$, for which we plot only 3.5 percent profit in general. The situation is extremely rare, yet we can infer that $+7$ points may mean a lot more near the end of the deck than early in the deck.

On the other hand, a counter illustration can be given for $+8$ points. If the last eight cards in the deck were all 10-value cards, the count would be high. Actually, all the player can do in this case is draw, with *his* 10-10 against the dealer's 10-10. (We are assuming one hand against the dealer, and excluding such subtleties as "end play," which will be taken up later.) Here we see the player's expectation in this apparently rich case is exactly zero percent profit. Thus, if all of the aces are gone, a high count due to 10s alone may be misleading.

The moral of the story is that the Wilson point-count system is not perfect. I do not claim that it is. Nonetheless, it is a *good practical scheme* for keeping rough track of the cards and for making bet changes that will in general be advantageous. There is nothing to prevent you from noting how far into the deck you are, and then allowing extra weight for cases near the end of the deck. You merely look at the dealer's undealt stack, and guess roughly what fraction of the deck remains.

The major advantage of the Wilson method is that you have to keep a running total on *one number only*. The method is ideally suited for the average card player who does not have a crackerjack memory for cards. It is simpler than other card-count techniques, where you have to keep track of *two* numbers and then mentally compute a ratio. In the Wilson method, there is also the extra advantage that you perform *addition* as you see each card dealt, and then subtract as you see aces and 10s at the end of the hand. Most other systems require subtracting continuously on two running numbers. Addition is a more familiar mental process, and fewer mistakes are likely to be made.

In summary, the chief appeal of the Wilson method is its simplicity. On this basis, it should attract the great majority of card players, who have neither the time, talent, nor inclination to go into the more complicated methods. On the other hand, the biggest shortcoming of the Wilson method is that it is less efficient than the more complex methods, that is, it does not win money at as fast a rate. Those who demand the greatest yield, and who are willing to put in the corresponding effort, should consider the methods discussed in the subsequent sections.

THE 10-COUNT METHOD

A better criterion for the richness of the deck is to keep track of the ratio of non-10s versus 10s (referred to hereafter as NT/T). Aces are included among the NT. The ratio value for a full deck is 36/16, or 2.25/1. As cards are dealt from the deck, fluctuations occur about this value. Not infrequently, NT/T drops to 1.5, and even occasionally to 1.0; such situations are "rich." On the other side, NT/T may swing up to 3.0 or 3.5, and even rather rarely to 4.0 or higher; these cases are "poor." As seen in Fig. 7-2, the great bulk of hands have ratio values at or near 2.25. Nonetheless, worthwhile deviations from this average value occur a reasonable portion of the time.

Dr. Edward Thorp, in his book, *Beat the Dealer*, has popularized the 10-count method, much to the chagrin of the casinos. He was the first to analyze mathematically the potentialities of this method with a computer. Testing a number of decks, which were either augmented with or depleted of one or more 10s, he determined the player's expectation as a function of NT/T. Using the correct basic strategy (and ignoring insurance for the time being), the expectation ranges from around +4 percent with a count of 1.0 down to about −4 percent with a count of 4.0. This is roughly the same spread as given for the Wilson point-count method in Table 7-3. The 10-count method is superior in that it gives a continuous measure of the *relative* richness, in contrast to an excess or absolute in the Wilson method. Consequently, the NT/T ratio has a more uniform meaning for varying depths into the deck.

A deficiency of the 10-count method is that aces are lumped in with the other non-10s. But Thorp has a cure for this. He estimates

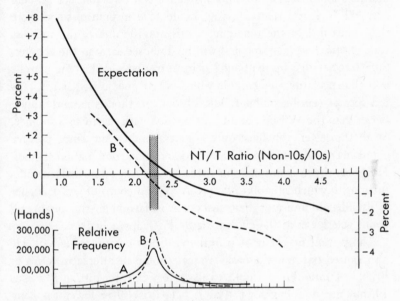

Upper Curves: Expectation as function of NT/T ratio.
Lower Curves: Relative frequency of various NT/T ratios.
  A: 1,400,000 hands played to depth of 46 cards in 1 deck.
  B: 1,400,000 hands played to depth of 160 cards in 4 decks mixed together.
  NOTE: Expectation curves fitted to computer data listings of Julian Braun, by means of *weighted* 4th degree polynomial; frequency curves faired in by hand.

FIG. 7-2.   Results of 10-Count Strategy

that you can figure the increment (or decrement) in expectation due to fluctuation in ace content as $(13A/N - 1) \times 4\%$. Here A is the number of unseen aces, and N is the total number of unseen cards. When $A/N = 1/13$, the number of aces is average, and the formula gives zero percent, as it should. When A/N is greater than 1/13, the deck is "ace rich," and the formula gives a number to be added;

when A/N is less than 1/13, the deck is "ace poor," and the formula gives a negative number. For the average player who finds it hard enough to keep track of NT and T, and to figure the NT/T ratio, the only practical hope is to try also to keep rough track of the aces and to "lean" in the right direction.

One of the great advantages of the 10-count method is that it indicates automatically whether insurance is a favorable bet. Whenever NT/T is less than 2.0, you should take insurance, since more than one-third of the remaining cards are 10-value cards, and the time is ripe. *Just how* ripe it is will be discussed later in the chapter. Suffice to say that up to about 2 percent can be added to the player's over-all expectation in a hand in which NT/T goes as rich as 1.0. This is a very perceptible amount. The 10-count method is patently much better than the Wilson point-count method with regard to insurance. With the latter, you have only a general indication, since positive count may be due to excess 10s or aces, or some combination thereof. However, if you count aces on the side, you can often make a judgment as to which situation prevails. A Wilson count of +5 or higher is usually an indicator that insurance is favorable; the qualifying count gets lower as the end of the deck is approached.

Thorp went one giant step further with his computer analysis. He also figured out how the basic strategy should be altered in terms of his NT/T ratio. For example, basic strategy calls for hitting 10 versus 10, but not doubling-down. But if NT/T is 1.9 or lower (as compared to the average 2.25 to which basic strategy applies), you should double-down. The deck is just enough richer in 10s to justify a reversal in basic strategy. A converse example is 11 versus 10. Here you normally double-down. However, if NT/T is higher than 2.8, you should just hit, and not double-down. The depletion of 10s at this point is such that the double-down no longer produces a higher expectation.

The critical ratio for one decision versus another can be evaluated for each type of player versus dealer situation. In fact, it can be calculated on either of two bases: (1) as applied to the count just prior to the deal, and (2) as applied after the player cards and the dealer up-card have been dealt. The latter case of a "running count" should, in principle, allow for all cards seen right up to the point of making the decision, including cards dealt to other players. The running count is more efficient than the prior count, especially at the end of the deck. However, a running count is harder to keep, and the NT/T ratios really do not differ much in the two cases. A chart of the NT/T ratios for running count is given in Table 7-4. For these data I am indebted to Julian Braun of the IBM Corporation, who ran a study that was a refinement of Thorp's original method. Many values of NT/T coincide with those on page 77 of Thorp's book.*

To commit all the numbers in this table to memory would be a staggering chore for most readers. To be able to recall any one of them within a few seconds, under the stress of fast casino play, would take more weeks or months of practice. Fortunately, that is not necessary. More than half of the available gain is achieved just by knowing the NT/T values that apply to the simple hard hands, and these fall into trends that can at least be remembered approximately without too much trouble. For those who wish to make the effort, the other groups, in decreasing order of contribution, are hard double-downs, splits, and soft double-downs. A number of the situations are so rare that one could play steadily for *days* without seeing them occur. Thorp himself admits that he does not succeed in remembering all.

What Profit Can the 10-Count Yield?

Is the 10-count method worth the trouble? Very definitely *yes*, for those who are persistent enough to master it. Again, I have the benefit of calculations by Braun to back this up. He programed it after many

---

* Certain refinements to the "basic" strategy in borderline cases can be inferred. Exact expectation (ε) calculations below illustrate this (e.g., hit 10-2 versus 3, but stand on 8-4). Where Table 7-4 leads to erroneous action, it is due to great sensitivity to particular card values. An especially instructive case is hard 16 versus 7. On a 4-card 16 with the highest card a 5 or lower, you should stand; same on a 5-card 16. Hard 16 versus 8 is similar, but less strongly.

Case	ε (hitting)	ε (standing)	Running NT/T Ratio
10-2 vs. 3	−0.220	−0.260	2.27
8-4 vs. 3	−0.230	−0.210	2.06
10-6 vs. 10	−0.507	−0.543	2.50
10-4-2 vs. 10	−0.550	−0.543	2.43
10-6 vs. 7	−0.377	−0.483	2.27
5-3-4-4 vs. 7	−0.487	−0.455	1.94

TABLE 7-4. STRATEGY AS A FUNCTION OF NON-10/10 RATIO

Normal Hit or Stand

		Dealer Up-Card									
		2	3	4	5	6	7	8	9	10	A
	18										
	17										3.1
Player	16	3.9	4.5	5.3	6.5	4.6		1.2	1.7	2.2	1.4
Hard	15	3.2	3.6	4.1	4.8	4.3			1.4	1.9	1.3
Total	14	2.7	2.9	3.3	3.7	3.4			1.1	1.6	1.2
	13	2.3	2.5	2.6	3.0	2.7				1.3	1.1
	12	2.0	2.1	2.2	2.4	2.3				1.1	1.0

(The table gives the "critical" ratios of NT/T. If the running count exceeds the entry in the table, then hit the hand. If it is equal to or less than the entry, then stand.)

Hard Double Down

	2	3	4	5	6	7	8	9	10	A
11	3.9	4.2	4.8	5.5	5.5	3.7	3.0	2.6	2.8	2.2
10	3.8	4.2	4.8	5.7	5.9	3.9	3.0	2.5	1.9	1.8
9	2.2	2.4	2.8	3.2	3.4	2.0	1.6			
8	1.4	1.5	1.8	2.1	2.1	1.0				

(If running count is equal to or less than entry, double down.)

Splitting of Pairs

	2	3	4	5	6	7	8	9	10	A
A-A	4.0	4.1	4.5	4.9	5.0	3.8	3.3	3.1	3.2	2.6
10-10	1.4	1.5	1.7	1.9	1.8					
9-9	2.4	2.8	3.1	3.7	3.2	1.6	3.5	4.2		1.6
8-8									1.6*	4.5
7-7							3.3			1.4
6-6	2.4	2.6	3.0	3.6	4.1	3.4				
5-5										
4-4	1.3	1.6	1.9	2.4	2.1					
3-3	5.5					1.1*	2.4*	4.2*	5.3*	
2-2	3.1	3.8				1.1*	3.8*			

(If running count is equal to or less than entry, split the pair—except if the entry is followed by *; in these few cases, the rule is reversed, namely split if the count exceeds entry.)

TABLE 7-4. STRATEGY AS A FUNCTION OF NON-10/10 RATIO (*Cont.*)

Soft Double Down		2	3	4	5	6
	A-9	1.3	1.3	1.5	1.6	1.6
	A-8	1.4	1.7	1.8	2.0	2.0
	A-7	2.0	2.2	3.3	3.8	3.5
	A-6	2.1	2.5	3.2	4.8	4.8
	A-5	1.6	1.9	2.5	3.1	4.0
	A-4	1.6	1.9	2.4	3.0	3.2
	A-3	1.5	1.8	2.3	2.9	3.0
	A-2	1.5	1.7	2.1	2.6	2.7

Soft Hands: In general, simply follow the basic strategy on soft hands. Only the
(Hitting or   case of soft 18 vs. A is marginal. If NT/T exceeds 2.2, hit soft 18 vs.
Standing)   A; if it is equal to or less than 2.2, stand as usual.

General note: Blanked areas in above tables imply that deviations which would call
for departure from the basic strategy are generally too rare to consider. (See
page 49 for the basic strategy.)

hours of effort and obtained raw data in his computer runs, which
he sent to me. I wrote a simpler program for smoothing the raw
data, and came out with curves that are plotted in Fig. 7-2. Braun
actually simulated the play of hands through the deck exactly as it
would occur in the casino. The computer kept a running count on
the NT/T ratio; also it had Table 7-4 in its perfect memory. Thus
did the IBM 7090 play millions of hands of flawless 10-count blackjack. The wins and losses were printed out, each listed in the appropriate NT/T category ranging from 0.5 to 7.0.

Braun's runs gave excellent statistical information on the expectation for any given NT/T value and also for the relative frequency of
that value. His results were in good concurrence with the curves and
tables given in Thorp's book, which were computed by an entirely
different method, namely, by direct probability.

With the 10-count system played according to basic strategy, with
neither insurance nor any correction for aces, and with some nominal
bet variation such as the 1 to 7 in Table 7-3, the yield is slightly
under 1 percent. Thus it is comparable with the Wilson count. But
with proper strategy variation based on the running NT/T value,

and with proper insurance and correction for aces, the yield is close to 2 percent, and a good 10-count play is about twice as productive as the Wilson count. As pointed out in Chapter 17 on bet sizing, with twice the edge, you can use bets twice as large for a given bankroll; then you can win at four times the rate.

10-Count Even Wins on a Flat Bet

Equally important, without any bet variation, the 10-count method with its attendant strategy changes, still enables you to play with a measurable advantage. Without bet variation, Wilson point counting is of much less value, and the edge drops almost to zero. Braun's simulations reveal that up to 1 percent can be squeezed out on flat bets by keeping a running 10-count and playing the appropriate hitting strategy, provided the deal goes almost to the end of the deck. Table 7-5 shows what can be accomplished as a function of depth

TABLE 7-5. PLAYER EXPECTATION AT FLAT BET AS FUNCTION OF "DEPTH" INTO DECK

(assuming *perfect* 10-count technique for strategy decisions)

	Percent
Minimum of 4 cards into the deck	+0.3
32	0.5
39	0.8
46	1.2

The deck is reshuffled whenever the number of cards used up by the end of the hand exceeds the indicated minimum. The minimum of 4 corresponds to only one hand, played "off the top" of the deck. In the 46 card minimum, if the deal actually reaches through 50 cards, a shuffle is made at this point.

into the deck. However, so that you will not jump to any conclusions about how easy this is, let these assumptions be clearly understood: (1) the player is head-to-head against the dealer (one hand only), for if more than one hand is played at a time, the relative frequency of the rich situations is reduced; (2) very high quality counting and adjusting of strategy is implied, since the computer played without error in working out these percentages. Dealer shuffleover, periodic introduction of new decks, presence of other players, and other factors may in practice seriously reduce this potentiality. Nonetheless, it is almost unbelievable to hear that a skillful flat-bet player can, under occasionally prevailing conditions, score up to a 1 percent advantage!

If You Can Master It, Play 10-Count

In the preceding sections, it has been definitely demonstrated that the 10-count produces a higher win rate than the Wilson point count. So, by all means, if you can master it well enough and do not become easily fatigued, play 10-count. I touted my own system early in the chapter because it is definitely simpler and easier to manage. Many players will choose to go no further. Personally, I prefer to play 10-count when I am in practice because it is the superior method. However, in my opinion, the counting procedure is improved if you count down on total cards rather than non-10s. Thus, you keep track of Total/T, and then for reference to the strategy table, you convert over by noting the simple relation $\text{Total}/T - 1 = (\text{Total} - T)/T = NT/T$. In fact, I should prefer to give the strategy table here in terms of Total/T, not just to be different from Thorp, but because I believe it to be better. Certainly this is true if you are taking the "prior count," for just as with the Wilson method, you can get this one accumulation out of the way immediately as the cards are first dealt. I would undoubtedly give the table this way were it not for the risk of confusing myself now that I have mastered quite a few of the NT/T values. For anyone starting out, I recommend adding 1 to all the NT/T values, and learning the table in terms of Total/T values. After you have had a little practice, you will appreciate why I think the "two-phase" technique is easier on the hard-working count player.

THE HI-LO METHOD

At the Fall Joint Computer Conference in 1963 (see page 99), Harvey Dubner presented a "hi-lo" point count method, which he claimed to be even more efficient than 10-count. The lo's consist of 2 through 6, and the hi's, of 10 through ace; excluded as neutral cards are the 7, 8, and 9. Dubner counts the following ratio: (hi's left − lo's left)/total cards left. On the basis of this ratio, a bet variation scale is prescribed in steps 1-5-10-20. No strategy alteration for hitting or standing, etc., has been worked out.

Dubner, an engineer at Simmonds Precision Products Company in Tarrytown, New York, doped out his scheme using a CDC 924 digital computer. He is a relative newcomer to the scene, his trip to the conference in Las Vegas being his first occasion for actual casino play; his system showed a win. It is clearly based on good general principles, since both ace and 10-value cards are considered as good cards, and the five poorest of the remaining eight cards are lumped in the poor group. He asserts that his calculations show that for each 0.10 in hi-lo index value, the player has 2.0 to 2.5 percent of advantage. For example, suppose 20 cards remain, composed of two aces, nine 10-value cards, five low cards, and four neutral cards. Then the hi-lo count is $(11 - 5)/20 = 6/20 = 0.30$, and the player advantage would be between 6 and 7½ percent. (Incidentally, the 10-count here would be $NT/T = 11/9 = 1.22$; Thorp predicts about a 6 percent edge.) Another typical result is that on 7 percent of hands, the player is calculated to have an advantage of 5 percent or more, provided the deck is not reshuffled until six cards from the end. Again, this is consistent with some of the simulations on 10-count play performed by Braun, with corresponding penetration into the deck.

Nonetheless, from our (limited) exposure to Dubner's description of his method of analysis, some of us at the conference concluded that his claims may be slightly exaggerated—particularly the allegation that hi-lo wins money almost twice as fast as 10-count. Insufficient allowance has been made, in my opinion, for the fact that you can shade the 10-count to bring aces into the picture. In any case, it is harder to keep a hi-lo count than a 10-count because you have to segregate out the 7s, 8s, and 9s from the low-card group. Furthermore, without additional information being carried along, hi-lo has distinct deficiencies as an insurance indicator: (1) aces are lumped in with the 10s in the high-card total, and (2) if only the hi minus lo numerator *difference* is remembered, then the *actual* number of high cards is not available for comparison with total card count in the denominator. Finally, to work out shifts in the hitting rules as a function of hi-lo count is far more complex than for 10-count. All the same, I have to hand it to Dubner for advancing so far in blackjack in such a short time!

THORP'S "ULTIMATE" POINT-COUNT METHOD

Contention over the relative merits of hi-lo versus 10-count is probably superfluous in the light of Thorp's "ultimate" strategy. Here he assigns a point value to each different denomination of card. Aces and 10s are at one end of the spectrum, and 5s and 4s at the other. The weight factor assigned to each card is proportional to the change in player expectation upon removal of one card of that denomination from a full deck. (More correctly, it is one-fourth of the change due to removal of four such cards, Thorp having made a number of computer runs with each denomination missing from the deck, one at a time.)

The "ultimate" strategy calls for keeping track of three numbers: non-10s, 10s, and points. As with the 10-count method, the NT/T ratio is used for insurance purposes and for changes in hitting rules. But the new point score gives a more accurate measure of the current player advantage (or disadvantage), and thus a better basis for selecting bet size. Also, it may reveal the exact value of an unseen card if the deal goes to the very end of the deck. Since the card point values involve numbers ranging from -9 to $+11$, and each denomination has a different number except for two that coincide, this ultimate technique is clearly for the person having *ultimate* mental agility! Nonetheless, Thorp estimates that this method wins at 2½ times the rate of the simple old 10-count.

REVIEW OF THE CARD-COUNTING TECHNIQUES

So far, this chapter has been devoted to the major methods of card counting. Each has been discussed as regards its attractive features and its drawbacks. You can take your pick as to which *you* have the capability of playing, ranging from the simple Wilson count to Thorp's "ultimate." If undue space seems to have been spent on my own system, it's because this is *my* book! Besides, I honestly believe the great bulk of players do not wish to exert themselves beyond the simplest available method that can turn a good profit. But my method can definitely stand improving. In fact, I confess that while using my system of counting, I have not always adhered to the basic strategy, but rather have made "intuitive" changes in hitting rules under occasional obvious circumstances. For example, if my count has gone way negative, I have hit 13 or 14 with the dealer showing 4 or 5. Conversely, if the count has swung strongly plus, I have found myself standing on 15 or 14 against 10. Thus I have used "flexibility" in applying my system.

Those who are seriously interested in the 10-count and the ultimate systems should read Thorp's book. It contains more detail than I could hope to include here even if my friend Thorp had no copyright objections. On the other hand, those who are content to read my coverage here may rest assured that a comprehensive summary of the best available information has been presented!

INTELLIGENT INSURANCE BETTING

In Chapter 5, we gave an introductory mention of insurance, and indicated that usually it is an unfavorable bet. But we have seen that with card memory, you can ferret out the favorable insurance situations and play them to your advantage. This subject has not been treated in any detail in published material, and appears here for the first time as a result of a short Fortran program which I wrote for an IBM 7094. It is a straightforward probability calculation, but without the aid of a computer, it would take days of hand computation; the computer took half a minute!

The key information is presented in Table 7-6 on page 128, and in Figure 7-3 on page 130. Two questions are answered:

I. What proportion of the time are more than one-third of the unseen cards 10-value cards?

II. What magnitude of yield can we expect in these favorable situations?

Answers to these questions can be given only if the playing conditions are specified. So we shall assume a reasonable set of conditions, but later shall consider variations. Conditions are: (1) The maximum number of unseen cards is 47, and the minimum is 5. The former implies that you can look at your own two cards and also those of a partner or neighbor; the latter implies that the dealer does not necessarily deal all the way down to the bottom of the deck. (2) The process of dealing and shuffling is such as to make all situations from 47 down to 5 unseen cards equally likely to occur. This may not be strictly true, but it is a good working approximation. (3) The bet size remains fixed.

The answer to question I depends very much on the number of unseen cards, but we can find an average value. One extreme is when most of the deck is as yet unseen. Here the fraction of the time that more than one-third of the unseen cards are 10-value cards is around 10 to 30 percent. This is shown nicely in Table 7-6. The decimal values that appear toward the bottom of the second column reveal this fact. (Examination of these figures reveals an interesting cyclic pattern, as the number of unseen cards changes by 3. This results from a 10 being paired off with two non-10s.) At the other extreme, most of the deck has been dealt out, and only a few cards remain unseen. Here the fraction of the time that more than one-third of the unseen cards are 10-value cards is much higher, around 30 to 50 percent. This dramatic increase is due to the fact that one or two excess 10s, above the average number, produce a much greater *relative* shift with a small number of cards than with a large number.

The average of these wide-ranging values is around 31 percent. (This is under assumption (2), namely, that situations from 47 down to 5 unseen cards occur with equal frequency.) Thus almost one-third of the time, more than one-third of the unseen cards are 10s. This clearly makes it worth while to keep track of the previously played cards, for purposes of knowing when the insurance bet is favorable.

Question II asks *how favorable* are these favorable insurance bets? Again there is a wide range of values, as may be seen in columns 3 and 4 of Table 6. When there are a large number of cards unseen, the expectation is in the neighborhood of 5 percent; with just a handful of unseen cards, it may be 25 percent, or even considerably higher. Again, a shift of one or two 10s near the end of the deck can swing the expectation greatly.

TABLE 7-6. TYPICAL DATA PERTAINING TO FAVORABLE INSURANCE BETS

Number of Unseen Cards	Fraction of Time that Insurance has + Expectation			Least Expectation for this Situation			Average Expectation for this Situation
6	.273			.500			.644
7		.381			.286		.460
8			.488			.125	.328
9	.289			.333			.468
10		.381			.200		.355
11			.475			.091	.265
12	.295			.250			.372
13		.378			.154		.290
14			.463			.071	.222
15	.296			.200			.308
16		.372			.125		.245
17			.452			.059	.190
.	.			.			.
.	.			.			.
.	.			.			.
42	.147			.071			.083
43		.206			.047		.059
44			.282			.023	.037
45	.090			.067			.067
46		.138			.043		.043
47			.210			.021	.021
48 or more		zero					

Among all situations where the insurance bet is favorable, the very least percentage in your favor is the 2.1 percent advantage that applies when there are 47 unseen cards and all 16 of the 10s are still out. There are two other situations where all 16 of the 10s must be among the unseen cards in order for insurance to be desirable; these are the cases of 46 and 45 cards. The advantages are $(+2)(16/46) + (-1)$ $(30/46) = 2/46$, or 4.3 percent, and $(+2)(16/45) + (-1)(29/45)$ $= 3/45$, or 6.7 percent, respectively. With 44 unseen cards, it suffices for 15 of them to be 10s, in which case the expectation works out to be 1/44, or 2.3 percent. Similar figures for 43 and 42 cards, with 15 of the 10s among them, are 4.7 percent and 7.1 percent. Again we see the cyclic pattern, in which the numbers move in groups of 3. (Incidentally, in these last three cases, if all 16 of the 10s are still left, the expectation is about 7 percent higher. However, sixteen 10s are somewhat less frequent than fifteen 10s in these cases.)

The expectation values quoted in the preceding paragraph are examples of "minimum expectation," that is, the smallest expectation you can have for a given number of unseen cards. As the number of unseen cards gets smaller, the minimum expectation increases. By the time that just a handful of cards is left, it can be very impressive. The minimum expectations for 8, 7, and 6 unseen cards, respectively, are 12.5, 28.6, and 50 percent! These apply when three of the unseen cards are 10s. As if these expectations were not high enough, there are appreciable contributions from cases where four or more of the unseen cards are 10s. When these various eventualities are considered according to their relative frequency of occurrence, we come up with "average expectation" values substantially higher than the minimum expectation. For the cases of eight, seven, and six unseen cards, these are a whopping big 33, 46, and 64 percent!

The foregoing information enables us to answer question III. What is the magnitude of yield that can be expected in the favorable insurance situations *as a whole?* The graph in Fig. 7-3 shows that the "average expectation" values range all the way from around 50 percent down to 2 percent. Subject to our earlier assumption (2) that all cases from 47 down to 5 unseen cards are equally likely to occur, an "average of the averages" may be figured. It works out to 18 percent. Thus, when insurance is a good bet, you may anticipate on the whole a profit of about one-fifth of a unit per unit of insurance wagered.

How Much Can Insurance Add to Your Profit?

The preceding situation sounds very rosy. However, let us bear in mind these facts: (1) The insurance wager is limited to one-half of the wager already placed. (2) The dealer shows an ace only one-thirteenth of the time. (3) Of these times, when insurance is offered, only about one-third of the time is it a favorable bet. When all the factors are combined, we find that the average available insurance profit, per unit of regular betting, is approximately

$$1/2 \times 1/13 \times 1/3 \times 1/5 = 1/390$$

or about 0.0025; that is to say, *at flat bets*, the over-all expectation of the basic game can be boosted by about 0.25 percent. (Technically speaking, the terms $1/3 \times 1/5$ should be replaced by the sum of the successive products of the entries in columns 2 and 4 of Table 7-6, divided by the number of entries. For simplicity, I have used the product of the two separate column averages, which is not exactly the same.)

While a boost of 0.25 percent is small, it should not be sneezed at. Furthermore, there is one very fortunate aspect of insurance

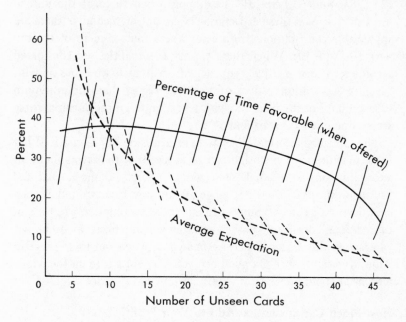

FIG. 7-3. Curves for Insurance Betting

betting. When the bet *is* favorable, the very smallest margin in your favor is 2 percent; often it is much more. Hence the fluctuation problem is minor, and you need very little additional capital on hand for the extra insurance bets.

When bets are increased with decreasing NT/T ratio, insurance can yield a higher profit. Assuming that playing conditions are such that assumptions (1) and (2) on page 126 are still valid, rough calculations show that something like 0.5 percent can be added to overall expectation when bets are boosted by around five, in mildly favorable insurance situations, and up to ten in more strongly favorable cases. This is twice as much improvement as applies in the flat-bet case.

My theoretical calculations are proved out by good agreement with the through-the-deck computer simulations of Julian Braun, in which he separately tabulated the frequency of occurrence of favorable insurance bets, and units won and lost therein. Accordingly, you have here in this section the best available information on the subject. In short, it pays to count 10s and to place smart insurance bets!

WHERE TO SIT AT THE BLACKJACK TABLE

A matter of potential importance to consider is whether any particular seat at a table is preferable when there are several players. The dealer usually passes out cards from his left, around to his right, and then to himself. Hence, the position at his extreme left has become known as *first base*, and that at the extreme right is *third base*. (No other analogies with baseball have been invoked for the other player positions.)

Many players prefer to sit on third base because they get to see more exposed cards before they have to decide what to do with their own hand. This is an unquestionable advantage, especially in cases where preceding players face *all* their cards, as in a split, double-down, or blackjack. When the preceding players do not have occasion to turn all their cards face up, which is the usual case, you must be careful with your inferences. The draw cards that you see are fine, but you must make allowance for the various possible card combinations that the player may hold in the first place and which may make him want to draw. These, of course, cannot be assumed as randomly distributed from among all the unseen cards in the deck. Many pairs of cards are possible, but many others are excluded because he would not need to draw to them.

Thus, the appraisal of the unseen cards of the other players can be a very subtle thing, especially if you do not know what strategies the other players follow. If there are any novices or just plain poor players at the table, their actions may deviate considerably from our recommended strategy. In view of this fact, and because of the speed with which play usually proceeds, I personally do not try much of this detective work. In any event, let the reader be warned of the possibility of bias error if he makes judgments solely on the basis of cards that are faced.

There is also a very definite advantage to first base when the dealer is kind enough to deal all the way down to the end of the deck. At a full table of six players, this advantage exists when there is a rich end-deck situation and less than 14 cards left to deal. If there are from 8 to 13 cards left, the player at the dealer's immediate left will take two cards from the rich pile, to the dealer's one card; if there are from one to six cards left, this player will draw one card from the rich pile, while the dealer will draw none. In either case, the dealer will have to fill his hand from the previously collected cards, which will be poorer than average. This is an advantage for the player on first base, provided he raises his bet in this situation; if he doesn't do that, then there is no advantage, since otherwise this situation just averages out with all the other end-deck situations.

Obviously this benefit exists to a lesser and lesser degree as you progress around from first to third base, just as the advantage of seeing previously played cards decreases as you progress around in the opposite direction. For my own style of play, I consider first base preferable to third, and ideally would choose to sit there. However, in practice, I often find it hard to see the cards of the third base player when they are turned over. Since it is essential in my card-count method to see all cards as they are faced, I usually try to obtain the seat next to first base. Thus, I am second on the deal, rather than first. In this position, there is usually little difficulty in seeing all the hands as they are turned over.

All this talk about seat preference is helpful only if you actually have a choice. If the tables are crowded, you take what you can get. If a better spot opens up after a while, either at the same table or a neighboring table, then it is advisable to move if you can avoid being too obvious about it. Your purpose in changing is probably less evident if you go to another table, since players are always roving from one table to another for a change of luck.

The true professional is not much concerned with the question of where to sit, since frequently he bets big and usurps all six places at the table for himself. When small fry are frozen out of the action, such a player may be in a position to employ a lucrative technique called *end play*. If the dealer goes to the end of the deck, and if the player has an accurate count, he may *modify* the number of hands he takes, so that he gets one card each and the dealer none. When all these remaining cards are high cards, the player gains a tremendous advantage, and reacts with a correspondingly high bet. (A "weak" version of this end play exists in the situation described on page 132, where the opportunist on first base is one of six players at the table.) Other variations on the end-play theme should occur to anyone with imagination. Certain card experts have won sizable sums in the past with this clever method, mainly, of course, against casinos that didn't think the player could have *that much* advantage. One of the most notable is the "little dark-haired guy from Southern California" who, according to Dr. Thorp, is alleged to have accumulated a quarter of a million dollars. Nowadays, casinos are reluctant to deal to the end of the deck in any such private games.

CARD-COUNT PLAY IN ACTION

Let us now take stock of the broad topics we have covered in this chapter. How to play winning blackjack has been approached on the following points: (1) point methods for card counting, (2) variation in bet size, (3) modification of hitting strategy, (4) intelligent insurance betting, and (5) optimum position at the table. All these factors enter into my own successful play at blackjack. The proof of my own particular method lies in my record, in Fig. 7-1. After some 10,000 hands, I had turned a profit slightly over $1000. Estimating between $100 and $125 thousand total amount bet, the yield is about 1 percent. To say exactly would be very difficult to do, for several reasons. A rigorous analysis would require having a record of the bet size and point count on each and every play. However, I had no desire to attract attention to myself with such unusual bookwork at the table. Hence, the only record that was kept was made in private at the end of each day, showing the bet range used, the number of plays, and the net profit or loss for the day.

Some accounting would have to be made for the occasional errors in the point count, which undoubtedly occurred, for then the bet size did not correspond to what the system really called for. (I found that it was necessary for me to work fast to avoid losing the count whenever a pretty cocktail waitress brought me a free highball at the table! Between thanking her, tipping her, and making sure not to spill the drink at the crowded table, I would sometimes lose sight of the cards that were being dealt at that instant.)

Sometimes the dealer shuffled the deck prematurely when a "rich" situation developed near the end of the deck. The removal of these choice situations made somewhat of a reduction in the calculated advantage. Strictly speaking, it would be most sensible to leave the table when this happens. However, sometimes the tables are so jammed that it is hard to find a seat at another table. Then there isn't much choice. You stay at the original table and hope it doesn't happen too frequently. Otherwise, you lose valuable playing time, and might just as well not have made the trip to the casino in the first place.

These various factors are mentioned to show that you cannot expect 100 percent operating efficiency with any system. It is one thing to play blackjack with pencil or computer, or even to play it with cards at a leisurely pace at home with your friends. It is quite another thing to play blackjack in the fast action atmosphere of a crowded casino, with some big-name band blasting away in the background, and with fatigue cutting down your accuracy. Theoretical calculations are wonderful for a guide to what you can expect to accomplish. But when all is said and done, it is the long-term profit you produce on the table that speaks for your actual skill in the game.

In playing my bet-variation system, there have been times when I could just *feel* it working for me—times when the point count would swing up, and I would hoist my bet, and then bang, a good hand. One of the most gratifying hands that I remember occurred with a point count of +14, with about a quarter of the deck left to be dealt. I flexed my maximum slightly and went to a $50 bet. The dealer very kindly tossed me a pair of aces, and of course I put up another $50 and split the aces. On the draw, I beat the dealer on both hands, and collected a nice $100. That one stands out in my memory, but there have been others almost as satisfying. One time I was playing two hands at a club in Reno. With a strong count, I pushed both bets up to twice normal, and—whammo! *Two* blackjacks! What's more, another player at the table collected a third one. Those blackjacks really popped out on that round! Another time, I hooked a pair of 9s on a $35 bet, with the dealer showing a lower card. Naturally I split, and then the dealer dealt me another 9. So I split again for a total bet of $105. Then I drew sweet 10s and 8s while the dealer went bust. Lovely.

Sometimes it is quite gratifying to win on a very low bet. With a high, negative, point count, I have dropped to my minimum $5.00 bet and landed say a two-card total of 14. With the dealer showing a low card, normal strategy would say to stand. But this is an abnormal situation. So I have modified my strategy in such "poor" situations, occasionally to my delight. It really makes me feel good to draw, say, a 5, and beat out the dealer who lands a total of only 17 or 18. There is a great sense of triumph in knowing you are smart enough to tell when the normal rules of strategy must be violated in order to avoid disaster!

On a few occasions, I have had such a remarkable succession of winning double-downs and blackjacks on higher-than-average bets that I have become uncomfortable over the attention that the winning streak was attracting. After piling up $300 or $400 in a short half-hour session, I have felt impelled to pick up my chips and move on.

But life is not always so rosy. There have been almost as many surges in the downward direction, for this is the nature of a random game. During one of my marathon plays in the summer of 1959, I was having just *rotten* luck at the casino in the Dunes Hotel. Twice in a row, with moderate bets, I pulled a pair of 10s, and the dealer drew to 21. So I shrugged my shoulders and accepted it philosophically. On the next hand, I again pulled a pair of 10s. Certain that I could not lose on my total of 20 for a third time in a row, I turned my cards over and *dared* the dealer to draw to 21. Then I sat there bug-eyed as he drew to a five-card 21!

That was the only time in my life that I have seen that happen. At the same sitting, further misfortune befell me. Two different times within 20 minutes, when I had my maximum bet out, he dealt me the last card—which turned out to be a nice juicy ace—and pulled it back as their dealing rules required, with a caustic comment like, "Nice card, for a big bet!" At times like those, you just cannot help feeling that the goddess of fortune has turned against you. I had worked my way out of the cellar at −$200, and then all the way up to +$900 the day before. I was hoping to level out at $1000 and then quit for a while. But after that rugged session at the Dunes, I had rocked back to +$500, and my morale was beginning to sag. So, if the reader wondered on page 105 why I folded up my tent and went home after 7400 hands and a $500 win, there is the answer.

Of course there is an understandable human tendency to take good luck for granted, as if proper strategy almost guaranteed it, and to remember bad luck only. I am sure that I have had a few hot winning sessions at the Dunes to compensate for that bad one. The rocketing climbs in the record of Fig. 7-1 were mighty spectacular, but the runs that stand out most vividly in my memory are those blood-curdling nose dives! Traumatic as they are, however, the fluctuations are but a test of the nerves when you arm yourself with sufficient capital and patience, and play for the long-term upward trend.

One of the best tributes to my system came from a dealer at the Stardust casino. I sat down to play one afternoon at a full table, in my usual position next to first base. The dealer was a sharp young man, who soon had me pegged. It wasn't long before he was dealing lickety-split, as fast as he could. The way he flashed those cards around, I was having a hard time keeping up with him. In fact, sometimes he lost me; but I just kept on playing, and didn't let on. After about 20 minutes of this whirlwind action, a player at the other end of the table got a hand on which he was undecided whether to stand or hit. Finally he said, "Heck, it's only a game of luck. Hit me." As the dealer gave him a draw card, the dealer replied, "No sir. It's not just a game of luck. There's a lot of skill to it." Then as he turned to make the settlement at my end of the table, he paid me a completely unsolicited compliment. Looking straight at me, he declared,

"You play a very fine game. And believe me, I don't say that to one person in 6 months!"

Naturally I felt quite flattered, for it is not often that a dealer will bestow such kind words on a skillful player. But I also knew that he was 100 percent right. My persistent winning record can only be a product of skill!

Will They Let You Win?

8

We have now set the stage for two very vital questions. (1) How do the casinos handle a winning skillful player? And (2), can you yourself, the reader, become a skillful player and win at blackjack? Question (1) must be answered before question (2). For, although we have discussed the important technical aspects of the game in considerable detail, we must also discuss some of the practical operating features of the game. In effect, the first question asks, "What can the casinos do to prevent a skillful player from winning?" After answering that, we'll come back to the second question.

THE DEALER'S ROLE

The attention that a dealer pays to a skillful player depends on how big his bets are and how big the casino is. Dealers, and the pit bosses behind them, are always watching for players who threaten to make any serious inroads on the casino bankroll. There are three classes of players who may do this: those who are lucky, those who are skillful, and those who cheat. The first class they tolerate, the second class they may or may not tolerate, and the third class they absolutely do not tolerate. Therefore, it is part of the job of the dealers and pit bosses to detect the class to which any apparent winner belongs.

Now a dealer can usually tell fairly quickly whether a player is any good. A poor player gives himself away with such boners as hitting on a stiff when the dealer has a low card, standing on a stiff when the dealer has a high card, splitting 10s, or taking insurance on his blackjacks. The casino cannot object to this player winning once in a while because most of the time he loses. With a 2 to 5 percent edge (or worse) against him, this player constitutes no long-term threat to the casino bankroll.

But the other two classes of players do present a threat. Skillful players can tap 1 or 2 percent profit over the long run, and cheaters can undoubtedly score much more heavily than this. (It doesn't take much imagination to see what a tremendous advantage there could be for someone who had marked the aces, say, and even a few of the 10s.) In any case, the casino must, for self-protection, be cynical about its customers and assume that everyone is guilty until proven innocent. This is regrettable, but it may as well be accepted. I have never cheated in any way whatever. Yet there have been occasions at some casinos, where after I have played at one table for 15 minutes or so and have had a small winning streak, the dealer has called for a new deck. When the dealer has given the old deck to the pit boss, the latter has stood right there behind the table examining the deck, to make sure there were no missing or extra cards, or signs of crimping or daubing the cards for identification.

Naturally, an honest player feels uncomfortable in this situation. I have always been careful to avoid any tinge of suspicion. I try to play with a minimum handling of the cards. My movements are deliberate, never fast or concealed. In the summertime, I wear short-sleeve sport shirts. My hands are usually immaculate, and especially the fingernails, which are clipped short. (Long, dirty fingernails are sometimes used by cheaters to conceal paint or other materials for marking cards.) I could rightly be accused of making a fetish of avoiding any suspicion. Still it doesn't do any harm. Let's face it. The house is up against it with the chiselers, and must wage perpetual war to screen them out. Anyone who has read the first 30 pages of *Scarne on Cards* knows the fantastic variations that are possible. That book should be required reading for every card player—not just blackjack players, but players of any card game under the sun. What an eye opener! He reveals countless ways of marking the cards, up-the-sleeve devices for slipping cards in and out of play, tricks for peeking at cards, etc. It is hard to believe that so many ways of playing dirty could be devised.

And every year some new trick comes along. Recently I read about crooked players wearing contact lenses especially designed to act as red filters for seeing markings on cards that would not ordinarily be visible to the eye. Who can blame the casino operators for being cynical? Although the actual percentage of blackjack players who cheat is probably very small, the casinos cannot afford to place anyone above suspicion.

The percentage of blackjack players who are skillful enough to win honestly in the long run is also probably very small. At least I judge this to be the case, after having sat next to hundreds and hundreds of mediocre and poor players over the years, and watching them commit countless errors. In fact, it is my impression that if a dealer or pit boss does get perturbed over a player having a short siege of winning hands, he is more likely to suspect dirty work than good play. For myself, I consider this an insult, which must nonetheless be endured. Whatever a winning streak may be attributed to, there are a number of perfectly honest countermeasures that the dealer can adopt to make it harder for the skillful player to win.

HONEST COUNTERMEASURES

The most effective countermeasure is the *shuffle-over*. The dealer simply shuffles the deck over at the end of any arbitrary round of play instead of dealing all the way to the end of the deck. The extreme in shuffle-over would be to shuffle at the end of each round. This would entirely remove the advantage of keeping count of the cards, and in effect would cause each hand to be dealt out of a fresh deck. This would reduce the entire play to the basic game, as discussed in Chapters 5 and 6. Since the basic game is essentially an even proposition, this would be a woeful state of affairs. Fortunately, I have so far seen very few cases of extreme shuffle-over.

Many dealers do not like the premature shuffle-over, on the grounds that it slows down the game. The fewer hands per hour that are dealt, they reason, the less they will take in. So they may prefer to employ some other countermeasure against the player. One almost as effective as shuffle-over is to deal and to pick up the cards extremely fast. The fast dealing can cause you to miss count, and generally ruffle you. The fast pickup can cause you to fail to see some of the cards and further foul up the count. Of course sustained fast dealing is hard on the dealer as well as hard on the player, and often it is only the younger dealers who have the energy to do it. It takes plenty of stamina for a dealer to run at 1½ to 2 times normal speed and not make mistakes on the settlements.

A popular alternative with some dealers is deliberately to handle some of the cards so that they are not seen by all the players. One time I played with a dealer who went out of his way to make sure I did not see the cards of the players at the other end of the table. The usual procedure on the settlement is for the dealer to turn over the previously face-down cards of any player and lay them momentarily face up on the table. However, this dealer would scoop the cards up and examine them while holding them in his hand, with the backs of the cards toward me. Needless to say, this was a very effective way of keeping me in the dark, and I soon moved on to another table.

There is another practice that the dealer can use on certain types of hands. One of these is used when the dealer has a blackjack. In this case, the dealer has an outright win, except against any player who also has a blackjack. Therefore, unless a player challenges the dealer with a blackjack of his own, the dealer may as well pick up the player's cards, sight unseen. Frequently, at a full table, none of the players will have such a tying blackjack, and the dealer, if so inclined, will pick up all six pairs of cards face down. (But he doesn't completely succeed when I am playing because I turn my two cards over for the other players to see.) Another instance of an obvious win for the dealer is when a player draws two 10s in a row in an attempt to improve a hand. The lowest total he could have is 22, so he has necessarily gone bust. Therefore, if the player has not turned over his original two cards, the dealer may be inclined to pick them up face down.

In these situations where the dealer collects all or some of the cards face down, he may not necessarily do it to prevent players from seeing cards. His purpose may simply be to avoid a wasted manipulation of the cards and thereby speed up the game. But the dealer's reason for doing this is irrelevant. The fact remains that this procedure does prevent the player from keeping a full tab on the cards.

Frequent changes of the deck are sometimes used as protection against cheaters who mark the cards. This may have some slight effect on card counters, by reducing the number of end-deck situations. However, as far as counting is concerned, the dealer can accomplish just as much with shuffle-over as with a complete change of the deck. In fact, insertion of a new deck into a game slows things down even more because the new deck usually has to be shuffled very thoroughly. (Some casinos even have a rule that a new deck must be shuffled some minimum number of times before being put into play.)

Some dealers make no bones about their dislike for players who keep track of the cards. There are even those who act as if they think it is a form of cheating. This seems irrational to me, for practically every card game that exists is a game of skill, to one extent or another. It is a very natural thing in a game of cards to keep track of the fall of the cards and to attempt to utilize this information to your advantage. Indeed, if you have played a game for a long time, it becomes almost automatic, and you would be hard put to prevent yourself from acquiring some remembrance of the pattern of play.

Barring a Player

The ultimate countermeasure that the casino can use against the skillful blackjack player is to bar him from play. It is just as tough to find out about this extreme measure as it is to find out casino policy on shuffle-over. However, I have it from an unimpeachable source that it does sometimes happen. I was told by Nick "the Greek" Dandolos, the all-time king of gamblers, who surely knows as much about American gambling operations as anyone. When Nick once told me that a "professional" eventually gets barred, I asked him what exactly constituted a "professional." In his wonderful, wry way of making a point, Nick replied, "If you're known, you're a professional; if you're not known, you're not a professional!"

The drastic move of barring a player is seldom invoked, however. (We are talking only of honest players here; those who are suspected of dishonesty can clearly expect their due desserts.) Since the shuffle-over and the fast deal are such potent weapons, it is not necessary to exclude skillful, honest players—unless they are personally obnoxious, or make a nuisance of themselves among the other players. Well-behaved players are likely to be barred only if they display the financial capability of winning thousands or tens of thousands with their methodical play. Such customers are few and far between!

DISHONEST COUNTERMEASURES

We have learned about the perfectly honest countermeasures that the dealer can use to discourage the skillful player, and now we turn our attention to dishonest tactics. The game of blackjack is by far the most vulnerable to cheating by the dealer. Of course mostly everyone will tell you that the casinos cannot afford to take the risk, that even a suspicion of cheating on the part of their employees would drive away their customers. They will argue that for the few extra dollars that could be gained, it would be sheer madness for a casino proprietor to put his cherished gaming license in jeopardy, and along with it his multimillion-dollar investment.

But these arguments are based on certain assumptions, which may or may not be valid, depending on certain influences. Before we accept them, we must consider other possibilities. (1) Is the Nevada State Gaming Control Board and all of its staff totally free of any corrupting influence from top to bottom? (2) Is it possible for such an organization, even if free of influence, to be effective in policing the casinos, in view of its limited budget and limited available manpower for rotation of duty? (3) If not effective for these reasons, would it have the courage to prosecute the complaint of a player against a large and powerful casino-hotel?

These are penetrating questions. It is hard to believe that where such huge sums of money are involved, money can have no influence on politics. Campaign contributions by casino-hotel owners are surely not made on a purely altruistic basis. Hence, the winning candidates may well find themselves obligated to make biased appointments to the regulatory agencies, which would please their benefactors if operations were questionable. Thus is the path open for graft at the top.

At the other end of the scale, the investigators generally make less than the dealers they are investigating, which is not a healthy situation. In any case, with only a few dozen investigators on the staff, it

is pretty hard for their faces not to become quickly well known, especially in a business where many of the casinos maintain a rogue's
gallery of hundreds of photos of known cheaters, professionals, and
"high-rollers." Pit bosses are frequently known for their ability to
instantly recognize any one of thousands of faces. Finally, if investigators were not effective in gathering evidence directly themselves,
would the board have the nerve to go before a judge and jury with
only the word of an offended player against a big casino? What jury
would shut down a multimillion-dollar operation on the testimony of
one intrepid player, who could readily be rejected as bitter and un-
reliable? Or with complaints accumulating against several casinos,
how could they ever decide which one of the big ones would take the
rap, until the heat was off, and it could re-open under "new management"?

The gist of the preceding two paragraphs is therefore to question
whether indeed a casino owner does risk his license if he encourages
or tolerates cheating by his dealers. The monetary morals of a number
of the big casino operators are certainly suspect, according to one of
the most unimpeachable sources in the nation, *The New York Times*.
In November, 1963, its western edition carried a week-long serial
describing how millions in untaxed Nevada casino profits give obscure
persons power that extends from the underworld to the government.
So-called *black money* is skimmed off the top by the simple expedient
of smuggling part of the daily take out of the vault before the take is
counted. (The vault is generally out-of-bounds to the revenue agents,
unless they have a special warrant.) An alternative practice is to collect debts from big-time players after they have returned to their
home states. I.O.U.'s are passed from hand to hand, unseen by the
eyes of the tax collector, and the cash payoff is carried out of this
country by corrupt agents to the Swiss-like banks of Panama. De-
posited there in nameless accounts, the funds are then free to return
to the United States via phony loans and other devices. In either
case, the black money eventually provides financial backing for various criminal enterprises—and also completely legal business ventures.
Nevada gambling operations are so lucrative that profits cannot be
absorbed in mere expansion, and other major outlets must be found

for this capital. This is not to impugn all or even a majority of the casinos, but such occurrences taint the whole industry. These comments on the conduct of some casino operations in Nevada are indeed tame in the light of the revelations of Reid and Demaris in *The Green Felt Jungle*.

The Crooks Come West

Any casino operator who indulges in such practices as just described clearly is not going to let his conscience be bothered by hard-to-prove crookedness on his blackjack tables. The subject of cheating was held up to public light in a nationwide television program in May of 1963. On his "Open End" program, David Susskind held a 2-hour panel on gambling; I watched it on Los Angeles station KTTV, channel 11. Participants included Michael MacDougall (well-known magician and card manipulator), George Ratterman (sheriff of Campbell County, Kentucky), Dr. Ed Thorp (author of *Beat the Dealer*), and Harold Smith, Jr. (son of Harold Smith, manager of Harolds Club in Reno). MacDougall indicated why the situation in Nevada has deteriorated in the past few years. Newport, Kentucky, used to be a big sin town, but reformer Ratterman put the lid on. Many of the unemployed card dealers migrated west to seek their fortunes; having worked in illegal gambling halls, many had special talents to offer. As MacDougall said to Ratterman on the program, "You chased them out of Kentucky, so they went out to Nevada."

One of the special skills was the "Kentucky step-up," a card stack that is *deadly* to the unsuspecting blackjack player; we shall say more about this presently. This was one of many forms of blackjack cheating that MacDougall helped Thorp detect when the former accompanied Thorp during a marathon blackjack play in Nevada in 1962. MacDougall also told the television audience that casinos were "95 percent honest in Nevada, and 95 percent dishonest outside of Nevada," the latter because graft had to be paid. (He told of investigating illegal casinos within a 50-mile radius of Baton Rouge, Louisiana. All were dishonest except one, which was owned by a sheriff!) Of course the statement "95 percent honest" would need further clarification. The interesting thing to me was that Harold Smith, Jr., made no attempt whatever to deny the things that MacDougall and Thorp said about cheating at cards in Nevada; one would have expected him to be in the know and to have put up some sort of defense of the casinos.

The Gaming Control Board has indeed closed a number of casinos over the years. Most of them have been very small. Occasionally there have been some moderate-sized casinos shut down, but invariably these have been on the verge of financial collapse, anyway. Never has a really big one been closed. (Fires of mysterious origin also assist in some closings, as with the El Rancho Vegas in Las Vegas, and the Golden Hotel in Reno.) Often a closed casino re-opens after a shuffle in management.

When cheating is given as the reason for closing a casino, almost invariably it is at blackjack, rather than any of the other games. About the largest operation halted because of dirty work on the blackjack tables was the Royal Nevada Hotel, on the "strip" in Las Vegas, in 1958. In the same year, the Senator Club in Nevada's capital, Carson City, was cut off for the same reason. In fact, Michael MacDougall was highly instrumental in the latter case. Acting as a special investigator for the Gaming Control Board, he posed as a tourist and trapped a dealer in the act. A play-by-play account of this incident is given in an article by MacDougall in *Look Magazine* for Oct. 28, 1958, entitled "Why Nevada's Gamblers Toe the Mark."

Frequently, the casino owners deny any knowledge of the cheating, but they are responsible nonetheless. There is hardly any excuse among the big casino operators, considering the elaborate protective measures at their disposal, including one-way mirrors, closed-circuit television, and platoons of detectives. If a dealer cheats for himself, he needs an accomplice, since it is mighty difficult for a dealer to secretly pocket any money off the table. The accomplice poses as a player and collects extra from the dealer. This can be accomplished by the dealer signaling his confederate what he has in his hand (for example, signaling him to hit in a situation where, with only the up-card to go by, the player would normally stand; or vice versa). Subtle signals, when not used too often, are hard to detect. Alternately, by stacking or other tricks, the dealer can give his buddy better-than-average hands. Either of these methods is, of course, much safer than for the dealer to make intentional "errors" and consistently overpay his accomplice.

Usually the management knows about how much it should be taking in on a given table during a shift. For a dealer to try to slice off an appreciable piece of this pie can be risky. So, the crooked dealer must cheat players other than his accomplice, and transfer the extra amount won to his accomplice. A friend of mine was once propositioned by a dealer at a large casino on the "strip." My friend was sitting quietly at a snack bar in the wee morning hours when the dealer plunked down next to him, gave him a sad tale about medical bills, and offered to split $1500 with him. The dealer was obviously looking for a fresh face that the pit bosses would not recognize. My friend declined.

So much for the fact that cheating does go on. The exact extent of it probably varies continuously, depending on such factors as the player's bet size, the length of a player's winning streak, the individual dealer, and the size and financial solvency of the casino. It is likely that the cheating is far greater than either the casinos or the Gaming Control Board will admit. A casino operator generally will claim that he is running a clean house, while professing not to be able to vouch for his competitors.

Common Cheating Techniques

For the reader's benefit, then, we should describe some of the more common techniques. Most of them are not new. Scarne's books on cards contain magnificent expositions of many of the tricks, complete with detailed photographs. Among the more popular forms are (1) stacking the deck, (2) reversing the deck, (3) dealing "seconds" (that is, dealing the second card from the top rather than the top card), (4) peeking at a card, (5) removing cards, and (6) the false shuffle. Some of these stand alone, and some must be used in conjunction with another. No better illustration could be cited than the case that closed the Senator Club. In that instance, tricks 1, 2, and 3 were used, in that order. The dealer picked up the discards in such a fashion that when placed on the bottom of the deck, the order ran alternately low and high. Just prior to dealing to himself, the dealer distracted the attention of the players, and at the same instant turned the deck over. Thus, the new top card was low, the next one high, the third low. If a low card helped the dealer's hand, he took the top one. If he needed a high card, he would second-deal. If he required two low cards, then a top-deal followed by a second-deal was the ticket.

It is intriguing to note the sequence of (1) low-high stacking, (2) reversing the deck, and (3) second-dealing, which the dealer employed in this case. Each of these steps contributed something essential to his technique. Alternatively, he could have substituted a peek at the regular top card for steps (1) and (2). This would not have been quite so powerful, since he would not have had knowledge of the second card. Nonetheless, the mere option of bypassing the top card if it did not help his hand would have boosted his chances of beating the player greatly. And peeking would be safer, since low-high pickup and reversing the deck might be spotted by someone who noticed that particular cards reappeared before the shuffle.

A Deadly Low-High-Low Stack

If anyone doubts the potency of the 1-2-3 punch just described, just consider the dealer's position if his low-high-low stack consists of 5-ace-7. If he has *any* two-card hand requiring a draw, all the way from 4 to 16, he can fix himself up with a sure 19, 20, or 21! In fact, in a great majority of the cases he can wangle the 21, and in only a few cases need he settle for a measly 19. The dealer's advantage is fantastic.

One form of the stack can be used to break any player who draws to a stiff. Say the dealer is working to a full table. Suppose the player on first base goes bust, and among his cards is a king. The dealer simply keeps track of this king in the discards, reverses the deck at the appropriate moment, and uses the same card to break a player drawing on third base. Chances are that the players at the two ends of the table do not see each other's cards well enough to know what is going on. If an alert player did notice that a certain card appeared twice in succession without a shuffle between, it would be his word against the dealer's. In case of a complaint, the player might very quickly find the bouncer escorting him to the door on the pretext he was just a sore loser.

Deletion of one or more cards from a deck is a dirty trick. The consequences are obvious, when these cards are aces or 10s. Unfortunately, when the dealer does not go all the way to the end of the deck, it is virtually impossible to establish this chicanery. By the time you can gather some statistics on several rounds, it is time for a new deck to be brought in. A friend of mine did spot a deck with only one ace at a small casino in Jackson Hole, Wyoming, one time. On drawing it to the attention of the dealer, he got the reply, "Yup. Short season, short deck!"

Occasionally I have run up against dealers who have a remarkable talent for getting an ace for either the bottom card or the buried card. (After the shuffle and the cut, the top card is "buried" on the bottom, face up against the regular bottom card, as if to seal the deck.) This effectively removes the ace from action and knocks about 0.6 percent off the player's basic expectation. Converse to the removal of cards from the pack is the possibility of *adding* cards to the pack. This is too risky in the single-deck game, of course, but with double-deck (or even better the multiple deck "shoe" type game), there is not too much likelihood of detecting a few extra low cards.

The Kentucky Step-up

The false shuffle and the phony cut are used to preserve a pre-selected sequence of cards. After the act, a clump of cards is left untouched, generally on the top or bottom of the deck. Some stacks require these manipulations to set them up. One particularly potent stack is the so-called Kentucky, or 7-card *step-up*. The dealer arranges a run that goes 7-8-9-10-10-J-Q-K-A; this is done in idle moments when there are no players at the table. If the dealer has the cards spread out face up on the table, sometimes you can detect this as you approach the table. Upon your arrival, the dealer scoops up the cards and prepares for action. He may not even bother to offer the deck for a cut, or if he does, he fixes it so that the stack gets back to the top of the deck. The 7 is burned, and you are dealt 8-10 to his 9-10, on the next hand you receive J-K to his Q-A. On the first two hands, you are automatically clobbered, and to add insult to injury, the deck is depleted of high cards.

Against two new players, the Kentucky step-up wins the first round from both players, but starts the next round with one high card to each player. Against three players, the step-up beats all three on the first round.

In a 30-page chapter in his book, Dr. Thorp describes numerous instances in which he was cheated at places all over the state of Nevada. Great detail is given, with only the names of the casinos and the dealers omitted. Presumably he does not wish to be sued over events that he cannot *prove*. The two of us have compared notes, and I can say positively that his book does not tell all of what he knows about the situation. At several places we have run up against the same conditions.

For example, his very first experience against a knockout dealer occurred at a large hotel-casino in Reno. I, too, was fleeced at this same spot in the summer of 1961. I sat down on first base, next to another man, to play against a woman dealer. Shortly after the play commenced, a young woman sat down next to him; I took her to be a shill, since the dealer provided her with the usual ten silver dollars. But I should have been more alert and asked myself why they needed a shill at a table that already had two players. Actually, she was an "anchor man" (or better, anchor woman, in this case); in any case, she soon sank me. The dealer was evidently peeking at the top card and signaling her confederate to take a hit when the dealer did not want the top card for herself. I was betting my usual scale of $5.00 to $35.00; within 20 hands I was clipped out of $300. I quit in disgust and never played there again. Despite this loss, I managed to clear $900 in less than 2000 hands during several days in the Reno-Tahoe area.

Another place where both Thorp and I have been clipped is in Las Vegas at a casino near the south end of the "strip." We have been subjected to some rather expert high-low stacking by a dealer of such unusual physique and features that it would be hard to forget him. He removed $350 from me in rather short order, at the same bet levels as mentioned before. That casino no longer gets my business. One half-hour lesson is enough.

One of the most damning experiences of cheating that I have ever heard of happened to Thorp at a major casino on the east side of the "strip." When he started to play at this place one time, he was immediately recognized as the "man who wrote the book." An obvious cheat dealer was brought in against him, so Thorp moved to another table. Whereupon that dealer was again moved to him. And he continued to follow Thorp to whatever table he went. Finally exasperated, the star said to the dealer, "Look, I have 17 silver dollars in change here. I'll play them one at a time. Why don't you give me a demonstration on how well you can cheat?" The dealer swiftly relieved our hero of his 17 dollars!

Why not complain to the State Gaming Control Board, you ask. If your objective is to win money, then don't waste your time on the Board. It's more practical to try to find a spot where the conditions are not hostile, at least for short periods of time. It may be a challenge to win money while you are *in* a casino, but it is a cinch you are not going to be winning any while you are *out* of the casino and talking to the Board.

How the Board Could Clean Up

Incidentally, if the Board wanted seriously to improve the blackjack situation, I believe the following would be the most practical procedure. Let them penalize a casino caught cheating by reducing the percentage of allowed blackjack tables, say, by 10 or 15 percent. But do not take the license away and shut down *all* the blackjack tables (let alone the whole casino). If all the tables were closed, then of course the reaction of the players would be to desert the other games, too, on the suspicion they were crooked also. This would force the casino out of business. But if just one or two tables were suspended, it could well pass unnoticed, especially if furniture were rearranged. Most of the players are tourists, and would not have the slightest awareness of such change. Even the locals could probably be given some plausible line.

The point is that it is just about impossible to expect any big hotel-casino operations to be closed down. The investments are just too great, and there would be no equitable way to select one for closing so as to give others a warning. But the gradual method I suggest would enable everybody to save face. Subsequent violations would lead to more percentage reductions, to the point where it would eventually be conspicuous and unprofitable; this, of course, would be the deterrent. By a prescribed, but sufficiently long period of "good behavior," a previously penalized casino would be permitted to regain its lost tables. Thus the industry could phase out the Kentucky step-up artists and the other light-fingered card sharks. Nevada, why not give it a try?

Meanwhile, the player should be on the lookout for cheating. It may occur only in a small percentage of cases, but the competent player who bets $20 to $50 or more may well find himself singled out for treatment. The more the player threatens to win, the more likely he is to be cheated at blackjack. This is especially true of the player who bets wisely and richly enough so that his winnings would support him. But caution must be observed at all bet levels, for even the dollar bettor, or lower, may run up against it.

PROTECTING YOURSELF

Unfortunately, for the player, the most popular forms of dealer cheating are those that are hardest to *prove*. They involve manipulation of the cards rather than marking or substitution. The latter two, as well as the first, are commonly used by shysters in private games. But marked cards, or extra cards, can be confiscated, and these constitute rather damning evidence. All six of the tricks listed on page 147 are pretty cunning; strictly speaking, they can be *proved* only with *motion pictures* as evidence (except for card removal). Stacking of the discards can be an especially subtle maneuver, and unless coupled with some other overt move, it may be very difficult for even an expert to detect. (In some casinos, the dealer is required to pick up each player's cards in the exact order in which he received them. This is done so that if the player complains that a mistake was made, the cards may be re-examined, and any error rectified. In such casinos, the player has the incidental advantage of protection against stacking.)

Most forms of skillful cheating take considerable practice to detect. A good "mechanic" can often *tell* an amateur exactly what he is going to do, and still pull it off unseen, right under the amateur's very nose. Nonetheless, it helps to know what tricks to look for, what the dealer is basically trying to accomplish. If you practice the tricks on page 147 a few times, you will get the idea. Then, in addition, observe the following precautions: (1) Watch the dealer's eyes. If he is looking where he should have no need to look, be very suspicious. (2) Note that the best opportunity the dealer has to peek at the top card in the deck is when his up-card is an ace or 10, and he must look at the down-card to see if he has a blackjack (5/13 of the time he will have this opportunity). The hand that probes the down-card may provide a perfect shield for the hand holding the deck. He may then do a "front peek," by pushing with his thumb to flare out the corner of the card closest to the table. Or he may do a "back peek," which is harder but safer. With the deck turned over, he bends in the corner of the card that is closest to the palm of his hand. It is virtually impossible for any player to see the card involved in the back peek, but the dealer's eyes may give it away.

(3) Watch carefully for signs of second dealing. It is easier to do this with cards that have a uniform crosshatched pattern than with cards that have a border. In the latter case, it is more apparent when the second card is pulled out from under the top one. You may also be able to detect a slight difference in the *sound* of a card pulled out from between two other cards, as compared to one flipped off the top. (4) Be alert for any distracting moves by the dealer (or by other players, who may actually be in league with him). The slightest diversion of your attention from the game gives the dealer golden opportunities for manipulation. (5) Keep your eye on the way he picks up the discards, to see if he is arranging them in a high-low pattern. (6) Beware of shills brought into the game, particularly if their hands are thrown in face down. They may be standing sometimes on 11 or less, or hitting 17 and higher, on signal from the dealer who wants to set up the right card for himself.

In addition to these six suggestions, which pertain specifically to the game, there is some worthwhile general advice to apply. (7) Play preferably at the large, plush casinos. Whatever your bet size, it is less of a threat to their bankroll than it would be at a small club. (8) Play only at tables where the illumination is good. Dark and dingy surroundings are an open invitation to skulduggery. (9) Avoid playing when you are tired and inattentive. When you are tempted to have a few more hands at 3 A.M., remember that you have had it for the day; the only place you belong is in the sack. But those dealers on the graveyard shift live that schedule every day; they're fresh and ready to go. (10) Stay sober when you play.

You must remember that many of the dealers and pit bosses have graduated from a tough apprenticeship in the illegal clubs elsewhere in this country. In many of those places, the operators try to get away with everything they can. When they come west, there is no guarantee of reform. As Nick the Greek once told me, "If they're honest, it's only because they have to be. Otherwise they'd steal you blind." On the other hand, it is reasonable to point out that in order to conduct a successful gambling operation, it can be a great asset to have survived the rugged underground training. There are so many ways for players (and dealers) to cheat the house that only the veterans can protect themselves.

At least one club has its own solution for avoiding dealers who have been contaminated in some previous school of hard knocks. This is Harolds Club in Reno, which runs its own dealer training program for raw recruits, untainted by prior experience. For all my chagrin over the roulette episode (see Chapter 3), I must commend that club for this practice. Of all places to play blackjack in Nevada, I should least expect to be cheated at Harolds.

CAN YOU WIN?

Now that we have thoroughly aired the subjects of honest and dishonest countermeasures, we return to question number (2) on the first page of this chapter: "Can you, the reader, become a skillful player and win at blackjack?" The answer is *yes*, provided you are willing to devote some effort to learning how, and also provided you do not antagonize the dealers. All you have to do is arm yourself with a reasonable bank-to-bet ratio and play patiently by one of the point-count methods advocated in the preceding chapter. Your rate of profit may range around 1 to 2 percent. But it is strictly a long-term proposition, and there may be substantial negative fluctuations before you pull away for good on the positive side. The graphs of my own experience show this only too well.

Let everyone recognize that 1 percent is a very small edge. We do not wish to delude anyone of limited means into thinking he can rush up to Reno or Las Vegas and parlay his capital into a fortune in a matter of days or even weeks. Any wishful thinkers would do well to recall that Hibbs and Walford had about a 20 percent edge on their roulette wheel, and it took them a solid eight days around the clock to parlay their $500 starting bank up to about $30,000. While it is true- that the lop-sided 35:1 payoff in roulette required a bigger bank-to-bet ratio than would be needed at blackjack, nonetheless a 20 percent win rate is positively *huge* compared to 1 percent.

Just to make expenses on this small edge obviously calls for a considerable bankroll. A basic bet of $5.00 would yield, at 1 percent, only 5¢ per hand. Yet I would not consider a basic bet of $5.00 without about 100 such bets in my wallet, or around $500. Simple arithmetic thus verifies the preceding emphasis on a "considerable bankroll." To compromise with the necessary bank-to-bet ratio is to invite disaster.

If a negative fluctuation reduces you to a level below the maximum bet size that your method calls for, quit playing and go for reserves. Otherwise you may deprive yourself of the opportunity to go your limit in a rich situation, which will definitely cut down on your expectation. I learned this little lesson the hard way, having allowed it to happen to myself a couple of times. The one that lingers in my memory was a case of betting my last $30 in a rich situation. I got two cards totaling 11, but did not have the extra $30 to double-down. It was nice when the dealer dealt me a 10, but it still burned my soul to think my lack of foresight had done me out of another $30!

Disguising a System

One of the conditions for winning at blackjack, which we have mentioned, is that you must not antagonize the dealer so that he uses countermeasures against you. If out-and-out point-count play meets with persistent shuffle-over or other actions, you may find it advisable to disguise your technique. By making it less apparent that you have a genuinely intelligent method of play and giving the appearance of being just another system-happy jerk, you may attract less scrutiny to your method of play. There are, in fact, some betting systems that are futile in other games, but which do have varying merit when applied to blackjack. In Chapter 16 it is pointed out that in a game in which the sequence of wins and losses is not purely random, there is justification for increasing the bet after a loss and decreasing after a win. This works best if you are playing alone against the dealer, and get eight or nine hands out of one deck. In that event, some type of pyramid or double-up system is intrinsically sound.

I once ran series of tests with such a system on a record of 1000 hands, which I had played and recorded at home, simulating one player against the dealer. The sequence just happened to be one in which the net profit on a flat bet would have been zero, that is, the player would have broken even. But the progressive betting systems, in general, fared better. Those with very modest bet ranges yielded a fraction of a percent profit. A double-up progression that went from a 1-unit minimum to a 32-unit maximum (that is, 1-2-4-8-16-32) yielded almost a full percent over an equivalent flat bet.

The general principle here is simple. We know that the player fares better when there are high cards left in the deck, and he fares poorer when there are low cards left. Inverting the logic, we say that if the player just won a hand, then on the average it is because a slight excess of good cards came out on that hand. The deck is accordingly now slightly poorer, and the bet should be reduced. On the other hand, if the player just lost a hand, then on the average it is because a slight excess of poor cards came out. The deck is now slightly richer, and the bet should be raised.

This is a very gross line of reasoning, and many violations can be found. For example, if the player just lost with a 10-10 against a dealer blackjack, the deck is actually poorer than before, and the bet should be reduced. Or if player tied dealer with a blackjack, the deck is definitely much poorer, rather than being essentially the same as before the tie, as implied above. The moral of the story is that for the same degree of bet variation, you can do much better with a more accurate scheme like the Wilson point-count method. Furthermore, the latter works regardless of how many players are at the table, whereas the progressive scheme described above is not much good with more than two players at the most, and is best when there is only one player.

Of course, with just a little imagination, you can make modifications on an outright progressive system to compensate for some of the more glaring errors that occur. Probably the most important thing is to start over when the end of the deck is reached, even if the highest bet level in the progression has not been reached. Unfortunatly, this tips off the dealer to the true nature of your method, and occasionally you may want to carry the sequence on around the end of the deck as if it were a pure progression.

Variations on this theme are endless. Regrettably, you cannot eat your cake and have it too. You cannot have the full power of a true point-count system and the full deception of an outright progression. Where you choose to compromise depends on your own little game of hide-and-seek with the dealer.

Guidelines

If you and I can win by using the basic strategy of Chapter 5 and the simple point-count system and bet-variation schemes of the preceding chapter, what is the future of blackjack? Can the casinos afford to support us? It seems they could not even afford to tolerate players who play the basic strategy with flat bets, and thereby break even, let alone tolerate players who use the methods of Chapter 7 and gradually win from them. But it is not as simple as that. There are many "ifs" in reply to the vital question of what the future holds for blackjack. Much depends on what percentage of all blackjack players eventually learn to play a decent game.

There is a wise old saying that, "you can lead a horse to water, but you can't make him drink." In blackjack, you can give a player plenty of good advice, but you can't make him follow it. There are a half a dozen "ifs" to successful blackjack, and every single one of them must be obeyed! Fall down on any one of them, and you won't be a winner very long. You can win in the long run:

1. *If* you are patient enough to learn the basic strategy of Chapter

5, and to follow a valid card-count and bet-variation scheme such as described in Chapter 7.

2. *If* you possess sufficient playing capital so that you can be indifferent to considerable fluctuations and are not dependent on winnings to pay living or travel expenses.

3. *If*, in addition to (2), you are willing to apportion your capital to a reasonably safe bank-to-bet ratio, as discussed in Chapter 17.

4. *If* you can avoid distractions while you play, and thereby devote sufficient concentration to the game.

5. *If* you can regulate those free drinks they offer you, and also avoid unwarranted fatigue.

6. *If* you can stay on sufficiently friendly terms with the dealer, so he won't employ serious countermeasures.

There you have six good reasons why expert blackjack players are few and far between, and why the casinos do not have much to fear. Most gamblers won't be bothered to make the modest effort required to play good blackjack. They mistakenly think you have to be an Einstein to grasp the concepts explained in the past few chapters. They fail to realize they do not have to be able to *write* a book like this; all they have to do is *read* it, and follow its recommendations.

Even assuming good playing technique, the normal player will not be content to limit his bets to a sufficiently small fraction of his playing capital. He looks at those gigantic fluctuations in Figs. 6-1 and 7-1, and thinks to himself, "Runs like that are extremely rare; Wilson must have been awfully unlucky," or "I'm not going to play that long, so I don't need to be prepared for such big oscillations." He reads Chapter 17 on bank-to-bet ratio, and says to himself, "That's a fine *theory*, but I don't really need *quite that big* a ratio, do I?" The closer it gets to his scheduled time of departure, the greater his suspension of good judgment. If he has lost a moderate amount, he thinks that with a couple of big bets he will salvage the week end and go home a winner. If he has been winning, then—boy oh boy, this is the time! Let's land a couple of whoppers, since it's their money anyway, and then we'll go home an even bigger winner! Ahead or behind, good sense is cast to the winds. Last-minute fever sweeps away any specific objectives that may previously have been set.

It is perfectly true that if the overwhelming majority of blackjack players learn to play the basic strategy reasonably well (much less master the bet-variation game), something will have to give. The casinos cannot afford to operate a game on which they barely break even. But it seems extremely unlikely that anywhere near a majority of blackjack players will learn to play a decent game for a long time to come. When the Baldwin book came out in 1957, I went around predicting that within six months the casinos would be forced to change the rules, and nobody would then be able to win any more. How wrong I was! Nothing of the sort happened. I don't know how many people bought the Baldwin book, but in any case it produced little more than a ripple in an ocean full of mediocre and poor players. In my own observation, the public as a whole is playing almost as bad a game of blackjack as it did five years ago.*

When you consider all the business the casinos get from the hordes who either won't bother or are incapable of learning how to play a good game, plus the additional business from beginners, drunks, and impatient gamblers of various sorts, it hardly seems that the good players could make much of a dent in their operations. Indeed, with books like mine boosting the popularity of the game, casino profits may actually be increased. For, although it is my obvious intention to help show players how to play a better game, it is by no means certain that any significant percentage of my readers will actually learn to win at the game. After all, I have no control

---

* In April 1964 the Las Vegas casinos did indeed temporarily change the playing rules. In a well publicized press conference, the Resort Hotel Association announced that doubling down would be confined to a two-card 11, and that a pair of aces could no longer be split. This move was attributed to the inroads which Dr. Thorp and the count players were making on the casino profits. However, within a few weeks, these changes were quietly rescinded, and all the casinos on the "strip" and downtown were dealing the game as before.

The effect of these temporary changes was to lower the player's expectation in the basic game from about +0.1 percent down to around −0.8 percent. (The card counter could still overcome this edge, but it was somewhat tougher than before.) The shift is readily computed from numbers given by Baldwin; namely, (1) loss of 10 double down, 0.52 percent; (2) loss of 9 double down, 0.11 percent; (3) loss of soft double downs, 0.09 percent; and (4) loss of ace pair split, 0.15 percent. In the event of future rules changes, these numbers, or others given here in Chapters 5 and 7, may be helpful. Simple empirical tests by dealing several hundreds of hands may also provide adequate rough estimates.

over how well you, the reader, master my recommendations and abide by the six "musts" given before.

There are so many variables involved that it is impossible to predict the impact of a book of this sort. The market covers two groups: people who play blackjack already, and prospective new players. In general, those who play already stand to learn how to play considerably better. Whether this means a net loss for the casinos, however, depends on how much these players improve and whether their new confidence causes them to bet more heavily than before. If they think they can win, but haven't really improved much, they may be in for losses. Despite a slower rate of losing, they may still lose total amounts that are as much as, or more than, before.

As for new players, similar arguments apply. If they have gotten the message, they will win in the long run; if not, they will lose. But even if two-thirds of the new flock succeeded, the remaining one-third could easily tilt the net balance to an added profit for the casinos. For, the best the winners will attain will be about a 1 to 2 percent advantage, whereas poor players can easily give the house a 3 to 5 percent edge. Of course the net balance would also depend on how much these two groups bet, but it is not hard to believe the casinos might come out ahead because of the new players lured in by books like this.

So, perhaps the casinos do not have much to fear from educational efforts like this. It depends on many factors, as we said before. Besides, the casinos always like to see a few spectacular winners, to help lure more suckers in to play. Perhaps at blackjack they will be willing to accept a slightly higher proportion of winners from among the ranks of the skillful players, rather than depend on the lucky but really bad players for such publicity.

Only the future can tell what will happen if the gambling public gradually plays a better and better game of blackjack. But there is one thing the reader had jolly well better beware of—dealers and pit bosses can read, too! *Their* reactions to books like this will play a big role in shaping the future of this fascinating game.

Meanwhile, when you know how to win, there's no harm in trying.

Good and Bad Advice in Other Books

9

The correct *basic* strategy has been available to the playing public since 1957, when the Baldwin book appeared on the market. Yet a number of books published since that time have recommended noteworthy departures from the proper strategy. Surprisingly, this has occurred with authors whom the lay public would have every reason to expect to be expert on the subject. For such erroneous advice I attribute one of three possible reasons:

1. The author is unsure, so he straddles the fence. He follows the advice of some predecessor in some instances, but also throws in some notions of his own.

2. The author strongly suspects that a previous mathematician author is right, but hesitates to copy him right down the line, for fear of copyright infringement.

3. The author gives generally valid advice, but purposely gives some bum steers. A writer who is associated with a casino management may reasonably be suspected of this approach, since he hurts his business by suggesting sufficiently perfect play that the player can either break even or win.

Blackjack is a complicated game to analyze, and only those having advanced mathematical training are qualified to do an independent evaluation of the over-all game. (Novices can do bits and pieces by trial-and-error methods, but the total concept requires a more sophisticated approach for a solution in a reasonable time.) This being the case, the only reliable credential for an author to write correctly on the percentages at blackjack is either that (1) he is mathematically trained himself, or (2) he draws upon the work of a mathematician. To date, only a few of the former have broken into print. So, in most cases, the reader must ask himself if an author has demonstrated that he satisfies the second alternative.

For example, John Crawford is a card expert and gambler par excellence. But he is not a professional mathematician. His book, *How to be a Consistent Winner in the Most Popular Card Games*, contains essentially error-free advice on the basic strategy for blackjack. This is because Crawford openly referred to the previously published work by Baldwin, *et al.*, and further availed himself of personal consultation with another scientist type.

On the other hand, John Scarne is also a world-famous gambling expert and counselor. He, too, is far from being a professional mathematician. His book, *Scarne's Complete Guide to Gambling*, contains numerous questionable statements on the basic blackjack strategy. Why? Either Scarne did not consult any bonafide mathematicians, or else his mathematicians made a lot of mistakes.

Table 9-1 is a summary of the coverage of blackjack in all of the books I have seen published on gambling in recent years. Notice that wide variations in the alleged house percentage have appeared in print. In general, the closer the quoted value is to zero, the better is the quality of what the author has chosen to write about the game. Please note that the books have been classified as to the "level of attempted coverage." It is only fair to point this out, since some authors mention the game only briefly. This is perfectly all right, and in most cases what is given fits harmoniously into the rest of their context. My purpose here is only to evaluate the correctness of whatever the author did choose to say on the subject.

Table 9-1 is followed by a more detailed scrutiny of the contents of these books.

1. *Oswald Jacoby on Gambling* is a recently published book that includes a section on blackjack. The famous bridge master upholds his reputation as an actuary and mathematician by correct statements in everything he says. Nevertheless, he could have said a great deal more, and I would have expected this of an expert on card games. Specifically, Jacoby gives the correct basic strategy, and several tables

TABLE 9-1. SUMMARY OF COVERAGE OF BLACKJACK IN RECENT BOOKS

Author and Title	Percentage Quoted	Level of Coverage Attempted			Quality of Coverage at Level Attempted		
		Moderate	Detailed	Very Detailed	Fair	Good	Excellent
Jacoby: *Oswald Jacoby on Gambling*	none given!	x				x	
Riddle & Hyams: *Weekend Gambler's Handbook*	—0.6% to —15.0%	x			x		
Goodman: *How to Win at Cards, Dice, Races, & Roulette*	none given!	x			x		
Thorp: *Beat the Dealer*	+0.1%			x			x
Scarne: *Scarne's Complete Guide to Gambling*	none given!		x		- x -		
Smith: *I Want to Quit Winners*	—2.5%	x			x		
Crawford: *How to be a Consistent Winner in the Most Popular Card Games*	—0.6%	x				x	
Baldwin: *Playing Blackjack to Win*	—0.6%			x			x

of calculations to support it. But he quotes no value for the net advantage to player or house in the basic game. Indeed he gives reference to no other authors in his book. It does not even have an index, let alone a bibliography.

So far as card counting is concerned, he asserts that you are not going to play a consistent winning game of blackjack unless you follow his advice to count the cards. But then he gives *hardly any* helpful advice on how to utilize such information. Aside from describing what a tremendous advantage the player has when he knows that the last eight cards consist of four aces and four 10s, and aside from a proper insurance commentary, Jacoby provides no other specific information.

2. Riddle and Hyams' *Weekend Gambler's Handbook* (1963) is one of three books written by a casino manager, Riddle being the president of the Dunes Hotel in Las Vegas (Hyams is a Hollywood columnist). It is written in a breezy, informal style; the coverage of blackjack strategy is fair, and there are some interesting, candid remarks about card-counting players and the possible future of the game.

The specific deficiencies that limit the coverage to being only fair are (1) the house percentage quoted against a good player is incorrect, (2) there are some errors in the recommended basic strategy, (3) the advice given on card counting is so vague as to be of little practical use, and (4) advice on the insurance bet is misleading. Furthermore, there are some remarks on "luck" that are downright meaningless and cast a cloud over everything.

Riddle asserts that card counting or "case down" players are not welcome in his casino. They win too frequently. This being the case, he is not about to give you any really significant tips on how to become a good one. He points out that his dealers are aware that the case-down player watches the cards more carefully than the average player, he increases his bets as the game proceeds, and he sits just to the dealer's right. But apart from suggesting that you keep track of 10s and 9s, he does not state explicitly how to use the information. Nor does he recommend any particular pattern of bet variation. In short, he indicates qualitatively that an advantage can be obtained by counting down, but he doesn't really tune you in on the details!

Riddle makes some very provocative statements about the current trend. He admits frankly that computer-generated strategy is making inroads. In fact, he states that if the average player followed the methods that computer experts have worked out, the casinos would be forced to discontinue the game of blackjack. This would be so, at least, if they stuck to the present rules of play. An alternative to this would be to alter the rules, by allowing the dealer some flexibility of play. Riddle claims that computer studies have shown that the dealer would be a sure winner if he could elect for himself whether to draw or stand, and that many Las Vegas casinos are seriously thinking of revising the rule. But until this comes to pass, he generously says the public is free to take advantage of his recommendations.

3. Next on the list is Mike Goodman's *How to Win at Cards, Dice, Races, and Roulette.* This is a 75¢ pocketbook type, which also came out in 1963. Oddly enough, Goodman is also associated with the Dunes Hotel, as a senior "pit boss." This should qualify him to write from the practical operating point of view. There is some good information in his book, but the title is misleading because he definitely does *not* tell you how to win at the games listed (other than occasionally by luck, for which you do not need a book).

Goodman's treatment of blackjack is rated as only fair because of the following defects: (1) no evaluation of the house percentage is given, (2) there are errors in the recommended basic strategy, (3) not merely is there no useful advice on card counting, but the author does his best to discredit the practice. His mistakes in strategy are sprinkled throughout various chapters and show up strongly in a partial summary on page 42 of his book. To Goodman's credit, he does make a blanket recommendation against the insurance bet: If you don't follow the cards, you shouldn't ever take it.

On the subject of card counting, he is extremely hostile; this, of course, is understandable, since he does not like to see his dealers losing to clever players. Goodman asserts that the gimmick of card counting is now "played out," and that shuffle-over will be applied to knock it out in his club. He pokes fun at the *faux pas* of beginning card-count players whose technique is not smooth, and runs down the professional.

4. The all-time sensation for a single book devoted entirely to the subject of blackjack is Thorp's *Beat the Dealer.* We have already made liberal reference to his contributions and experiences, first in Chapter 6 in the section covering the whole chain of scientists who have worked on blackjack, and then on the subject of card-counting by "10-count" and by his "ultimate" strategy, and finally in the section on cheating by the dealer. Consequently, we shall devote less space here to his amazing book than we would if he had not already received plaudits elsewhere.

Thorp's first announced value of the player's expectation at basic blackjack was −0.2 percent, but in his book he makes amends. In a footnote he quotes my results, which I had communicated to him, and acknowledges that his refinement of the Baldwin method still contains a bias. From this point of departure, he explains in considerable detail his 10-count method for modifying the strategy. This is by far his most important contribution to scientific blackjack play. Although his results again are limited by computational feasibility to certain inaccuracies, their general validity is well confirmed in his description of a spectacular win in the Reno-Lake Tahoe area. First described in an article in the *Atlantic Monthly* for June, 1962, entitled "A Prof Beats the Gamblers," the story also appears as a chapter in his book.

Other items in his 225-page masterpiece include some of the finer points of play, an extensive 30 pages dealing with the cheating situation in Nevada, and certain tables useful to those who wish to conduct their own independent analysis of the game. Altogether, he has put out a most authoritative book on blackjack.

5. Scarne's *Complete Guide to Gambling* has some 40 pages devoted to blackjack. Certain aspects of the coverage are quite good, such as the description of the mechanics of the game, the photographs of how a dealer can cheat, and the breath-taking account of the huge $250,000 win in the Cuban casinos in 1958. Yet many of Scarne's statements on the mathematical odds in the game are misleading and erroneous.

The particular shortcomings of Scarne's coverage on blackjack can be summarized as follows: (1) He makes numerous mistakes in specific strategy recommendations, (2) he makes a gross error in claiming that the player who never hits a total over 11 gives the house a 21.5 percent advantage (it is more like 5 to 6 percent), (3) he claims that he is going to tell the reader the "Blackjack dealer's exact percentage take," but strangely he never gets around to even an approximate quote on this vital figure, (4) he pans the bridge experts as poor blackjack players, yet Scarne's strategy recommendations are definitely inferior to those of bridge champion John Crawford, who published more than a year before Scarne, and (5) he gives no credit whatever to anyone else as having advanced the understanding of blackjack through scientific analysis.

There are too many erroneous recommendations in Scarne's book to attribute them to oversights or to errors in transcribing the manuscript. I bought the book when it was hot off the press. Immediately after reading it, I fired off a challenge to him. I offered to bet him $1000 that it is more to the player's advantage to split a pair of 9s against a dealer 6, than to stand on the total of 18 as recommended by Scarne. I proposed to win this bet either by proving it to him mathematically, or by the play of hands, at Scarne's option.

Not receiving any reply within two months, I wrote again. I reiterated the first challenge, and added a second one. This was also a $1000 bet, to the effect that Scarne was wrong in claiming that the house enjoys a 21.49 percent advantage against the player who never hits a stiff. Specifically, I offered to wager that the advantage was at least 10 percent less than he claimed. Again I proposed to prove it either by mathematics or by play of hands. In the latter case, I would play against him; he would be banker, and I would be a player standing on all stiffs, but with the proviso that on each play he would return 15¢ on each dollar wagered. Thus he would still retain a healthy 6.49 percent advantage as dealer, *if* his figure was right.

Scarne never did reply directly to these challenges. Eventually one of his associates accepted my challenge, but only on condition that I accept his $5000 challenge to a man-to-man blackjack *freezeout*. Supposedly, Scarne was to pay all my expenses to go to Puerto Rico to make this play. Since I do not claim to be a top memory expert, and quite possibly Scarne's confederate is one, I wisely declined this proposition.

Actually, I have never contended that Scarne himself might not be able to play a winning game against the casinos, when all factors such as card counting and bet variation are taken into account. But I do contend that a number of his recommendations on the basic game are incorrect, and therefore his basic point of departure presents him with a larger inherent edge to be overcome by techniques like card count and bet variation than is mathematically necessary. (Incidentally, his book reveals virtually none of his alleged "secrets" on these two techniques. They are "too valuable.")

The hardest thing for me to accept in Scarne's book are these sentences: "I decided it was high time someone figured out the exact percentage in the bank's favor. I spent several months on the mathematical calculations this required; you will find, for the first time anywhere, the correct percentage in favor of the bank or blackjack dealer on pages 325–329."

The closest that Scarne comes to figuring "the exact percentage" is a statement that the player who simply mimics the dealer is bucking an edge of 5.90 percent. (Note that on page 47 of this book I show this to be about 4½ percent.) But Scarne does not say how much can be knocked off of this, using a proper fixed strategy for the various player options. Using his strategy recommendations, and his numbers, the final expectation would be between 1.5 and 2.5 percent, which is a lot worse than the 0.6 percent that Baldwin published *six years earlier*.

Nor should Scarne lament that he did not have the aid of an electronic computer; Baldwin didn't have one either. Actually, much can be done with approximations and rough estimates, given sufficient time, but in several cases Scarne simply did not put the numbers together correctly. This appeared to be due to misconceptions in basic probability fundamentals.

Scarne has a wide reputation as a gambling authority. Considering that his handbook in general gives a magnificent coverage of the American gambling scene, it is regrettable that the blackjack section is so deficient.

6. The celebrated autobiography of Harold Smith should not go unmentioned. Entitled, *I Want to Quit Winners*, it is a fascinating account of the life of a casino proprietor—all the more so because Harold and his father built Harolds Club from scratch, and now it is one of the largest casinos in the world. His story runs the gamut of human emotion, and I found myself completely absorbed as I read it. It is the saga of a gambler, too, for Harold is a high-roller himself when he sallies forth from his own fortress and beards the other lions in their dens.

Harold has a short chapter called "My Primer of Gambling." I rate his four pages on blackjack as fair. His advice contains a curious mixture of partially correct hitting rules, and some playing philosophy which certainly deserves some discussion. His most serious misstatement in strategy is in suggesting that aside from certain (unstated) exceptions you should never hit a stiff. Whenever the dealer shows 7 or higher, which is 8/13 of the time, you normally *should hit* a stiff. Accordingly the hitting of a stiff should be done more often than not, and this can hardly be considered as an "exception." His advice, while not literally untrue, is very misleading.

Harold's book is loaded with questionable statements about luck, some of which are quite inconsistent with each other, and none of which in my opinion has scientific merit:

1. The expert gambler believes implicitly in the supernatural and develops his extrasensory perception to its ultimate keenness.
2. You can take chances one day that you couldn't on another.
3. The great majority of players do not capitalize on their luck when it is running.
4. If I have a strong hunch that a non-breaking card will come, I do hit a stiff hand.
5. You can soon discern how the cards or dice are running.

Item (2) actually appears in a passage that says, "I always watch the trend of the cards as other cards are hit. They may indicate, on this evening, that only 10s are coming on my 12s, but they may also indicate 4s and 5s are falling to my 16s. You can take chances one day that you couldn't on another." This statement does not make sense. If you want to maximize your chance of winning, you have to play the best known strategy for the long run. It is one thing to base a strategy for drawing or standing on 12 by the temporal consideration of whether you have consistently drawn 10s on your previous 12s during the preceding hours of play. It is quite another to base it on a count of cards remaining in the *immediate present* deck, and the knowledge that more than the normal proportion of 10s remain in the deck. The former, which is what Harold intimates, is a strictly irrelevant consideration of previous decks. The latter is highly relevant.

Item (5) appears on the *same page* as a statement, "The chances on each succeeding bet are exactly the same as they were on the first." Clearly these two statements are mutually contradictory. Statement (5) might make some sense if it were rewritten as follows:

"You can soon discern how the cards or dice *were* running, within the plays just previously observed." Unfortunately this information doesn't tell you whether a streak of wins or losses will continue into the future.

The other items in the list are equally as dubious as the ones on which we have expanded. The whole thing reflects Harold's impulsive attitude toward a bet. But of course impulsive bettors are just what support the casinos, in contrast to scientific bettors. In connection with the latter, Harold gives absolutely no advice on counting the cards at blackjack. As usual, one would not expect such assistance from a casino operator.

Harold does not try to deceive any player into thinking he has much chance of making a coup at Harolds Club. His book tells of far more big losers than winners. Indeed, Harolds is the *only* club in Nevada that has signs posted to gently remind you, "You can't win all the time. Harolds Club urges you to gamble only what you can afford." Such a nice place to lose!

7. John Crawford came out in 1961 with a revision of a book he first published in 1953 and entitled, *How to Be a Consistent Winner in the Most Popular Card Games*. His coverage includes a page or so of qualitative remarks on keeping track of the cards, varying bet size, and adjusting your hitting strategy. This material is not sufficiently quantitative to be of any real help. So on an over-all basis, I rate John Crawford's treatment as "good," but not excellent.

8. The first authoritative book giving the correct strategy for the basic game of blackjack appeared in 1957. Written by the Baldwin team at Aberdeen, it was titled, *Playing Blackjack to Win*. For the most part, it was a magnificent little book. Not only did they give a nearly flawless basic strategy, but they also showed the price of not following their strategy in various cases. The one serious error in the Baldwin book was mentioned on pages 61 and 92.

The book also made an attempt at a policy for using the exposed cards to improve the hitting strategy. It did not have the finesse of methods like 10-count and its attendant NT/T ratio, but it was a step in the right direction. Baldwin and company deserve much credit for getting the scientific treatment of blackjack off the ground!

MAGAZINES ARE EVEN LESS RELIABLE THAN BOOKS

If you have to be discriminating about believing what is written on the subject of blackjack percentages and strategy in books, it is even more necessary in the case of magazine articles. Misinformation is the rule rather than the exception, for magazines ranging all the way from the prominent national weeklies and monthlies down to the grubbiest of the pulps. We give here a smattering of excerpts to demonstrate the range of quality (correctness) in published articles. The list is not intended to cover all articles published or to probe in depth as we did with the books, but just to illustrate typical writing.

1. *Look Magazine*, March, 1963. "The Weird World of Gambling." This one quotes 6 percent advantage for the house at blackjack, although it does mention Dr. Thorp's claims to be able to beat the game. The remarks about the latter's method are rather disparaging, however, implying in effect that only a rare combination of perfectionist and superintellect could succeed at it.

2. *Glamour Magazine*, January, 1963. "Fearless Man: Ian Fleming." Here we have 7 percent for the house, stated by the famous British writer of mystery stories. Fleming is supposed to have spent a bit of time in the casinos of the world during his colorful career, but nonetheless his information on blackjack is misleading.

3. *Climax*, September, 1961. "How to Beat the Blackjack Odds," by Jeff Poland. This one quotes 1 percent for the house. The article goes into enough detail so as to actually recommend a hitting strategy; it is fairly close to Baldwin strategy, but no credit is given to Baldwin. Errors include recommendation against splitting 2s, 3s, and 6s; against doubling down on soft 18; and against doubling down with 11 against ace. No mention is given to counting cards, and varying bet size. Therefore, the title, "How to Beat the Blackjack Odds," is not justified.

4. *Man's Conquest*, August, 1961. "How You Can Win at Blackjack." This is one of those "as told to" articles, namely, as told to Michael Davis by an alleged professional Las Vegas gambler by name of Lance Parker. He, too, recommends essentially a Baldwin strategy, without benefit of references to the latter.

As with the preceding article, nothing is said about counting cards and varying bet size, and the title, "How You Can Win at Blackjack," is unsubstantiated.

5. *Argosy*, August, 1961. "Counting the Cards." Alfred Sheinwold runs a regular one-page feature in Argosy magazine, entitled, "It's in the Cards." This issue deals with blackjack. Sheinwold is a genuine card expert, well-known for his books on bridge, and as an editor of "The Bridge World." In this relatively short feature, he summarizes the percentage situation in basic blackjack, and makes some instructive but strictly qualitative remarks about card counting.

Sheinwold has written something that is more free from error than most magazine articles on blackjack, but it could have been stronger in many ways. In addition, he ought to give the reader at least one reference on where to find the gross strategy and its refinements in print.

6. *Playboy*, March, 1960. "On the Town in Las Vegas." (No author's name given.) Here we find "4 to 5 percent" quoted for the house, in an article that gives a colorfully photographed and well-written spread on entertainment, gambling, and the personality of Las Vegas, but which attempts to give no facts on blackjack play.

7. *Monsieur*, September, 1960. "Why You Lose When You Gamble," by Eli Camellan. This one doesn't say anything profound. You lose, reveals the author, because the house has a big fat advantage at every game. Specifically at blackjack, the house takes all busts, stands off all ties, and never passes the deal. For these reasons, Camellan says "the odds are 17 percent with them, i.e., on every $100 wagered, the bank stands to win $17."

8. *Las Vegas Playground*, January, 1964. "Basics of 21," by F. Robert Louis. After laying out the rules of the game, the author proceeds to present simultaneous advice from three different books. Thorp, Goodman, and Scarne are *all* quoted, "in the interests of neutrality," on such strategy decisions as straight hit or stand, double-down, and split. Wherever conflicting advice occurs, the reader is invited to take his choice, or even to inject ideas of his own.

Gradually the magazine coverage has gotten a little better, but misinformation continues to be propagated. I believe this occurs because writers either will not be bothered to track down what is written by competent mathematicians, or else they are incapable of absorbing even the essence of what is written. Change comes slowly. Even those supposedly unimpeachable authorities, the encyclopedias, cannot be trusted. Recently the *Britannica* stated that the dealer has an advantage, but if the game is played honestly, it is not an exorbitant edge (quoting consultant A. Morehead). When eight books, eight magazine articles, and an encyclopedia make strongly conflicting statements and present almost as many views as there are authors, on a topic on which there is only one mathematically correct position, it is time to sit up and take notice. Those who wish to be correctly informed must choose carefully among the available informers.

Slot Machines

10

The most popular form of casino gambling is with slot machines. The lure of the "jackpot" payoff on a token investment is irresistible to many. Further, there is a great advantage—you don't have to learn any rules of play. Just drop a coin in the slot and pull the handle. This makes it especially attractive to the newcomer, who doesn't like to admit that he or she is ignorant of how to play the complicated gambling games. This person can immerse himself in the forest of slot machines and go to work. Since the forest is so thick, there is bound to be somebody winning a moderate payoff every few minutes. The attending clamor serves to spur all others on. Since someone else has just won, each sucker figures his turn is next!

The slots are particularly popular with the fair sex because they can play by themselves. In this way, a woman can avoid sitting at a gambling table, populated mostly by men, who may register disapproval if she makes a mistake in play. She thus prevents the occasional risk of sneering glances or unkind remarks on the part of inconsiderate males. But a more important reason for women preferring the slots may be that they are more emotional than men, and love the opportunity to jump with joy when they hit a payoff! The slot machine has high entertainment value for some.

THE ODDS ON THE SLOTS

All slot machine players, men or women, suffer from the disadvantage that it is seemingly impossible to find out the correct odds against them on any one machine. Ironically, it is a cinch to compute these odds, *if* you have access to certain basic information about the machine. Unfortunately, this information is not generally available. All it amounts to is knowing how many symbols of each type appear on each of the three reels in the machine. But this can be determined only if you see the machine disassembled, since the machine is designed to show only one of the 20 symbols at a time. It could also be determined by statistical sampling of the relative frequency with which each symbol appears in the window. For a reliable answer, 200 or more trials might be advisable, and not many people would have the curiosity or patience to make a scientific investigation like this. Ironically, though, there are plenty of people who would *play* a machine for several hours—more than the required sample time.

The evaluation of the house percentage for a representative slot machine is shown in Table 10-1. The first part of the table lists the

TABLE 10-1. SLOT MACHINE HOUSE PERCENTAGE

Symbol and Abbreviation		Number of Symbols on Reel		
		Reel 1	Reel 2	Reel 3
Cherry	(C)	5	6	3
Plum	(P)	5	2	2
Orange	(O)	5	6	4
Melon	(M)	1	2	8
Bell	(B)	3	3	2
Bar	(#)	1	1	1

Winning Combination	Payoff in Coins	Number of Possible Ways	Contribution
C - C - *	2	5 × 6 × 10 = 300	600
C - C - M	5	5 × 6 × 8 = 240	1200
C - C - B	6	5 × 6 × 2 = 60	360
O - O - #	10	5 × 6 × 1 = 30	300
O - O - O	10	5 × 6 × 4 = 120	1200
P - P - #	20	5 × 2 × 1 = 10	200
P - P - P	75	5 × 2 × 2 = 20	1500
B - B - B	100	3 × 3 × 2 = 18	1800
# - # - #	200	1 × 1 × 1 = 1	200
(Jackpot)			
		799	7360 Net Return
			—8000 Investment
			— 640 Net Loss

* This means any symbol except M or B.

number of symbols of each type on each of the three reels. The second part gives (1) the winning combinations, (2) the payoffs on these combinations, (3) the number of ways each combination can be formed out of the total 8000 possible combinations ($20 \times 20 \times 20 = 8000$), and finally (4) the contribution from each winning combination. The numbers in this last column add up to 7360. This is the number of coins you would get back, on the average, for each 8000 coins invested on this particular machine. The net loss is 640, and the house advantage is thus $640/8000 = 0.08$, or 8 percent.

The figure of 8 percent house advantage on the machine cited here is simply for purposes of illustration. The actual casino percentages are rarely publicized by the operators. Some casinos would like you to believe that their machines are more generous than the figure shown in the table. In an article about Harolds Club in 1953, Richard Donovan told of an interesting incident at that casino. A hardy optimist kept plunking one nickel after another into a 5¢ machine. At first he had a positive spurt, and was at one point almost $7.00 ahead. Then the tide turned, and 4 hours later he was $13 in the hole. Having counted a total of around 7800 plays, he was completely disgusted, and hauled off and smashed his fist into the machine! This foolish act earned him some medical attention, plus a soothing lecture from the club manager. Now the interesting fact to me was that the player had put in 7800 coins and had gotten 7540 in return. The loss of 260 coins implied a house edge somewhere around 3 percent, a figure that agreed with that I had heard about from one of the casino employees. But this was before some of the taxes went up in Nevada, and should be regarded cautiously. Certainly, many Nevada slot machines are far less generous than this. Major A. Riddle, in 1963, quotes 10 percent to 50 percent, and he ought to know something about the subject, since he is president and managing director of the Dunes Hotel on the Las Vegas "strip."

There is a certain tantalization in the arrangement of symbols on the reels. In general, the less likely a combination is to occur, the greater the payoff. On the machine described here, there is only one jackpot combination, paying 200 for 1; conversely, the most likely winning combination can be formed 300 ways, and pays only 2 for 1.

But the rule is not hard and fast. Many relatively unlikely combinations do not pay off at all, as for example, bar-bar-bell.

The melon is not productive unless teamed with two preceding cherries. It is worth while to note that there is only one melon on the first reel, two on the second, but eight on the third. Suspense can be readily built up as the symbols successively fall into place, with a potential winner lined up on the first and second—only to have it wiped out with a dud in the third! Note also that there is some sort of payoff in 799 out of the possible 8000 combinations. This is about 10 percent and is typical of the slots. That occasional winner once every ten times (on the average) keeps a lot of players on the hook!

Many players find it hard to believe that a mechanical device like a slot machine can produce an essentially random sequence of results. Yet this definitely appears to be the case. The notion of a machine being "due" after it has failed to pay a jackpot for a long time is fallacious. Long streaks between wins on the slots are analogous to streaks between numbers winning on a roulette wheel, and all that was said in this respect in Chapter 3 applies here. A very telling illustration of the monotony with which a slot machine can grind out its percentage for the owner is the experience of my friend Philip Fox, at the University of Wisconsin. As a professor in the School of Commerce, Fox has been interested in odds for many years. In his office he has a slot machine, which was set by its previous owner to yield 25 percent; when this device was confiscated by state authorities while in illegal operation, Fox persuaded them to let him have it in the interests of science. Since 1940, an endless succession of students have pulled the handle and tallied up the result (without benefit of payoff, of course). During the collection of some 200,000 samples, the cumulative record showed that never once did the machine deviate from the set percentage return by more than 1 percent!

CHEATING THE MACHINES

Countless ways of cheating the slot machines have been tried over the years. There seems to be a never-ending battle of wits, the ingenuity of the crooks challenging the defensive measures of the operators and of the machine designers. Over the years, various models of the machines have had some vulnerability, some fatal flaw, which could be capitalized upon. Early cheats devised spoonshaped rods to stick up the payoff tube, analogous to jimmying the coin return tube on a pay telephone. The cure to this proved to be the use of a zigzag path in the tube, preventing the insertion of any object that could get a purchase for prying. Magnets have been used in various and sundry ways, until the location of parts and the materials they were made of rendered them useless. Some cheats have been bold enough to improvise keys to open up the back of the machine and fiddle with the mechanism in such a way as to set up a big payoff for a confederate playing the machine; of course the man with the key is gone from the scene when the player claims his jackpot.

An even bigger team effort has been employed by a trio, with the first man using a small drill concealed in the palm of his hand to bore a tiny hole at a critical spot, the second man slipping a thin wire through the hole to rig the mechanism, and the third to collect on this chicanery. A slab of boiler plate along the inside wall at the right spot has foiled this operation. Many naïve subjects have tried slugs or low-value foreign coins, only to find themselves spotted and subsequently penalized by law, which prohibits their use. All these tricks are more or less obvious to someone with a larcenous mind. Their application is largely a question of the existing "state of the art" of mechanical technique. Usually, the proprietors react swiftly to any new twists. It is pretty hard to put something over on an experienced casino operator, especially if he has the advantage of constant surveillance from behind one-way mirrors or viewing ports!

RHYTHM PLAYERS

About a dozen years ago, an attack was launched on the slot machines, which soon had the operators quivering in their boots. Someone discovered that by proper manipulation of the handle, he could control the drop on one or more reels. Now, just to be able to select a good symbol on the first reel, and thereby exclude those that offered little or no payoff prospect, was an enormous advantage. Any further selection ability meant profits even more huge. One of the pioneers is said to have won tens of thousands in the first year, playing not only the legal slots in Nevada, but also illegal slots elsewhere in the nation. Presently a corps of artists sprang up, called the "rhythm players," for indeed the style of pulling the handle required variations from the usual regular pattern of the ordinary player. Proper timing was a skill that took many hours of practice, and indeed the artists varied in their ability to perform. The true virtuosos made a mint.

The success of the method was dependent upon the design of slot machines in use at that time. In principle, there was nothing dishonest about the method. Eventually, the star performers became persona non grata at the casinos, and then proceeded to continue to cash in on their talent by training others. A brochure appeared on the market, explaining the method for a mere $5.00. The more enterprising experts set up a school in Las Vegas, with the tuition fee in the hundreds of dollars; their thesis was that the novice could learn it right only by personal instruction from a master. The swarms of additional rhythm players who developed through these various media began to make serious inroads on the profits of the operators. The loss of revenue ran into many millions. Finally, the slot machine makers figured out how to amend the design, and by injecting an additional element of randomization into the clocking mechanism, they put an end to their troubles. But for a few years there, they were really sweating!

Even more quickly than they had been clobbered themselves, the operators turned the tables on their adversaries. One highly successful rhythm player in Reno, having earned a healthy yield in a short few weeks, decided to lay low for a while. He took a vacation trip to Mexico. When he came back, lo and behold—his system didn't work any more. The machines had all been changed!

So much for the highly intriguing "rhythm method." To my knowledge, it was the only honest yet scientifically valid approach for defeating the slots that had ever been used. Otherwise, the slot machine situation can be summed up by saying it is sheer poison to all who play. The casino percentage is quite severe, and there is almost no likelihood of a player being lucky enough to parlay a substantial win over a short period of time. The casinos make tremendous publicity about *how many* jackpots they pay out per day or week. But they never, never say *what proportion* of the players have this success, or *how much* they have poured down the chute on the average to win a jackpot; these things, of course, are what really count. I have never heard of any present-day player who is ahead on the slots. Have you?

An intriguing sidelight in slot machine operations is the recent introduction of an electronic computer system to monitor the operations of all the slot machines in a casino. Such a system has been installed at the Fremont Hotel in Las Vegas, which has hundreds of slots. Costing several hundred thousand dollars, it is referred to as an automatic coin-counting and payoff-indicating system. It provides a 24-hour typewritten summary, giving each machine's number, income, amount paid out, amount retained or lost, and the payout as a percentage of income or loss. Also, it supplies a historical record of a machine's performance. This device, made by Video Corporation in San Diego, California, cuts *days* off the accounting lag prevalent in manual methods of tabulation.

The casino will gain an interesting side benefit from this automation. They expect a sharp reduction of their losses to wayward jackpot-payoff girls. In the past, the casino had to rely on their own security force, operating behind one-way mirrors, to check up on the honesty of these employees. But now the payoff girl's tally at the end of the day will have to agree with the computer, or else she will be immediately suspected of overpaying a confederate. Enforced honesty will thus be a benefit of the electronic marvel!

Craps

11

Craps is the game that gets the biggest money play in the casinos. The action is fast, and a player can rip loose from his inhibitions. He can shout and wave his arms, and in general, raise enough turmoil to draw more attention to himself than in any other gambling game! Extroverts love it. The majority of such players know how to figure the odds for the various simple propositions. But it is surprising how many experienced players do not really know the correct percentages on some of the even-money bets that they make all the time (although these crap-shooters must be given credit for being generally aware that the house percentage approaches a low value on these bets). There is also considerable ignorance and confusion in the matter of *taking* and *laying* the odds, wherein the house cut is reduced even lower. Yet many writers omit this subject completely, and others scarcely mention it in passing. All of these percentages are readily computed, and we give here a brief but thorough coverage.

A SIMPLE COMPUTATION OF ODDS

Craps is played by tossing two dice. Since each of these has 6 faces, there are 36 possible combinations. The least likely totals are 2 ("snake-eyes," 1-1) and 12 ("boxcars," 6-6); the most likely total is 7 (6-1, 5-2, 4-3, 3-4, 2-5, 1-6). As typical cases, we can work out the expected return on a couple of bets that have a large percentage favoring the house. For example, the house offers 8 for 1 on a wager entitled "any craps." Here you bet that on the next roll of the dice, the total will be 2, 3, or 12. The chance of winning is $1/36 + 2/36 +$

$1/36 = 4/36$, or $1/9$. Thus, the correct odds are 8 *to* 1 against it, but the payoff is only 8 *for* 1, or 7 *to* 1. (In an 8 *for* 1 payoff, the casino keeps the unit you bet, but pays 8. With 8 *to* 1 the casino lets you keep your unit, and also pays 8. Watch carefully whether the word *to* or *for* is used.) The expected return on this bet is

$$+7 \cdot (1/9) - 1 \cdot (8/9) = -1/9 \text{ of a unit}$$

This amounts to 11.1 percent against you—a very healthy edge!

8 the Hard Way

As a second example, we shall figure one of the "hard way" propositions. Take the case of 8, the hard way, which pays 9:1. Here you are betting that you will roll a double 4 before you roll any other combination totaling 8 or before you roll a 7. Of all the 36 combinations, only one of them is a 4-4. On the other hand, there are four other ways to total 8, and six ways to total 7. Thus, there is one way to win, and ten ways to lose. If you roll any of the other 25 combinations, they do not count. So, the odds are 10 *to* 1 against winning on 8 the hard way. With a payoff of 10 *for* 1, or 9 *to* 1, the expected return is

$$+9 \cdot (1/11) - 1 \cdot (10/11) = -1/11 \text{ of a unit}$$

This is 9.1 percent against you, which again is a hard percentage to beat.

BETTING ON THE PASS LINE

All other center propositions are easy to figure, using the same lines of reasoning we have employed in the previous two examples. Now we move on to the basic play on the "pass line." Here the analysis takes just a few more steps, but each step in the logic is just as simple as those we have already used. The pass line bet is an even-money bet. On the first roll of the dice, called the *come-out* roll, three possible things can happen:

1. A *natural* (7 or 11) may be thrown; this is an outright win, often called a *pass*.

2. A *crap* (2, 3, or 12) may be thrown; this is an outright loss, often called a *miss-out*.

3. A 4, 5, 6, 8, 9, or 10 may be thrown; in this case, the number that you have rolled is your "point," and you then continue to roll until either of two things occur:

(a) your point is thrown again, in which case you win;

(b) a 7 is thrown, in which case you lose.

Table 11-1 shows the probabilities of all various eventualities. The second column gives the probabilities of initially rolling the totals indicated in the first column. If a point is rolled on the first toss, then the subsequent probabilities of win or loss on that point are shown in the next column. For example, with point 4, there are three ways to win (1-3, 2-2, 3-1), but six ways to lose, with a total of 7, as enumerated previously. The entries in the "net win" and "net loss" columns are obtained from products of the third column times those of second column. Thus, the chance of originally throwing 4, and also subsequently winning on it, is $3/36 \times 3/9 = 1/36$; by the same token, the chance of throwing a 4 and then losing on it is $3/36 \times 6/9 = 2/36$. The same numbers apply to point 10, since the number of combinations totaling 10 is the same as for 4.

TABLE 11-1. PLAYER'S EXPECTATION ON THE PASS-LINE BET

Probability of Initially Rolling a Given Total		Probability of Outcome on Point (Win)	(Loss)	Net Win Probability	Net Loss Probability
2	1/36				$1/36 = 55/1980$
3	2/36				$2/36 = 110/1980$
4	3/36	3/9	6/9	$1/36 = 55/1980$	$2/36 = 110/1980$
5	4/36	4/10	6/10	$2/45 = 88/1980$	$3/45 = 132/1980$
6	5/36	5/11	6/11	$25/396 = 125/1980$	$30/396 = 150/1980$
7	6/36	....	....	$6/36 = 330/1980$	
8	5/36	5/11	6/11	$25/396 = 125/1980$	$30/396 = 150/1980$
9	4/36	4/10	6/10	$2/45 = 88/1980$	$3/45 = 132/1980$
10	3/36	3/9	6/9	$1/36 = 55/1980$	$2/36 = 110/1980$
11	2/36	....	....	$2/36 = 110/1980$	
12	1/36	....	....		$1/36 = 55/1980$
				976/1980, or $244/495 = 0.493$	1004/1980, or $251/495 = 0.507$

Expected return: $+1 \cdot (0.493) - 1 \cdot (0.507) = -0.014$, or -1.4 percent.

The House Percentage on the Pass Line

By analogous reasoning, the probabilities for the other point values may be computed. The final step is to convert all fractions to the common denominator of $36 \times 55 = 1980$, so that two net totals may be obtained. When the last two columns of Table 11-1 are added up, it is evident that in 1980 trials, you can expect 28 more losses than wins. Since the pass-line wager is an even-money bet, the house advantage is therefore $28/1980 = 7/495$. As a decimal, this works out to 0.0141414, or roughly a percentage of 1.4 percent. This is indeed one of the lowest percentages available in the casino, and explains why craps is so popular among the high rollers. (But, of course, this is nowhere near as good as blackjack, as we have already seen in Chapters 5-8.)

This same percentage also applies to the *come* bet, which in reality is just a delayed pass-line bet. The whole purpose of it is to enable new players to get immediately into the game while another player is holding the dice and shooting for his point.

Betting on the Don't-Pass Line

Instead of betting that the dice will *pass*, you can bet that they will *not* pass. In this case, you put your bet on a space marked *don't pass* (or if the action has already started, on a space labeled *don't come*). Now you are apparently betting *with* the house, *but there is an important exception.* Double 6 is barred on the come-out roll; it is neither a winner nor a loser, but a standoff or tie for the don't-pass bettor. In every 1980 trials, on the average, the don't-pass bettor gets 949 wins, 55 ties, and 976 losses. There are 27 more losses than wins, and the house advantage is $27/1980 = 0.01364$, or 1.364 percent. This is slightly lower than the 1.414 on the pass line, though to the nearest tenth, they both round off to 1.4 percent. Most players take the pass line: is this superstition or distrust?

The above method of computing the house advantage is consistent with that used for baccarat in Chapter 13 (but note blackjack is yet another matter, due to splits and doubles). Alternatively, we may compute it as $27/1925 = 0.01403$, in effect using *relative* probabilities p' and q' rather than *absolute* probabilities p and q (see page 289).

Thus a tie is not really regarded as such, but as a momentary interruption, forgotten in seconds as the dice are tossed again. The emphasis differs from that in card games where draw of extra cards up to the final tying total may occur, and where a new hand must then be dealt out. It all hinges on your definition of the word *trial*. Here I choose to ignore the tie as a trial, so I shall use 1.403 percent.

TAKING THE ODDS

Many players think that the foregoing 1.4 percent is the irreducible minimum, below which you cannot go at craps. However, numerous casinos permit an additional bet at exactly correct odds (no advantage to house or to player), and this effectively reduces the house advantage on the total amount bet.

There are two cases to consider, *taking the odds* and *laying* the odds. We shall take them separately, in order. The first one applies if you are playing the pass line. On the come-out roll, if you roll a point, the house may allow you to take the odds for an amount equal to what you have already bet on the pass line. You place an additional bet outside the layout behind the pass line. You are betting that you *will* make your point, and in the event that you do, the payoff is at correct odds. Thus, point 6 or 8 pays 6:5, point 5 or 9 pays 3:2, and point 4 or 10 pays 2:1. The effect this has on the expected return is easy to figure. As our previous calculations have shown, you will roll a point on two-thirds of the come-out rolls. Thus, 1320 out of the 1980 plays will be on the point. This means that you have another 1320 bets on which the advantage is neither plus nor minus. The expected return computation should therefore be revised as follows:

$$\frac{+1 \times (976) - 1 \times (1004) + 0 \times (1320)}{976 \quad + \quad 1004 \quad + \quad 1320} = \frac{-28}{3300} = 0.008484$$

As a percentage, this is 0.848 percent, which is a substantial reduction from 1.4 percent. An alternate way of expressing the situation is to say that, on the average, you are betting another two-thirds of a unit, but with the same *absolute* expected loss as before. Hence, the *relative* loss will be reduced by the factor $1/(1 + 2/3) = 3/5$. When 1.414 percent is multiplied by $3/5$, we get 0.848 percent.

LAYING THE ODDS

If you are playing the don't-pass line, and a point is thrown on the come-out roll, the house may allow you to lay the odds. You place an additional bet outside the layout behind the don't-pass line. You are betting that the point will *not* be made, since you are betting *against* the dice. If the shooter "sevens" out, you will be appropriately paid at 5:6, 2:3, or 1:2, depending on what the point is.

There are two distinct cases to consider in figuring the expected return on laying the odds. First, we shall suppose that your additional bet is equal to your don't-pass bet. (Dollar-wise this imposes certain limitations if the casino has a rule about paying in round dollars. The smallest bet that would work is $30, in which case you would be paid $25, $20, and $15, respectively, in the cases cited in the preceding paragraph.) Referring to our previous calculations, and bearing in mind that double 6 is barred on the come-out roll on the don't-pass bet, it is evident that the shooter will roll a point on 24/35 of the meaningful come-out rolls. (This is in contrast to the 24/36, or 2/3, on the pass-line bet.) Applying the same reasoning as in taking the odds, we can say that on the average you are betting another 24/35 of a unit, but with the same absolute expected loss as before. Hence, the relative loss will be reduced by the factor $1/(1 + 24/35) = 35/59$. When 1.403 percent is multiplied by 35/59, the result is 0.832 percent. We see that this is a little less than the corresponding result for taking the odds on the pass line (0.848 percent).

Very often the casino allows you to lay the odds with a *larger* bet than what you have on the don't-pass line, larger in amount such that, if you win, the payoff to you equals your initial don't-pass bet. In a way, this simplifies payoffs, but it slightly complicates the computation because the additional bet is no longer a single amount, and depends on what the point is. For example, if your don't-pass bet is $10.00, you will find yourself laying the odds with $12, $15, or $20, depending on the point. In terms of a one-unit don't-pass bet, these odds bets will be 6/5, 3/2, or two units.

The details of this computation are left as an exercise for the reader. The final outcome appears in the summary tabulation in

Table 11-2 as 0.691 percent. Some of the clubs in Reno even permit twice as much to be wagered on the odds bets. The corresponding house edge is shown in the bottom line of the chart.

TABLE 11-2. SUMMARY OF LINE-BET PERCENTAGES AGAINST
PLAYER AT CRAPS

	Pass, %	Don't Pass, %
Basic percentage	1.414	1.403
IF free bets allowed	(Taking the odds), 0.848	(Laying the odds),* 0.832 or 0.691
IF *double* free bets allowed	(Taking *double* the odds), 0.606	(Laying *double* the odds), 0.591 or 0.459

* See page 186 for reason why two different values are given for "laying" the odds.

SUMMARY

The competition between casinos for the big money play is the only thing that leads to permitting bets with such low percentages as you have on taking or laying double the odds. After all, 1 percent on $500 is $5.00, which is a lot more than even 10 percent on $1.00. The operators can also hope, and often expect, that in the heat of the action, those big money splurgers will take some of those atrocious 10 percent hard-way bets and other propositions. They may *claim* that it is the dollar bettor who supports the casino, but man, how they lick their chops when a high roller walks in the door!

At this point, we have accomplished the basic objective of this chapter. This was to show how to go about figuring the odds on craps, particularly for the pass-line and similar bets. Great emphasis is placed on the so-called free bets, or taking and laying the odds, since these are the very best bets on the crap table. We have not even attempted to compute the odds for *all* the various bets at craps, simply because there are so many of them, and because all can be figured by methods we have used in this chapter. A book that shows you *how to go about* figuring some of these things *for yourself* is far more instructive than one that simply catalogs all the results! People generally have far more confidence in facts that they can check for themselves than they do in facts they have simply memorized. There is no pretense that a complete coverage of craps has been made in this chapter. We have concentrated only on the most important facts.

Keno

12

It will always be a great mystery to me that, in ten years of active interest in all published material related to gambling, I have seen only one presentation of the odds for keno. They just aren't that hard to figure. I first got interested in keno while clocking a roulette wheel at Harolds Club. Nearby, they were installing a keno. Since our bets were low on the marathon roulette, it was a little dull, and I got to wondering about the prospects of a bias in keno. In particular, if some of the numbered balls were lighter than others, they might have a greater tendency to come to the top of the cage and then get drawn out as winners. Or perhaps if the mixing process were not complete, the balls that were put back into the cage might have a greater or smaller chance of being drawn the next time. Other factors could be at work. As with the roulette, such a bias could be detected by making a statistical analysis of the winning numbers.

How big a basic house percentage would the bias have to overcome? Nobody could tell us. We understood right away how to figure it, but it did look as though exact results would require lengthy calculation. So I made a rough estimate while clocking the roulette. It took me about a half-hour, and my result was a whopping 20 percent! Clearly, any casino employees who knew this did not go around broadcasting to the hapless players.

DESCRIPTION OF KENO

In the standard keno game, the operator draws from 80 numbered balls in the cage. Drawings are scheduled for specific times. Prior to the next drawing, a player gets into the game by purchasing one or more tickets. On each ticket he marks his selection of ten numbers which he hopes will win. When it is time for the drawing, everybody gathers round to watch. The operator makes a great fuss over whirling the cage, so that all the players are satisfied that the balls are thoroughly mixed. Then, one by one, he draws a total of 20 balls from the cage. The winning numbers are called out, and these numbers are lit up on the conspicuous electric *keno board*. With bated breath, each player compares his ticket with the board, hoping against hope that all of his 10 numbers are among the 20 which have been picked, for if he is so lucky, he wins a fantastic payoff of 25,000:1! The chance of hitting such a jackpot, is only about 1 in 9 million. But there are other combinations that are not quite so improbable, although they return a smaller amount. Picking nine numbers will bring a payoff of 2800:1; here the chance is about 1 in 160,000. And so on down the line, to picking five numbers, which pays 2:1 with about 1 chance in 20 to happen. Thus, if five or more numbers are picked, there is a payoff. But if four or fewer numbers are picked, there is none.

Technically speaking, keno is a *lottery*, so the payoffs quoted here are *maximum* payoffs. Thus, the *most* that a $1.00 bet can bring is $25,000. But if two lucky players were to write simultaneous ten-number winners in the same game, they would have to share the $25,000 pot, along with those who wrote lesser winning tickets.

The fatal fascination of a game like keno is, of course, the possibility of the gigantic payoff. Players allow themselves to be hypnotized by this, and utterly disregard the tiny chance of occurrence. Indeed, the game is artfully designed to produce lots of "near misses," so the player is enticed to try again. It is a great game for the small-money suckers, who dream of sudden wealth. In form, it is identical with the Chinese lottery. In magnetic lure, it resembles the numbers, or policy game, and other lotteries that are deeply entrenched in many of our larger cities and which presumably operate unmolested by the law. The principal difference in the illegal games is that the payoffs are much lower, and the operators' cut is far higher. In the slums of our major cities, the policy operators prey on the poor and ignorant, who know that the only chance of quick escape from their miserable circumstances is to win a bonanza.

A WHOPPING BIG HOUSE PERCENTAGE

The procedure for computing the chance of picking any particular number of winners is explained in Appendix A. This chance is listed in the middle column of Table 12-1. In order to assess the expected return on the ticket, we must multiply the chance of each possible number of winners by the corresponding payoff. Hence, the payoffs are listed in column 4, and then the resulting contribution to the return is listed in the last column. We see that all contributions total to 0.809 on a 1.000-unit ticket. Thus, the expected return on a $1.00 ticket is about 81¢, and the house advantage is then 19¢ on the dollar. (Actually the house advantage is slightly larger than this, owing to the limited liability that the house assumes in any one game.)

To consider an interesting extreme, suppose a syndicate of the world's richest men came to a casino and purchased *all possible* 10-number tickets. This would mean all combinations of 80 things taken 10 at a time, which is

$$\binom{80}{10} = \frac{80!}{10!\ 70!} = 1.6(10)^{12}$$

This number is more than a million million, and it would require a huge syndicate to put up the money at $1.00 per ticket! (Rockefeller reputedly amassed a fortune of $2 billion, or $2 thousand million, but even with this fortune he would be able to buy only a fraction of these tickets.) This sum exceeds the annual gross national product of the whole United States. If the keno tickets were compressed to stacks of 1000 tickets per inch and bound like a bundle of newspapers laid on their side, the bundle would circle the globe! Or if the dollar bills to buy them were laid end to end, they would reach from here to the sun! Yet the return on this purchase would be $25,000, a fantastically small fraction of the cost.

For a full understanding of the game of keno, you should look at more than just the expected return. Table 12-1 shows, for example, that there is a probability of 0.935 that you will not get paid at all on your ticket; thus, the odds are about 14:1 that you will not collect. Of course this is just the price you pay to get a crack at those big,

TABLE 12-1. EXPECTED RETURN ON A TYPICAL KENO TICKET

Number of Winners (x)	Odds Against This Number of Winners	Chance of This Number of Winners		Payoff	Contribution to Return
10	8,910,000 : 1	0.000000112	×	25,000	0.0028
9	163,000 : 1	0.00000612	×	2,800	0.0171
8	7,390 : 1	0.000135	×	1,400	0.189
7	621 : 1	0.00161	×	180	0.290
6	87.1 : 1	0.0115	×	18	0.207
5	19.4 : 1	0.0514	×	2	0.103
4	6.8 : 1	0.147 ⎫			0.809
3	3.7 : 1	0.267 ⎪ Not paid			
2	3.4 : 1	0.295 ⎬ (Totals 0.935.)			Expected return
1	5.6 : 1	0.180 ⎪			on a 1.000-unit
0	21.8 : 1	0.046 ⎭			investment

1.000 Total probability

juicy payoffs. But the important thing to observe is that the chance of hitting three or four winners is considerable. These are tantalizingly close to five and six winners, which do produce a payoff; the 2:1 payoff on five winning numbers is not much to shout about, but the 18:1 payoff on six-winner is rather nice. The average player, when he picks four winners, figures that with just *a little more luck* he could have picked five winners for a payoff; and with just a little more luck than that, he could have picked six winners, for a nice substantial reward. The truth of the matter, as revealed by our table, is that it takes *a lot more luck* to get one or two more winners. Odds of 87:1 against you picking six winners are mighty strong odds!

Other Tickets

The 10-spot ticket, for which we have computed the detailed odds, is only one of a wide variety of keno tickets that can be purchased. In some operations, you can buy tickets ranging all the way from an elaborate 15-spot down to a lowly 1-spot. But the payoffs are all so adjusted that you can expect just about the same 80¢ return on the dollar. A typical schedule of payoffs for the 8-, 9-, and 10-spot tickets is shown in Table 12-2.

TABLE 12-2. TYPICAL SCHEDULE OF PAYOFFS AT KENO*

8-SPOT RATE

Spots	$2.60 Ticket	$3.20 Ticket	$6.40 Ticket	$12.80 Ticket
3	0.25	0.35	0.70	1.40
4	3.95	5.00	10.00	20.00
5	37.15	46.45	92.90	185.85
6	258.70	323.40	646.80	1,293.60
7	2,500.00	3,000.00	6,000.00	12,000.00
8	7,500.00	8,000.00	16,000.00	25,000.00

9-SPOT RATE

Spots	35¢ Ticket	70¢ Ticket	$1.05 Ticket	$7.00 Ticket
4	0.15	0.30	0.45	3.00
5	1.80	3.60	5.40	36.00
6	17.80	35.60	53.40	356.00
7	110.70	221.40	332.10	2,214.00
8	1,250.00	2,500.00	3,750.00	25,000.00
9	2,750.00	5,500.00	8,250.00	25,000.00

10-SPOT RATE

Spots	25¢ Ticket	50¢ Ticket	$1.00 Ticket	$5.00 Ticket
5	0.50	1.00	2.00	10.00
6	4.50	9.00	18.00	90.00
7	45.00	90.00	180.00	900.00
8	350.00	700.00	1,400.00	7,000.00
9	700.00	1,400.00	2,800.00	14,000.00
10	6,250.00	12,500.00	25,000.00	25,000.00

* $25,000-limit, each-game aggregate payoff.

The one-spot is the simplest ticket sold. On the $1.00 ticket, if the number you pick to win is right, you collect $3.25 for your trouble. Obviously, your chance of choosing the winner is 20/80, or 1/4. On the average, then, you will win once for every four plays. So, it costs $4.00 to win $3.25, or the return on the $1.00 bet is a little over 81¢. This makes the one-spot keno ticket just about the dumbest bet in the whole casino. The only conceivable justification for playing keno in the first place is the potentially high payoff. But the one-spot ticket hardly pays any better than 3:1, and you can get low odds like this in lots of other games without giving the house near so much the best of it.

Is 20 Percent a Reasonable House Cut?

On the surface, 20 percent may seem to be an outrageous house cut. The managements may justify it on the grounds that the turnover is not rapid and that the game requires extensive paraphernalia and a crew of operators. Nonetheless, one cannot help wondering if they are not taking advantage of the player's ignorance of the odds against him. If an enlightened public were to engage in a boycott of keno, the operators would probably quickly oblige with more generous payoffs.

It is interesting to note that keno is pretty much a game for the hoi polloi. It is rarely found outside the downtown, supermarket-type casinos. The resort hotels, with their plush casinos, do not stoop to this bourgeois game. Of the dozen odd hotels on the Las Vegas "strip," only one has keno. And even there, it is tucked into a corner where it will not be conspicuous. Traditionally, the lotteries appeal to the small-money bettors who tend to gravitate to the downtown clubs. There, with quiet desperation, they dream of hitting the great jackpot, and being lifted gloriously out of their financial abyss.

THE CHINESE LOTTERY

We mentioned early in the chapter that the game of keno is identical in form with the Chinese lottery. This brings up an interesting diversion that is not directly related to the Nevada casino games, but which is worth treating as a matter of general information. One of the strongholds of the Chinese lotteries is in San Francisco, which has a concentrated "Chinatown" section. While I was a student at the University of California in nearby Berkeley, the lotteries began to extend their operations to other sections of San Francisco. This finally evoked an order from the police chief to "shut them down."

At that time, there were some 25 different lotteries operating in

Chinatown, each with two drawings per day. The estimated amount of money wagered in these lotteries came to $10 million per year. The lottery ticket contains 80 Chinese characters, rather than the numbers 1 through 80 found on the keno ticket. These 80 symbols form an ancient poem, and indeed many a ticket "runner" has tried to wangle his way out of arrest by claiming to be a student of literature or publisher of poetry! The most popular ticket is the 35¢ nine-spot, for which the payoffs are somewhat less than the corresponding keno payoffs shown in Table 12-2. Actually, the payoffs for four-, five-, six-, and seven-symbol winners are essentially the same; but with eight-number winners, the lottery pays only $373.50 instead of $1,250, and with the nine-winner jackpot, the lottery returns only $738 instead of $2,750! These reduced payoffs on the long shots give the lottery operators a *theoretical* edge of around 26 percent, which is noticeably higher than the keno percentage that we worked out. Furthermore, the word "theoretically," which is emphasized, is not to be taken lightly. Since the lotteries are illegal to begin with, the player has no assurance whatever that the game is conducted fairly.

In fact, there is every reason to suspect skulduggery. What the operators fear most is many players writing identical tickets. This is much more likely to happen in the Chinese lottery than at keno because of the use of symbols on the tickets. On the first day of spring, for example, there may be an undue concentration of betting on the character for spring. Thus, the curious ways of superstition may cause the selections of many players to coincide, and if their particular choice hits eight or nine winners, the lottery company can go broke. Just as the keno operators protect themselves with a certain limit, the lottery companies guard against catastrophe by abiding by a simple rule: "When a company goes broke, the capital will be divided by the company in percentage to the winners." It is not hard to imagine what abuses this loophole may lead to. Since new companies invariably spring up when old ones go broke, there is the ever-present possibility of the old company holding out on a big payoff and using the remaining capital for the formation of a new company.

Such stratagems may not even be necessary, however, because of a scientific technique for lowering the odds, which they allegedly employ. This technique uses X-rays! The day's tickets are stacked, and an X-ray picture is taken of the lot. This reveals which numbers have the heaviest concentration of play. Then, all they have to do is to punch the master ticket where the concentration is lightest! What chance does the poor player have against this dirty trick?

Needless to say, the average chump who squanders his money on the Chinese lotteries does not even know where the drawings are held. For a long time it was rumored that the drawings were so secret that they were held in a moving car! This notion was particularly prevalent just after the Oakland police raided a warehouse and apprehended two Chinamen in the midst of bales and bales of tickets.

The language barrier, of course, is one of the principal factors that prevents the police from tightly shutting down the lotteries. The best the law can do is drive the operations back into Chinatown. The extreme difficulty of getting one Chinaman to testify against another in an American court of law almost precludes the possibility of any legal prosecution. In a tightly knit community like Chinatown, the inhabitants adhere to their own inherited code of ethics. The situation is not likely to change until there are fewer ties with the old country, and our Chinese-American citizens become more thoroughly assimilated into our Western culture and learn to speak the English language more fluently.

When a local newspaper undertook an exposé, it could find no published scientific information pertaining to the odds on the Chinese lottery. Eventually, the problem was taken to the statistical laboratory at the University of California in Berkeley, near Oakland. The awesome complexities of the lottery were attacked by research mathematicians. Thus, from California's unfailing fountainhead of wisdom, the paper was pleased to report, an authoritative answer soon was issued. Actually, I heard about it from one of my friends in the statistics department. Nobody wanted to work on such a trivial problem, and it was passed down the line until it could go no lower. The young graduate student from France who got stuck with the job had to spend a few hours bending over an electric hand calculator, groaning all the while that it was sheer dog work, fit only for a lowly engineer or an accountant!

FINAL REMARKS

My interest in keno died suddenly as soon as I estimated the basic odds. It seems utterly improbable that any mechanical effect could be sufficiently pronounced to overcome that 20 percent edge. So, in fact, I have never even bought a keno ticket in my life. It is positively the worst sucker game in the house.

Baccarat and Chemin de Fer

13

For sheer spectacle, baccarat and chemin der fer take the prize. Imports from France, these games have a certain zing that none of the standard American games possesses. The aura is frequently enhanced by stakes of sufficient size to cause the operators to rope off the playing area. It is nothing to see players presiding haughtily over huge stacks of $100 bills. The players, often attired in formal evening dress, seat themselves around a large, oval-shaped table. Seats may accommodate up to a dozen players. The game is played with six or eight decks of cards, one card at a time being drawn from a shoe. Cards are passed from dealer to player on a fancy wooden scoop, or palette. The action is accompanied by expressive French words like "Banco" and "La Grande." Altogether, the atmosphere is one of high society, and rich plungers have been known to wager tens of thousands of dollars in an evening.

The games of baccarat and chemin de fer have been called twins because they are so closely related. The play of the hands is nearly identical, and it is only in the supervision of the bank that the principal difference occurs. In baccarat, the house has the permanent role of banker. In chemin de fer, one of the players assumes the role of banker, and this role may pass from player to player, according to the state of their fortunes.

The game mathematically favors the banker. In baccarat, therefore, the house has a natural edge. In chemin de fer, the house taxes the winnings of the player who is acting as banker. So, in either case, there is effectively a house percentage. Indeed, at chemin de fer, the house takes no risk whatever, since the players are pitted against one another and the house continually takes a cut out of the money that is being wagered. On the other hand, there are certain operating advantages to baccarat. The principal one is that the game can be started with merely one player. This is in contrast to chemin de fer, where prospective players may have to wait around for hours until enough players show up to get a game started.

OBJECT OF THE GAME

In baccarat and chemin de fer, the player's objective is to get a hand that is closer to 9 in value than the banker's. Initially, two cards are dealt to the player and two cards to the banker, all face down. (There is only one player at a time who receives cards; other players at the table may bet on his hand or on the banker's hand.) The game is played modulo 10, that is, if the total in a hand exceeds 10, then 10 is subtracted from this total. Thus the value of a hand always lies between 0 through 9, inclusive. Ace counts 1, two counts 2, etc., up through nine counts 9, but 10 (also jack, queen, or king) counts 0. Table 13-1 indicates the player's and the banker's action on any two-card total. Some explanation is also given in the next few paragraphs.

If player (or banker) has a two-card total of 8 or 9, he turns his cards over immediately. The other must do likewise. The total of 8 is "La Petite" (that is, the little one), and 9 is "La Grande" (that is, the big one). A 9-value wins over any lesser total, and if neither player nor banker has a 9, then 8 wins over any lesser total. Tied 9s or tied 8s are a stand-off; no money changes hands.

If the banker does not show 8 or 9, then the player stands on a total of 6 or 7, and draws one card (face up) on a total of 5 or lower. Then it is the banker's turn. With a total of 7, he stands. With 6 or lower, his selection of drawing or standing is dictated by dual consideration of his two-card total and the value of the card that the player drew. The rules for the banker's action are shown in the table. When the banker's action is completed, the two hands are compared, and the higher one wins. The payoff is even money. If both totals are the same, it is a draw, and no money is exchanged.

TABLE 13-1. RULES FOR BACCARAT*
PLAYER

Value Held	Action
1-2-3-4-5-10	Draws a card
6-7	Stands
8-9	Turns cards over

BANKER

Value Held	Draws When Giving	Does Not Draw When Giving
3	1-2-3-4-5-6-7-9-10	8
4	2-3-4-5-6-7	1-8-9-10
5	4-5-6-7	1-2-3-8-9-10
6	6-7	1-2-3-4-5-8-9-10
7	Stands	
8-9	Turns cards over	
10-1-2	Draws a card	

* Picture cards and 10s count zero.
NOTE: Boxed numbers show departures from the "symmetrical" game.

In baccarat, the play in all situations is clearly spelled out by the rules. There are no options for either player or banker. In chemin de fer, however, certain options exist. These relatively minor variations constitute the only difference in the playing of the hands in the two games. The options will be mentioned later.

The rules may look involved, but they stem from simple considerations. It is reasonable for the player to want to draw if he has a greater chance of raising his total than of lowering it. Consider an initial total of 7, for example. Two draw cards will improve this hand (ace and 2), four cards will leave it unchanged (10, J, Q, K), and seven cards will make it worse (3 through 9). Clearly, the player should stand on 7. A similar argument applies to 6, where the odds of *improvement/no change/deprovement* are in the ratio 3:4:6.

For a total of 5, these odds would appear to be 4:4:5, suggesting that the player stand. However, gross odds no longer serve to tell the story. It must now be borne in mind that the banker definitely does not have a two-card total of 8 or 9 (for, if he had, he would already have turned those hands over), and this fact exerts a strong compensation. So, in baccarat, the player is required to draw to 5. In chemin de fer, this draw is optional and leads to various interesting strategies. When the player's hand is worth 4 or less, in either game, he is more likely to do better, and therefore draws in all these cases.

To sum up, the player stands on 6 or 7, and draws on 5 or less. Now, if the banker were to follow the identical rules, the game would be "symmetrical," and neither side would have an advantage. To provide an edge for the banker, certain alterations are made so that the banker's choice depends on the player's draw card. As we have seen, the mere fact that the player has drawn gives a clue to the player's original two-card total, and hence an indication of his final total. Accordingly, it is easy to work out, for any given case, whether it is to the banker's advantage to draw or to stand.

Take for example the case where the banker's two-card total is 3, and the player has drawn an 8. With a low total like 3, it might seem reasonable to expect the banker to draw. But it turns out that the banker is better off if he stands. If he draws, he has a 6.3 percent advantage, but if he stands, he has a 6.7 percent edge. Supporting calculations are shown in Table 13-2. The crux of the explanation lies in the fact that, in just standing pat on his 3, the banker will beat the player more often than not. The banker's hand requires improvement only when the player's total is 8 or 9, but the banker must then draw 5 or 6 to accomplish any good. Since the chance of so doing is relatively slight, the possible gain is overcome by the chance of the banker getting a worse hand than he had to begin with, and thereby losing to a player total that he would otherwise have beaten.

On the other hand, where the banker's total is 3, and the player has drawn anything but 8, the banker is better off if he draws. In all such cases he has a greater advantage, or at least a lesser disadvantage (money-wise, this amounts to the same thing). Numerical values are shown in Table 13-3. All calculations have been performed on the

TABLE 13-2. COMPARISON SHOWING BANKER SHOULD STAND ON
TWO-CARD TOTAL OF 3 WHEN GIVING 8 TO PLAYER
AS DRAW CARD*

Player Total	If Banker Draws			If Banker Stands		
	Loss	Tie	Win	Loss	Tie	Win
9	—	1	12	—	—	1
8	1.5625	1.5625	$11 \times 1.5625 = 17.1875$	—	—	1.5625
3	6	4	3	—	1	
2	10	1	2	1		
1	11	1	1	1		
0	12	1	—	1		
	40.5625	9.5625	35.1875	3	1	2.5625

BANKER EXPECTATION

If banker draws:

$$\frac{40.5625 - 35.1875}{40.5625 + 9.5625 + 35.1875} = \frac{5.3750}{85.3125} = \frac{86}{1365} = 0.063$$

If banker stands:

$$\frac{3 - 2.5625}{3 + 1 + 2.5625} = \frac{0.4375}{6.5625} = \frac{91}{1365} = 0.067$$

* Since player has drawn, he must have had a two-card total of 0-1-2-3-4-5, and upon drawing 8, will have 8-9-0-1-2-3.

NOTE: Relative weights of 1 and 1.5625 correspond to two-card combinations that *do not* involve and *do* involve totals of 10 on two cards, respectively. Associated probabilities are 16/169 and 25/169, which are in the ratio 1:1.5625.

assumption of an infinite deck, that is, assuming fixed probability 1/13 of a nonzero-value card, and 4/13 for a zero-value card. In view of the many decks used in the game, this is a very reasonable approximation. In all cases, the basic calculations follow the same pattern as illustrated for banker total of 3 versus player draw of 8.

TABLE 13-3. VALUES OF BANKER EXPECTATION

Illustrating that Banker Should Generally Draw on a Two-Card
Total of 3 When the Player Draws, Except for 8

	Player Draw Card			
	6	7	8	9
Banker Draws	—0.204	—0.053	+0.063	+0.144
Banker Stands	—0.390	—0.086	+0.067	+0.067

NOTE: The upper line is more positive than the lower line, except for the case where the player draws 8.

In general, the rules of the game call for a departure from "symmetrical" play when departure benefits the banker. This is *almost invariably* the case. One interesting and simple exception is that the banker does not draw to 6 when the player stands on his initial two-card hand. Here, the player must have a total of either 6 or 7, since these are the only instances when the player neither turns his cards over (8, 9) nor draws (0 through 5). With the banker standing on 6, he has a clear tie if the player holds 6 also, and a clear loss if the player holds 7. These possibilities are equally likely. Thus, the banker's expectation per unit bet is simply $\frac{1}{2}(0) + \frac{1}{2}(-1) = -\frac{1}{2}$, or -0.500 unit. On the other hand, if the banker were to draw, he would risk trading the tie against 6 for a loss more times than a win, but he would also stand to trade the sure loss against 7 for an occasional win or tie. The expectation for the draw may be shown readily to be $-11/26 = -0.423$ unit. Stand or draw, the banker obviously has a losing situation, but he would have a lesser disadvantage if he were to draw. Strangely, the rules do not call for it. When the frequency of occurrence of this situation is taken into account, it can be shown that the banker could add another 0.138 percent to his basic percentage with this option.

HOW TO FIGURE THE BANKER'S PERCENTAGE

The sample computations given thus far in this chapter have been selected for a specific purpose. They serve to illustrate the sort of analysis that must be conducted in order to figure out the net advantage which the banker attains by departing from the symmetric game. Each basic situation must be weighted according to its proper relative frequency of occurrence, and then from the weighted advantage (or disadvantage) for each situation, a grand result may be obtained by addition. This is similar to what we have done to find the house advantage for other games such as, for example, keno and craps, but here there is an important difference. Because there is action (receiving of cards) on the part of both player and banker, many situations cancel by symmetry, and need not be included in the figuring. As a matter of fact, 91 percent of the time, the hands are of the cancel-by-symmetry type, and only 9 percent of the time is the banker's play not a mirror image of the player's action in holding the same cards.

There are 13 situations in which the banker's action departs from symmetrical play. This is a sufficiently small number so that hand calculations are feasible. A typical case has already been given in Table 13-2. The calculation is straightforward but lengthy. Therefore, only the results of the other 12 calculations will be given here.

Accordingly, there are 13 individual terms to be written down and added up, in order to figure the banker's edge in baccarat. Each term has the form of a product $A \times B \times C \times D$, where the contributing factors are spelled out below. A, B, and C are the same in all cases, and only D varies from one case to another:

$A = 16/169$ = chance that banker holds specified two-card total.
$B = 105/169$ = chance that player does not have a satisfactory two-total (that is, does not have total of 6, 7, 8, or 9).
$C = 1/13$ = chance that the banker gives specified card as a draw card to the player.
D = difference in banker's expectation between standing and drawing in this specific situation.

It turns out that the most convenient denominator to use for D is 1365. For example, in the case when banker holds 3 and gives 8, the value of D is $91/1365 - 86/1365 = 5/1365$, as indicated in Table 13-2. For simplicity, then, we shall assume $D = N/1365$, and list the values of the numerator N.

The final tabulation is shown in Table 13-4. All but one of the entries in the column N have positive values, showing that the banker gains by standing rather than by drawing in the indicated cases for banker two-card totals of 3, 4, and 5; conversely, he gains by drawing rather than standing in the indicated cases for a banker two-card total of 6. I can offer no satisfactory explanation for the one exception of banker two-card total of 4 and player draw-card of 1 (ace), where the N value is negative, showing that the banker actually does the wrong thing in this instance. Perhaps someone miscalculated on this one a long time ago, and it has stuck ever since. In any event, the banker loses very little as a result of this error.

TABLE 13-4. DIFFERENCES IN BANKER'S EXPECTATION DUE TO
DEPARTURE FROM SYMMETRICAL PLAY

Banker Two-Card Total	Player Draw Card	N
3	8	+ 5
4	1	−5
	8	+ 165
	9	+ 215
	10 (= 0)	+ 105
	J (= 0)	+ 105
	Q (= 0)	+ 105
	K (= 0)	+ 105
5	1	+ 315
	2	+ 205
	3	+ 95
	8	+ 165
	9	+ 375
	10 (= 0)	+ 425
	J (= 0)	+ 425
	Q (= 0)	+ 425
	K (= 0)	+ 425
6	6	+ 5
	7	+ 45
		+3710 − 5 = 3705

Final Calculation of Banker's Expectation

$$\underset{A}{\frac{16}{169}} \times \underset{B}{\frac{105}{169}} \times \underset{C}{\frac{1}{13}} \times \underset{\text{Sum of }D}{\frac{3705}{1365}} = \frac{4560}{371{,}293} \quad \text{(lowest fraction)}$$

$$= 0.01228, \text{ or } 1.228 \text{ percent}$$

HOW TO FIGURE THE HOUSE PERCENTAGE

The final calculation reveals a percentage of 1.23 percent in favor of the banker. Note carefully that we have not referred to this as the *house* percentage. As pointed out at the beginning of the chapter, we must distinguish between the games of baccarat and chemin de fer, and in the case of baccarat, we must also distinguish between a player betting against or with the house.

In baccarat, the house has the role of permanent banker, and as such enjoys the stated edge of 1.23 percent against the player who bets against the banker. (The 1.23 percent reflects the difference between the 44.62 percent probability of winning and the 45.85 percent probability of losing, there also being 9.53 percent probability of a tie.) But the player can also bet *with* the banker; here, his winnings are taxed by the house, so that the apparent advantage of betting with the banker is nullified. The tax is commonly 5 percent. Thus, on betting 1 unit, this player may either gain 0.95 unit if he wins, or forfeit 1 full unit if he loses. Clearly, the true percentage for this player is $+0.95 \times 45.85\% - 1.00 \times 44.62\% = -1.06\%$. Evidently, it is slightly better to bet with, rather than against, the banker when the tax is 5 percent. Variations in the amount of tax or the way in which it is levied may occur, but the edge may be refigured by the same principles used here.

In chemin de fer, the role of banker passes among the players. The player who is momentarily the banker has an edge of 1.06 percent against him (assuming 5 percent tax), while the edge against him as an ordinary player is the usual 1.23 percent. The *average* edge against the player depends on the relative amounts of money he risks as player and as banker. The simplest and most plausible case to consider is where all players wager the same amount, except for the player-banker, who necessarily covers them all. If there are $N + 1$ participants, including the player-banker, then he risks N times as much when player-banker than when he is an ordinary player. But on the average, he is banker only $1/N$ times as often as he is an ordinary player. Thus, he risks the same total amount as player-banker as he does as ordinary player, and the average edge against him is simply $(1.23\% + 1.06\%)/2 = 1.15\%$.

Since the 5 percent tax is prevalent, we can summarize things by saying that the edge against the player at either baccarat or chemin de fer is usually around 1.1 to 1.2 percent. This puts these games in a category slightly better than craps, with its approximate 1.4 percent on either the pass or don't-pass line.

SIDE BETS

As in craps, there are additional side bets offered to the player, which are substantially more unfavorable to him. There is a bet that pays 9:1 if the banker's two-card total is 9. The correct odds are about 9.56:1, and the house enjoys a little over a 5 percent advantage on that one. A similar bet pays 9:1 if the total is 8, and the house percentage is essentially the same as for the bet on 9. Finally, a 4:1 payoff is offered if the banker's two-card total is either 8 *or* 9. Again the same percentage applies.

These percentages are rather simple to figure. We illustrate by discussing the two-card total of 9. The probability that the banker *has* this total may be taken as 16/169, and that he does *not* have it, as $1 - 16/169 = 153/169$. Hence, the player's expectation is

$$(+9)(16/169) + (-1)(153/169) = -9/169 = -0.053, \text{ or } -5.3\%.$$

The probability 16/169 used in this computation denotes the fact that there are 16 chances out of 169 that the total is 9. Combinations that give a total of 9 consist of pairs such as 9-K, K-9, 9-Q, 9-10, 8-1, 1-8, and 7-2. There are 16 of these combinations. Both the first card and the second are assumed to have probabilities of 1/13. Thus, $1/13 \times 1/13 = 1/169$, and then $16 \times 1/169 = 16/169$. For simplicity, the draw of the second card is assumed unaffected by the draw of the first. Since numerous decks are shuffled together into one big pack at baccarat, this is approximately correct. With eight decks, for example, the true probability value is $32/416 \times 32/415 = 1/13 \times 32/415 = 32/5395$ instead of 1/169. This leads to odds of 9.537:1 and a house edge of 5.10 percent rather than 5.33 percent. The difference is very small. On the other hand, some authors have calculated the side bet percentages by assuming only one deck. Their results are low or high by around 1½ percent.

CAN BACCARAT BE BEATEN BY CARD COUNTING?

When I was first introduced to baccarat some years ago, I wondered if it were possible to count the cards, as in blackjack, and gain an advantage by betting on player or banker side, whichever was momentarily more favorable. My rough estimates showed, however, that fluctuations were not generally sufficient to overcome the approximate 1 percent house advantage. The hitch lies in the fact that the game is too "balanced." The 13 departures from symmetrical play cited in Table 13-4 simply do not produce great enough deviations, nor does the fact that the player draws first have significant effect. In this respect the game is different from blackjack, where the player has a number of options that the dealer does not. Blackjack is much less symmetrical.

But what about the side bets? Here, the basic percentage to overcome is greater (−5 percent), but the concentration of particular cards enters in, and this, combined with the high 9:1 ratio on the payoff, makes it seem conceivable. The situation is similar to the insurance situation at blackjack, in which the basic edge is unfavorable (−6 percent), but in which fluctuations can give rise to occasional very favorable bets (see Table 7-6). In single-deck blackjack dealt to the bottom of the deck, favorable insurance bets arise about 30 percent of the time. In baccarat, with eight decks dealt nearly to the bottom, favorable side bets on 9 and 8 occur more than 10 percent of the time. This did not appear to me to be feasible because I did not believe the casinos would permit plunging in with *high* side bets that were positive, after a long string of *low*, waiting bets on the main wager that were negative.

Ed Thorp had the audacity to think differently, and profited to the tune of several thousand dollars. He and a partner did the necessary calculations and trained themselves to keep track of the required cards. They tried it out in two casinos in Las Vegas. In the first one, they got away with it for a whole week of evenings, mainly because the house could not believe that anyone could remember the cards that well; hence, they concentrated on looking for other gimmicks, that is, cheating. Finally they caught on, and used some unfriendly method of getting rid of him and his partner. At the second casino, they did not have much opportunity to play before they were barred. Subsequently, one of the casinos eliminated its side bets.

Thus do we have one more illustration that you can beat the game, but you can't beat the house. Ironically, the side bets were grafted onto the French version of baccarat by greedy American operators who saw what rich dividends these side bets reap at craps. But now they may be scared into dropping them.

CONTINENTAL BACCARAT

In baccarat as played in France and some other countries, the player may stand or draw on 5, as he pleases. Furthermore, the banker's draw is entirely optional (except that he naturally turns over 8 or 9). Thus, the game differs from the American version with its fixed rules, as prescribed in Table 13-1. Such options, particularly those of the banker, sound pretty wild, and one might think that the two versions of the game differed drastically. But it turns out that, in most cases, it is to the banker's advantage to do what the fixed rules require. As a matter of fact, regardless of whether the player stands or draws on 5, the best choice of action for the banker is the same in all but four cases.

Consequently, baccarat with options does not differ greatly in practice from the fixed-rule game. Intelligent exercising of any combination of the options does not lead to as much as ½ percent being added to or subtracted from the fixed-rule percentage in favor of the banker. Space does not permit discussion of the details of the Continental game in this book.* Nonetheless, some mention should be made because no other book published in the English language has yet given any real mention of the matter. In essence, baccarat becomes a genuine two-person game of strategy, since the player's action in certain cases depends on what he thinks the banker is going to do, and vice versa. Each party must employ a mixed strategy, standing part of the time and drawing at other times.

Mixed strategy details are given in a paper by Kemeny and Snell (see references list). The important point to understand is that when a mixed strategy is called for, this does not necessarily mean the mixing should be 50:50, that is, to do one thing half the time, and the opposite the other half of the time. Several writers on baccarat have fallen into the 50:50 fallacy, including the original and prolific French author Marcel Boll, who treated baccarat in great detail in 1937 in his book, *La Chance et Les Jeux de Hasard*. In the analysis of games in which each party tries to outguess the other, clear thinking is required. Many years of controversy passed before accepted mathematical thought crystallized to a correct viewpoint toward this seemingly simple game of baccarat.

---

* A subtle variation on the game exists in which *two* player hands and a banker hand are dealt. Banker strategy can then well depend on the relative amounts bet on the two hands. For details, see the book by Culbertson, Morehead, & Mott-Smith.

Other Games

14

BINGO

Bingo is a first cousin to keno, and the house percentage is probably at least as atrocious, and quite possibly even worse. The nature of the game makes it difficult to obtain accurate facts about the house cut. Furthermore, it is supported primarily by women, who generally have much less awareness of the odds than do men. This makes it easier for the operators to get away with a big cut. (I do not intend to cast any aspersions on women's general intelligence, but it is a fact that in our culture, men tend to learn more mathematics than women. Also, gambling is considered as more of a masculine pastime, and hence men have more opportunity to learn about it.)

Practically everyone knows how to play bingo. You buy a printed card that bears a five-by-five array of numbers, except that the middle square in the array is a free square. Otherwise, the first column contains five different numbers chosen at random from 1 through 15, the second column contains five chosen from 16 through 30, etc. You may buy more than one card if you wish. The game commences when all the participants have armed themselves with all the cards they want, plus a pile of markers. Numbers between 1 and 75 are drawn at random, often by the use of the same type of device used in keno, that is, numbered plastic balls in a whirling cage. As the winning numbers are called one by one, you place a marker on any winning number that appears on your card. The object of the game is to be the first person to get five in a row, either horizontally, vertically, or diagonally. Suspense builds up as you reach three and then four in a row. You hope and hope—and then suddenly somebody shouts "Bingo!"

I once watched the action in a Reno bingo parlor for about half an hour, to get an estimate of the operator's percentage. In a game with a $10.00 payoff, cards were sold 2 for 10¢, 4 for 20¢, etc., up to 11 for 50¢ (in the latter case, one card was "free"). It was early on a week-day afternoon, and the attendance was moderate. I counted about 40 players, most of whom had a big spread of cards in front of them. If we suppose that each of the players purchased 50¢ worth of cards, then a total of $20 would have been paid in. The $10.00 return makes it look as if the players were getting only a 50 percent return for their investment, and if there had been more players, it would appear to be even worse. But we must also take into account the various "bonuses" that are paid out in such a game. For example, one of the 24 numbers on each card was designated as a special jackpot number. If you won the bingo, and if your jackpot number was in your winning combina-tion, you could collect a bonus ranging from $10.00 up to a couple of hundred dollars. The large bonus was paid only once a day, and the smaller one more frequently. In addition, there were occasional bonuses granted in the form of winning free play for an hour, a day, or even a week.

Since the number of players in any game varies, and the number of cards bought by each player varies, and since the bonuses and jack-pots vary from one bingo parlor to another as they compete for the customers, it is plain to see that a direct computation of the house percentage is well nigh impossible to make. But inasmuch as the game is very much like keno in many operational respects, it seems reasonable to infer that the cut must be somewhere in the neighbor-hood of that for keno, which is 20 percent.

Running a bingo game calls for a substantial layout. The parlor that I observed in Reno had seats for at least 100 players, and it was one of the smaller places. At the Showboat Hotel in Las Vegas, the daily bingo game is a celebrated event, and is held in a moderate-sized auditorium. Since bingo calls for a large crowd, by comparison with the other gambling games, it is even more of an intermittent affair than keno. The size of the layout, the number of employees involved, and the intermittent operation may all be used by the operators as a justification for charging a high cut.

But for the player, it is unquestionably a sucker's game. Just as in keno, there are enticing prizes and many tantalizing near-misses. If the gentle ladies who populate the bingo sessions would pause to add up all they have invested in the game and compare the total with all they or their friends have won, they would soon realize that they are paying a mighty high price for their entertainment!

WHEEL OF FORTUNE

There is no gambling device for which it is easier to figure the odds than the wheel of fortune. You can do it *mentally*, just by looking at that giant wheel as it turns lazily on its axle. It is so simple, we shall not even bother with the odds for the half-dozen different available bets, except to marvel that they ever get anyone to play that greedy device, what with a house cut of more than 10 percent staring the player in the face! True, a couple of the payoffs are somewhat tempting: 40:1 looks rich, but with only 1 chance in 48, you are giving the house 7/48 or about 14½ percent. Yet, surprisingly, these stately old wheels seem to get enough business to sustain them in a number of casinos. It must be the tourists, who feel they simply must take a fling at each and every different game. For this reason, probably, you usually find the wheel right next to the entrance to the casino. It lends an aura of Wild West nostalgia to the place, and helps entice the tourist. But no self-respecting professional would favor a wheel with a second look as he strides by to his favorite poison beyond.

If it weren't for the tremendous house advantage to overcome, the wheel of fortune might present interesting possibilities for bias analysis. It is hard to believe that the manner in which the leather flapper rides on the pegs, and finally picks one segment to land in, can be entirely identical for all 48 segments. To be sure, the Nevada casinos have wheels that are much fancier and more carefully constructed than the suspicious, crude kind you see in a traveling circus. (The latter you would assume rigged until proved otherwise.) Still, no mechanical device is perfect. And just as with chuck-a-luck, there would appear to be strong potentialities for the operator to exert *some* influence on the outcome of the spin. If he could guarantee the final resting position to within even a quarter of a revolution, he could always bar the maximum payoff of 40:1, since the two segments "Flag" and "Joker" are 180 degrees apart; but how could you ever *prove* that a dealer was doing such a thing?

It may be all very unlikely, but as long as a possibility existed, it would bother *me*. Altogether, I find the wheel of fortune singularly unattractive! Don't *you?*

CHUCK-A-LUCK

Here is a game in which the naïve player thinks that he has the best of it, but actually there is a substantial margin against him. Such a situation pleases the house no end, since beginners may plug away at it for a while until the truth dawns on them.

Chuck-a-luck is played with three dice in a cage. There are several different types of bets in the game, of which we shall first consider the most beguiling. The player may bet on a number from 1 to 6. If his selected number appears on all three dice, he is paid at 3:1. If it appears on two of the three dice, the payoff is 2:1, and if it shows on one of the dice, the payoff is 1:1. If none of the three dice bears his number, he loses. The sucker reasons erroneously that, on the average, his number will appear half of the time; hence, with occasional better-than-even payoffs, he is bound to come out ahead. Actually his number will show up only 91 times in 216 tosses of the three dice, and the house has practically an 8 percent advantage. Let's work this out, to see how the phony reasoning can lead you so far astray. This is a simple but classic example.

Although the three dice are tossed simultaneously, the outcome on each one is quite independent of the others. Accordingly, we could just as well regard the situation as if one die were thrown three times in succession. Whichever way we look at it, the mathematical analysis proceeds along the same lines. On each die, there is chance 1/6 that the selected number wins, and chance 5/6 that it does not. The chances for various possible outcomes on the three dice are readily figured by using our now familiar binomial distribution:

$$(1/6 + 5/6)^3 = (1/6)^3 + 3 \cdot (1/6)^2 \cdot (5/6) + 3 \cdot (1/6) \cdot$$
$$(5/6)^2 + (5/6)^3$$
$$= 1/216 + 15/216 + 75/216 + 125/216$$

The number 216 enters as a common denominator in these fractions because each die has six faces, and hence there are $6 \times 6 \times 6 = 216$ different ways in which the three dice can turn up. You can easily verify this by writing down all numbers from 111 to 666 that contain only 1s through 6s. There are 216 of them.

We see that of the 216 possible arrangements, only one contains the selected number on all three dice; 15 of them contain the selected number on two of the dice but not the third; and 75 of them show the selected number on only one of the dice. In 125 cases, the selected number does not appear on *any* dice. Note that half of 216 is 108, so that *more* than half of the time, the selected number does not show up.

The expected return on a one-unit bet is found by the same method that we have applied in numerous other games; we simply find the sum of each payoff times its respective chance of occurring:

$$+3 \cdot 1/216 + 2 \cdot 15/216 + 1 \cdot 75/216 - 1 \cdot 125/216 = -17/216$$

This reduces to 0.079 as a decimal, or a 7.9 percent edge against the player. Often this comes as quite a jolt to a player who thinks he has better than a 50:50 proposition. But when you examine the facts of the matter *correctly*, this illusion soon vanishes. We see that, of 216 plays on the average, you win 91 and lose 125. Of these 91 wins, 15 are paid off at one unit more than even money, and one is paid at two units more than even money. This adds 17 units to the 91, for a total of 108, but you are still 17 units shy of balancing out the 125-unit loss. It is fairly obvious that this bet definitely does not pay.

There are other wagers at chuck-a-luck in which the edge is even simpler to figure. These range from the *high* or *low* wager, at slightly less than 3 percent against you, to the *jackpot* bet at 13.9 percent. In addition to the already stiff house percentage, there is always the possibility of operator control (a skill acquired through long practice) or outright rigging. While the latter may not be found in the Nevada casinos, an electrical fix should be taken for granted in illegal gambling joints and fairs around the country. For all these various reasons, plus the lack of player participation, it is not hard to understand chuck-a-luck's general lack of popularity.

FARO-BANK

Faro is a fast-vanishing game, played now mainly by the oldtimers. Yet, 100 years ago it was one of the most popular games in the West. Great sums were won and lost at faro. The eclipse of this one-time king of gambling games has been due to a combination of two factors: when honestly run, faro has a rather small percentage for the house; and casinos have definitely gotten more honest than they used to be. In the Gold Rush days, cheating at faro was common. So, despite an apparently small percentage, the operators were actually collecting a very healthy cut. Today, only a few of the downtown clubs in Reno and Las Vegas run faro games. Since it is probably on the level, they must hope for substantial bets in order to support the game.

Essentially, faro is a guessing game. For example, you may bet that the second of two cards drawn at random from the deck will be of a particular denomination, say, Q (queen). If neither of the two cards is a Q, no decision is effected, and you wait for the next two cards to be drawn. If the first card is not a Q, but the second is a Q, you win and collect at even money. If the first card is Q, but the second is not, you lose at even money. If *both* cards are Qs, the house collects half your bet. Since the latter situation (called a *split*) happens infrequently, the game is not too far from an even game. In general, the house has somewhat less than 2 percent advantage.

Actually, for any particular type of wager, the edge can change as the deck is dealt out. Typical values will be demonstrated below. They are relatively simple to compute, provided you understand what you are trying to evaluate, and the assumptions you are making. This appears to be a big *if*, for I have never seen another book that shows how to compute the odds at faro (except for the trivial end-deck proposition on *calling the turn*, mentioned later).

But before showing how to figure the odds, we must describe the action so that the basis for the figuring is plain. Cards are dealt face up from a dealing box, one card at a time being exposed at the top of the box. A single deck of 52 cards is used. The suits have no significance in this game; only the denomination of a card is important. As the cards are dealt, a man known as the *casekeeper* keeps a running tally. With an abacus-like device, he records the number of cards of each denomination that have been played. Thus, player and dealer alike have complete knowledge of the prior play.

The first card, called *soda*, is inactive. Then cards are dealt in pairs. The first of the pair is the losing card, and the second is the winning card. The losing card is drawn from the box and placed immediately to the side in the losing pile. The winning card stays momentarily in the box. After the settlement of this hand, or *turn*, the winning card is put to the opposite side in the winning pile. Then another pair of cards is drawn, as before. The process continues until 24 pairs have been played, totaling 48 cards, plus the original soda card.

This leaves three cards in the box, the identity of which is known by the casekeeper. At this point, the separate wager of *calling the turn* may be made, that is, guessing the order in which the last three cards will appear. There are six possible orders (when the three cards all have different denominations), but the payoff is only 4:1. A fair payoff would be 5:1, since those are the odds against a correct guess. Accordingly, the house has an edge of 1/6, or 16⅔ percent on this particular proposition.

Getting back to the regular succession of turns through the deck, a typical wager is made on a certain rank card to win. Numerous other bets are also available, such as odd or even, high or low, and various combination bets. The method of figuring the odds is similar for all, however, and we shall demonstrate only the betting on a certain rank to win.

Suppose you are betting on Q to win. The odds are figured as follows: As the deck is played through, eventually a Q will appear. The two cards on this turn may be X-Q, Q-X, or Q-Q (where X stands for any denomination other than Q). There are four ways to pick a Q from the 52 card deck, and 48 ways to pick an X, in forming the combination X-Q. The same holds true for the formation of Q-X. On the other hand, in forming Q-Q, there are four ways to pick the first Q, but only three ways to pick the second Q. The 4 is a common factor throughout, so the relative chances of the three possible events are 48:48:3. This may be further reduced to 16:16:1.

To recapitulate, then, the probability of the wager on Q to win being terminated by the outcome X-Q is 16/33; likewise for Q-X. For the outcome to be Q-Q, the probability is 1/33. Accordingly, the player's expectation is

$$+1(16/33) -1(16/33) -\tfrac{1}{2}(1/33) = -1/66 \text{ unit}$$

per unit wagered. This is about 1.5 percent. (More complicated approaches, correctly performed, yield the same percentage.)

This figure applies if your selection is made without regard to knowledge of what the soda card is. Thus, with the 52-card deck used in this computation, if the soda card were known to be a Q, as you placed your bet at the beginning of the game, the house percentage would be smaller because the chance of a split would be smaller. There would be only three ways to pick the first Q from the remaining 51-card deck, and the relative chances of win, lose, or split would work out to 48:48:2, or 24:24:1. The expectation would be $+(24/49) - 1(24/49) - \tfrac{1}{2}(1/49) = -1/98$, or -1.02 percent. This is a significant improvement over the basic -1.5 percent.

On the other hand, if the fraction of Qs left in the deck were to exceed the normal 1:13 ratio, the odds would be worse. For example, suppose there were 21 cards left to be dealt, including three Qs. Suppose at just this point you came up to the faro table and placed a bet on Q. The relative chances would be 18:18:2, and the expectation $-\tfrac{1}{2}(1/19) = -1/38$, or about $-2\tfrac{1}{2}$ percent.

It is apparent that the best situation would exist if all but one Q were already dealt. Then a split would be impossible in the remaining hands, and the odds would be strictly even. Understandably, the faro operators try to discourage players from betting exclusively on a *case* card, as this situation is called. The player may, for example, be required to place one or more bets at nominal odds before being permitted to take the dead-even bet. By this method, the casino assures itself some net advantage over each and every player.

To the uninitiated, faro is an intriguing game. Many of the crusty chaps who haunt it take secret pride in knowing that this is a game that only the long-time gambler knows how to play! The betting paraphernalia is unusual, to say the least. Besides the dealing box and casekeeper, which have been mentioned already, there is the fancy layout on a green-felt table, with the 13 separate cards of the spade suit on which to place your wagers. To make the various multiple bets, you have to learn the special conventions for placing your stake upon the betting layout. Finally, there is the *lookout*, who sits on a chair on top of a box, to oversee the bets and payoffs, and to act as peacemaker in the event of disputes. In this quaint atmosphere, it is easy for the gambler to imagine himself transported back to the late 1800s, to the heyday of the Comstock Lode, when gentleman and outlaw alike found it sport to "buck the tiger"!

But the modern-day gambler is so overwhelmed by other razzle-dazzling games that he scarcely pays any attention to this relic of the past. So, faro is fast fading from the scene, and the only real justification for covering it in this chapter is for the sake of completeness. Although the correct odds are quite easy to figure, as the preceding discussion shows, they have not appeared before in print. The few authors who do give figures are patently uncertain about them, and quote mysterious numbers such as 1.15 percent (attributed to "Graveyard Schultz," an old-time dealer) and 2 percent (given by Scarne), numbers that do not appear to be directly related to any numbers worked out in this chapter. The *Encyclopaedia Britannica*, which generally draws upon the services of competent mathematicians for information of this sort, states in the 1957 edition that, "it is empirically estimated that the house retains 2.5 percent of the amount bet." On the other hand, *Colliers' Encyclopedia* in 1962 makes the rash statement that, "the bank's advantage is apparently at least 4 percent, but expert mathematicians believe it to be nearer 15 percent."

With such rampant confusion, it seems high time for someone to set the tiger straight. Since this is the first time that calculations have broken into print, we hope they will be accepted in lieu of all the previous erroneous guesses. The intelligent faro player has no worse than 1.5 percent against him, and frequently the edge is substantially less.

POKER, AND OTHER HOUSE-POT CARD GAMES

Many casinos operate card games in which the house serves as banker only and the players compete against one another. Chief among these are draw poker, stud poker, low ball, and pan, the latter being somewhat similar to gin rummy. In these games, the house has a sure thing, since it takes a fixed percentage out of the pot. Accordingly, a smart player does not get involved in one of these games unless he is definitely more skilled than most of the other players. A long game between evenly matched players is likely to end up with everyone losing except the house! For example, a 5 percent tax on the pot may sound like just a small bite, but if the game rocks back and forth for a mere 20 hands, the house has collected a full-pot size at no risk to itself. As players drop out, chances are that the stakes go up and the house continues to make money just as fast as before, or faster. The final winner *may* wind up with little more than a moral victory.

Poker is the king of all card games—a true gambler's game! A reasonable mastery of the odds is a necessity, but by no means a guarantee of success. This is but a fraction of the total skill required to win in stiff competition. Your betting strategy must be based on a penetrating psychoanalysis of your opponents' play and mannerisms while you simultaneously strive to give no clue to your own plan of action. Bluff and counterbluff. It all adds up to nerves of steel, tortuous patience, facial control like an actor, accurate knowledge of the odds, and a sizeable bankroll to back it all up. These are the ingredients of the successful poker player.

How to develop and mix these ingredients so as to make your game dynamite to all comers is the subject of various excellent books. Needless to say, only an expert in poker can write such a book, someone who has played for years and who knows all the angles. This author knows precious little about poker and has the sense to refer you immediately to the works of others if you are interested. Among the books that have a substantial coverage of the game are: John Scarne, *Scarne on Cards*; Oswald Jacoby, *Jacoby on Poker*; Herbert Yardley, *Education of a Poker Player*; John McDonald, *Strategy in Poker, Business, and War*; and Horace Levinson, *The Science of Chance*. No attempt is made to rate these various books, nor is there any intention to slight other titles that we do not happen to have heard of. If you acquire a substantial grasp of the content of *any one* of these five books, you are well on the way to being a better than average player.

Scarne minces no words over the fact that you have to be a lot smarter than the other players if you are to hope to show a profit in a casino-operated game. Despite this fact, poker and the other games that we are considering under this heading enjoy a wide popularity in certain of the casinos. The real professional (or semiprofessional) gambler, having long since given up on craps and having been barred as an expert at blackjack, sticks to these games, for these are the only real games of skill in the casino. By a curious coincidence, these games are played principally at the "downtown" places. You do not find them in Reno at the plush hotels, nor in Las Vegas on the "strip," again with one exception. The absence of the poker games in the resort hotels is probably due to the fact that they cater to a different type of clientele.

The patrons of the downtown clubs are a curious lot. Many, of course, are tourists (including servicemen from near or far, on weekend or longer leave), with varying personal reasons for concentrating on the downtown spots. They may feel that these casinos have more of the "Old Wild West" flavor to them, or they may feel that they are not properly dressed for the resort hotels, or they may want to play lower bets than the plushier casinos allow. There is no denying that socioeconomic factors govern the casinos at which people play, just as they determine what restaurants, hotels, and places of entertainment they frequent. But aside from the tourists, the downtown clubs have more of a corps of "regulars." These are local tradesmen and housewives, pensioners, and workers from the surrounding territory who are in town for a bit of relaxation, plus a horde of drifters, whose mode of support may not be readily apparent.

It is questionable that very many of this crusty crew are genuine experts. Yet they all have one thing in common—plenty of experience! For this reason alone, the neophyte should steer clear. To sit down with these grizzled veterans would be as dangerous as for a lamb to jump into a den of wolves. Better to learn your poker from tried and true friends—and even at that, be careful!

The Law of Averages

15

A general idea that many people hold goes something like this: The longer a series of chance events goes on, the more likely it is that things will "even up." For example, the longer you drive a car, the more likely you are to have your share of flat tires. The more children you have, the more likely you will have an equal division of boys and girls (assuming an even number of children). The longer you flip a coin, the more likely the number of heads and tails will equalize.

Actually, the latter two examples are identical, if certain simple assumptions are made. In the case of the coin, we shall suppose that the coin is "fair," so that on any one flip, head and tail are equally likely. In the case of the children, we shall rule out twins or other multiple births, and shall assume that the parents do not have any tendency to produce children of one sex as preferred to the other. Of course there is the practical consideration that one can flip a coin a lot more times than a woman can bear a child. So, it is more natural to use the coin for purposes of illustrating large samples. But for small samples, there is something unique about each child, which makes the family a marvelous illustration for stressing certain points.

THE LAW OF LARGE NUMBERS

I have never actually seen a statement of a *law of averages* as such in any book on probability or statistics. However, I have seen references to a *law of large numbers*, which in rather loose language could be expressed this way: The greater the number of trials, the *smaller* will be *percentage fluctuations* away from the expected (or average) number of successes, but the *larger* will be the *absolute fluctuations*. Note carefully that this deals with *fluctuations* about the expected number of successes, and *not* with the expected number itself.

Let's see how this applies to our example of children in the family (or to the flipping of a coin). We shall consider the various boy-girl combinations that can occur in successively larger families, starting with 2 children, and ranging on up through 4, 6, 8, 10, 100, 10,000, and 1,000,000. In the last three cases, we shall, of course, switch over mentally from children to coins. We shall find these examples very instructive!

At each birth, there are two possibilities for the sex of the child, B (boy) or G (girl). In a two-child family, therefore, there are $2 \times 2 = 4$ possible orders in which the two children are born. These are indicated in Table 15-1.

TABLE 15-1. DISTRIBUTION OF BOY-GIRL BIRTHS
IN TWO-CHILD FAMILY

	Both Boys	Equal Division	Both Girls
		B-G	
	B-B	G-B	G-G
Chance	1/4	2/4	1/4
As a percent	25%	50%	25%

Now we move on to the four-child family. There are $2 \times 2 \times 2 \times 2 = 16$ possible orders. (A more compact way to represent this is 2^4, which means 2 to the power 4, or the product of four 2s.) These 16 possibilities tabulate as in Table 15-2.

TABLE 15-2. DISTRIBUTION OF B-G IN FOUR-CHILD FAMILY

4 B	3 B and 1 G	2 B and 2 G	1 B and 3 G	4 G
B-B-B-B	B-B-B-G	B-B-G-G	B-G-G-G	G-G-G-G
	B-B-G-B	B-G-B-G	G-B-G-G	
	B-G-B-B	B-G-G-B	G-G-B-G	
	G-B-B-B	G-B-B-G	G-G-G-B	
		G-B-G-B		
		G-G-B-B		
1/16	4/16	6/16	4/16	1/16
6¼%	25%	37½%	25%	6¼%

Notice in Table 15-2 that in the four-child family, there is less chance of an exactly equal boy-girl split than in the two-child family. It is 37½ percent versus 50 percent.

The next case is that of the six-child family. There are $2^6 = 64$ combinations. These are simple enough to write down, but they are too numerous to spend the space on here. However, we can at least make a tabulation of the relative numbers involved (Table 15-3).

TABLE 15-3. THE SIX-CHILD FAMILY

6 B 0 G	5 B 1 G	4 B 2 G	3 B 3 G	2 B 4 G	1 B 5 G	0 B 6 G
1/64	6/64	15/64	20/64	15/64	6/64	1/64

We see that the chance of an exactly equal boy-girl split is again less than in the previous case. Here we have 20/64 or about 31 percent.

As we move on to larger families, the numbers tend to pyramid. The information for all cases up through ten children is now summarized compactly in Table 15-4.

TABLE 15-4. DISTRIBUTION IN TEN-CHILD FAMILY

Children	Distribution of Combinations	Total Combinations
2	1- 2 -1	4
4	1- 4- 6 -4 -1	16
6	1- 6- 15- 20-15 -6 -1	64
8	1- 8- 28- 56- 70-56 -28 -8 -1	256
10	1-10-45-120-210-252-210-120-45-10-1	1024

In each case, the center entry in the pyramid, divided by the corresponding number of total combinations indicated in the right-hand column, gives the chance of an exactly equal boy-girl split. In the ten-child family, this chance is 252/1024, or about 25 percent. As our sample gets bigger, it is quite clear that the probability of an exactly even split gets progressively smaller.

Now let's get back to the law of averages, this notion that the more trials we have, the more likely it is that things will "even up." We have just convinced ourselves that the larger the sample, the *less* likely is an *exactly even* split. But what about an *almost* even split? We shall now proceed to explore this.

The Binomial Distribution

Anyone who has had intermediate algebra in high school will perhaps realize that our pyramid is nothing more than what is called a *binomial expansion* of $(1 + 1)^N$, where N is the number of children in the family. The numbers in the pyramid are nothing more than the *binomial coefficients*, and the actual probabilities referred to are obtained by dividing the whole scheme by the total number of combinations, 2^N. Alternatively, these probabilities may be obtained by the expansion of $(\frac{1}{2} + \frac{1}{2})^N$. (Incidentally, the entire method is equally valid for odd values of N, but we have purposely ignored these because you could not get an exactly even split of boys and girls if there were an odd number of children.)

Now these calculations may be extended for however large a value of N we please, but it turns out that for values of N much bigger than 10, the labor involved in an exact computation gets prohibitive. For example, 2^{10} is 1024, which is a reasonable number to work with. But 2^{100} is the same as 1024^{10}, or *ten* 1024s multiplied together; *this* product has more than 30 digits, and is therefore somewhat difficult to handle. Fortunately, complete exactness is neither necessary nor desirable. Reliable approximations will be entirely satisfactory for our purposes.

In Fig. 15-1 are given graphs of the chances of having various numbers of boys and girls in families of various sizes, or alternatively, the chances of having various numbers of heads and tails in flipping a coin. All these graphs have two characteristics in common: (1) they *peak* in the middle, corresponding to a maximum chance of an even split; (2) they are *symmetrical* about the middle, since at any one birth the chances of boy or girl are equal.

The "Normal" Distribution

This bell-shaped curve is called by the mathematicians a *normal distribution* curve, or a *Gaussian* curve (in honor of the famous mathematician, Gauss, who first worked with it). The binomial

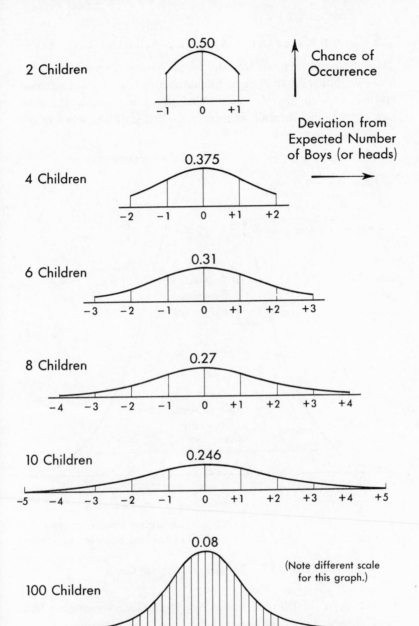

FIG. 15-1. Binomial Distribution Curves

distribution, which is what we started out with here, gradually blends into the normal distribution as the number of trials is indefinitely increased. Incidentally, this bell-shaped curve is probably *the most important* single distribution used in applied statistics, whether one

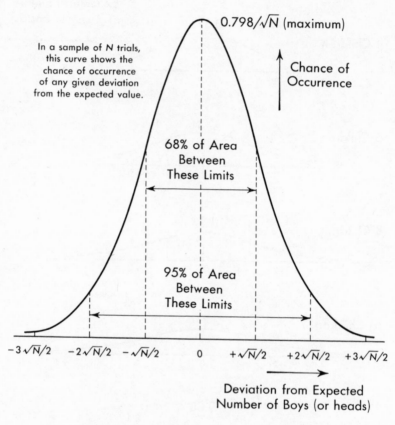

In a sample of N trials, this curve shows the chance of occurrence of any given deviation from the expected value.

0.798/$\sqrt{N}$ (maximum)

Chance of Occurrence

68% of Area Between These Limits

95% of Area Between These Limits

$-3\sqrt{N}/2$ $-2\sqrt{N}/2$ $-\sqrt{N}/2$ 0 $+\sqrt{N}/2$ $+2\sqrt{N}/2$ $+3\sqrt{N}/2$

Deviation from Expected Number of Boys (or heads)

Fig. 15-2.   Normal Distribution Curve

is working in the fields of census bureau studies, economics, education, biology, physics—or games of chance!

This curve is drawn again in Fig. 15-2 to a much larger scale and in more general terms. The purpose is to show more clearly the potent information that it contains. As in Fig. 15-1, on the horizontal is plotted to the right the excess of heads (over an even split), and to the left the deficiency of heads (or excess of tails); on the vertical is plotted the chance of such an occurrence. Values on the horizontal are plotted in multiples of what is called a *standard deviation*. This has the numerical value $\sqrt{N}/2$. We shall soon see how this is used. On the vertical, the central value is largest, being equal to $0.798/\sqrt{N}$. The values then fall away on either side, as the curve indicates. It is important to note that both the horizontal and vertical values depend on the number of trials, N. As N is increased, the numbers on the horizontal *increase* as the square root of N and the numbers on the vertical *decrease* correspondingly.

The numbers for the bottom graph in Fig. 15-1, for the case $N = 100$, were computed from these formulas. Since $\sqrt{100} = 10$, these computations were simple. The standard deviation is $10/2$, or 5. The central value is $0.798/10$, or 0.0798, which is about 0.08, or 8 percent. You will notice that individual lines are drawn for each value of excess ranging from 1 to 10, but it is apparent that as the value of N is increased, the lines will get closer and closer together. Eventually, the lines will become indistinguishable from their neighbors, and the whole thing will blur into one continuous figure.

This brings up an important point. The sum of the chances of all the various combinations in each case is 1. The entries in all tables here readily show this, and so do the vertical values in the graphs. We have pointed out that as N increases, the lines get closer together, but get smaller in value. It is reasonable to suppose that the blurred, continuous figure that we eventually get has exactly one unit of *area*. We shall not introduce any fancy mathematical terminology and attempt to *prove* this. We shall simply take it for granted.

Significance of the Standard Deviation

The significance of the area relationship is readily shown in the following interesting example. Suppose we draw vertical lines at the $+1$ and -1 standard deviation points in Fig. 15-2. Theory shows that 68.3 percent of the area of the figure lies between these two lines. This tells us that, in a given sample, there is 68.3 percent chance that the result will lie within these limits. The implications are revealed in Tables 15-5 and 15-6.

TABLE 15-5. ONE STANDARD DEVIATION, FOR VARIOUS SAMPLE SIZES

Number of Trials	Expected Number of Heads	Range of values for +1 or −1 Standard Deviation	Standard Deviation Value	Deviation as Percent of Expected Number
100	50	45–55	5	10.0
10,000	5000	4950–5050	50	1.0
1,000,000	500,000	499,500–500,500	500	0.1

Now, 68.3 percent is about two-thirds. So, we see that in about two samples out of three, the number of heads will lie within the limits shown in Table 15-5. For +2 and −2 deviations, the area under the curve is about 95 percent; and for +3 and −3 deviations, it is 99.7 percent. These are the chances that the results will lie within bands that are respectively two and three times as wide as the previous case.

TABLE 15-6. ONE, TWO, AND THREE STANDARD DEVIATIONS

68 Percent Chance for Results Within This Range	95 Percent Chance for Results Within This Range	99.7 Percent Chance for Results Within This Range
45–55	40–60	35–65
4950–5050	4900–5100	4850–5150
499,500–500,500	499,000–501,000	498,500–501,500

Of course fractional values of a standard deviation, and the corresponding percentage areas, may be employed. For convenience, we have used round numbers and percentage values that are often quoted by statisticians.

Percentage Deviation Is What Counts

The last two columns of Table 15-5 reveal a principle that is of utmost importance in understanding the law of averages, or better, the law of large numbers. The greater the number of trials, the smaller the *percentage* deviation, but the larger the actual (or *absolute*) deviation value. In the table, each time we multiply the number of trials by 100, we *multiply* the absolute deviation value by 10, but we *divide* the percentage deviation value by 10. Herein lies the reason why we have no right to expect the number of heads and tails to equalize after many trials. It *is* true that if we flip silver dollars with someone, after many trials we may be closer to an even split *percentage-wise* than we were after a few trials, but *dollar-wise* we may be *much, much* further away from an even split than before!

"LUCK" AND FLUCTUATIONS

The percentage deviation cannot be stressed enough. It refutes the notion that one's luck is "bound to change" (after having been *bad* for a while, since nobody ever prepares for *good* luck to change). One's luck can just as well *keep on* being bad as it can take a turn for the better. The longer one plays, the bigger the fluctuations that should be anticipated in *either* direction. It may seem somewhat mysterious that the most probable division of heads and tails is an even split, but we seldom get it, in a large number of plays. The point is that the larger the number of plays, the greater the number of *other* possible divisions of heads and tails that are *almost as likely* to happen as the even split!

To illustrate: In the normal distribution curve, the vertical height at 0.2 of a standard deviation is almost as high as at the center of the curve. Referring to mathematical tables (not given here) from which the curve can be plotted, we find the vertical height is about 2 percent lower than at the center. This is only slightly less, and on a drawing it is just about imperceptible. But in the case of a million trials, the standard deviation is 500, and 0.2 of this value is 100. Hence, we see that the curve is so flat near the middle that all possible outcomes ranging from an excess of 100 heads down to a deficiency of 100 heads are about equally likely. Yet there are many people who like to think that the law of averages is being violated if they lose $100 in a million flips of the silver dollar. Actually, our graph has shown us that there is a considerable chance that we shall be *quite a few hundred* dollars ahead *or* behind after a million trials! Indeed, there is a 5 percent chance that we shall be more than two standard deviations off center, and therefore ahead, or behind, by *more than* $1000!

It may seem very repetitive to keep emphasizing the distinction between percentage fluctuation and absolute fluctuation, but it is extremely important to have a clear understanding of the fact that one can become smaller while the other becomes bigger.

All this talk about the normal distribution and the absolute and percentage deviations associated with it must not be thought of as just a lot of fancy mathematical theory. In *countless practical applications*, these things have been verified remarkably well. Figure 15-3 is a graph illustrating typical agreement between experiment and theory. A coin was flipped 2000 times. A record was kept for each group of 10 flips. The labels on the graph indicate that 55 groups had 5 heads and 5 tails (deviation 0 from the expected number), 39 groups had 6 heads and 4 tails (deviation 1), 17 groups had 7 heads and 3 tails (deviation 2), etc. The steps on the graph show the experimental results. The circles indicate the values predicted by theory. As an example, we saw previously that the chance of an even split is 24.6 percent. Therefore, in 200 groups, theory predicts 200 × 0.246, or 49.2 groups yielding an even split; this compares quite reasonably with the experimental value of 55. A glance at Fig. 15-3 shows that sometimes experiment gave bigger values than those predicted by theory, and at other times smaller. But on the average, the trend predicted by theory is very well borne out. If a greater number of trials had been conducted, say, 2000 groups, we could well have expected that the *step diagram* would have more closely followed the dotted theoretical curve.

WHO WILL LEAD MOST OF THE TIME?

We have seen that larger and larger absolute deviations may be expected as more and more trials are undertaken. Accompanying this is a related phenomenon that seems almost to be a fantastic paradox. In a simple coin-tossing game, many people would be inclined to guess that it is very likely that heads would lead half of the time and tails the other half. This appears to be consistent with the notion of "things tending to even up." Amazingly enough, this is the *least likely* thing to happen. It is far more likely that either heads will be in the lead for most of the game or that tails will. (When we say that heads is leading tails at some point in the game, we mean, of course, that up to that point, there have been more heads than tails tossed.)

There is a simple explanation for this behavior. If one side gets off

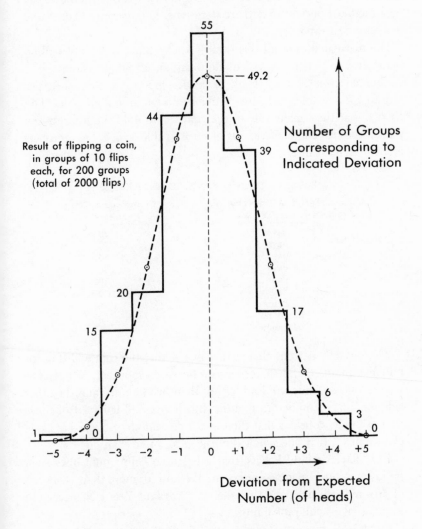

Result of flipping a coin, in groups of 10 flips each, for 200 groups (total of 2000 flips)

Number of Groups Corresponding to Indicated Deviation

Deviation from Expected Number (of heads)

Fig. 15-3. Typical Comparison of Experiment with Theory

to a moderate lead, then minor oscillations about this point will continue to leave the one side persistently in the lead. This was certainly borne out in my experiments at basic, fixed-bet blackjack, as shown in Fig. 6-1. At the end of 25,000 hands, I had won approximately 12,550 units and lost 12,450. The wins exceeded the losses by a mere 0.4 percent. Yet there were long, long periods when I was nowhere near even.

The mathematics of all this is fairly sticky, and no attempt will be made here to present the calculation. But an intriguing example will be quoted from Feller's book. Consider flipping a coin once per second for a whole year; this would be about 31 million flips. The chance that the lagging side of the coin would hold the lead for less than a certain length of time is given in Table 15-7.* The numbers are truly remarkable.

TABLE 15-7. LEAD ADVANTAGE POSSIBILITIES

Maximum Length of Time Lagging Side of Coin Holds Lead	Corresponding Chance of Occurrence, Percent
154 days	90
100 days	70
53.5 days	50
19.9 days	30
2.2 days	10
1 day	6.6
13.5 hours	5
2.2 hours	2
32.4 minutes	1

There is a 90 percent chance that one side of the coin will lead for only five months, and the other side for seven months; a 50 percent chance that one side will lead for less than two months, and the other side for the remaining ten months. But if you find it hard to believe that example, consider that there is 6.6 percent chance, or about one chance in 15, that one side will not lead for more than one day.

Few players would believe that a balanced coin would obey such fantastic trends. Imagine not getting the lead for more than 1 day out of 365 and still believing that the coin was fair! Yet, 1 chance in 15 is not at all a small probability.

* William A. Feller. An Introduction to Probability Theory and Its Applications, I (New York: John Wiley & Sons, Inc., 1957), p. 251.

Only those players who have kept a *written* record (preferably in graphical form) over long, long sequences of play can expect to acquire any true appreciation of the fluctuations that can occur in a game of chance. The record must, of course, be written, for the human memory is quite incapable of reproducing a long train of events. Even after compiling the record, it is easy to lull yourself into believing that you have now seen the ultimate in fluctuations and to think that hardly ever would one see sequences more wild than those you have already witnessed. Something about the concept of a phenomenon that diverges without bounds is beyond our puny finite minds!

Summing up, we have learned in this chapter some of the facts of life about fluctuations in games of chance. Let them serve as a strong warning to those who think things will "even up" if they just wait long enough. This erroneous notion is the basis of countless so-called gambling systems, which we take up in the next chapter.

Fallacies and Gambling Systems

16

There are countless betting schemes by which players delude themselves into thinking they have overcome the odds against them. Many of these are based on misconceptions about the so-called *law of averages*. In this chapter we shall explore some of these schemes and amplify the brief remarks on systems, which we made in the chapter on roulette.

BETTING ON A REVERSAL IN TREND

One of the most popular betting schemes is to bet that there will be a reversal rather than a continuation of some momentary trend. In roulette, for example, this may take the form of betting on a number or on a color that has failed to win in some preceding short period of time. For example, there is the practice of playing "cold" numbers, with the supposition that they are now "due." This is plainly ridiculous. In fact, the playing of a cold number is probably the *worst* possible bet on the wheel, since if there exists any *mechanical* reason for its being cold, then it is a subnormal number on which you can expect to lose money even faster than on a normal number. In the light of the mechanical considerations, it would be far better to play a "hot" number, in hopes that it will continue to be hot.

As we have seen in the preceding chapter, there is no tendency for the number of wins and losses to "even up." The longer we play, the greater the deviations that can be expected. If a number has lost 100 times in a row, this does not reduce its chance of losing another 100 in a row, or another 100 after that. In our marathon clocking of those two wheels at Harolds Club, we watched numerous numbers stay out for over 300 rolls in a row, and a few for over 400.

Nor is the practice of playing a "cold" *color* or *section* of the wheel any more sensible. Listen to this tale. One morning when we were playing marathon roulette, a prosperous-looking businessman strolled up to the table to play. Noticing that we were keeping track of the numbers, he inquired how the colors had been going. We had been interested in individual numbers only, having soon realized that a mechanical bias sufficient to enable us to win consistently on a whole block of numbers (such as the 18 numbers of one color) was out of the question. Nonetheless it was easy enough to check the record over the past hour and give him the answer. We found that red had been going like a house on fire. It had actually been winning two times out of three for at least 1 hour. Some of the other players and the dealer chimed in that red was really "hot."

The businessman promptly announced that black must be "due." He bought $7000 in hundred-dollar chips and began to play black. His bets ranged from one or two chips up to ten chips, the latter hitting the house limit of $1000. Red continued to roll, and he went through his $7000 quickly. Then he bought another $5000 in chips, but fared no better. By now he was beginning to take his bad luck hard. He muttered comments about the honesty of the wheel (although we had sat by that wheel for several weeks and had never the slightest suspicion that the dealers were manipulating it). When those chips were gone, he went to the cashier's cage and got credit for $4000 more, but he lost that, too, and finally quit—having lost $16,000 in less than 2 hours.

After he had left, we surveyed the tally sheet to see what had transpired. We found that during the splurger's play, there was a sequence in which black had failed to win 20 times in a row. In this sequence, there were 18 red wins and 2 green wins. A run in which one color loses 20 times in a row is not likely to happen more than once a month. And that poor fellow sat down at the wheel at just the wrong time of the month!

DEFINITION OF A SYSTEM

Now we shall pass on to the intriguing topic of the gambling *system*. This word is used to describe a method of varying your bets so that in a sequence of play there is a large chance of winding up with a small win, and a small chance of suffering a large loss; you then hope that the latter does not happen. If the latter has not happened after a number of such sequences, you have succeeded in making a series of wins. Thus, it seems as though you have overcome the basic odds against you, and have magically devised a way always to win.

There are two classes of system players: (1) those who play a system for fun, but who recognize full well that they cannot win in the long run, and (2) those who play in earnest, with the conviction that they have a guaranteed method of making a consistent profit, and a risk of loss that is totally negligible. I have no bone to pick with the first class. If you are going to play a gambling game for an hour or two, it is fun to have a method that keeps you in the black unless you encounter that one nasty sequence that puts you completely out of action. But the realistic system player knows that when his system is played for any length of time, the nasty sequences will take away more than he has won in small profits. Unfortunately, there are probably many more people in the second class. These poor souls are just deluding themselves.

The system may assure a good chance of a modest short-term win, but in the long run, it is impossible to come out ahead. And show me the gambler whose intentions are really limited only to the short run! I will then show you a liar, or a self-deceiver, who is planning to add those short runs together into a long-term play.

THE MARTINGALE, OR DOUBLE-UP PROGRESSION

One of the most popular systems is some form of *progression*, or *Martingale*, if called by its more elegant European name. The basic idea is that whenever you lose a bet, you progress (or increase) your bet size until you make a glorious win that wipes out all your previous losses and leaves you with a profit. The most widespread of these progressions is the *double-up system*, which is used against even-money propositions such as red and black on the roulette, or on the pass and don't-pass lines at craps. The idea is simple. You initially bet one unit. If you lose the first bet, you then bet two units. If you lose that one, you bet four, and so on, doubling each time you lose until you finally win a bet. The final winning bet has a value one more than the sum of all the previous losses. So you wind up with a net profit of one unit, and start all over again.

It sounds easy as pie. There is only one hitch. An unbroken series of losses may very quickly lead to preposterous bet sizes. Starting with $1.00 and doubling ten times in a row, you reach a bet of $1024. And doubling 20 times in a row, your bet would exceed $1 million! Remember that we *saw* the color black lose 20 times in a row on a roulette table!

There are two immediate limitations. Only a few casinos permit a maximum bet of $1000; in many the limit is $500, or even $200. While it is true that occasionally a casino will raise the limit, each casino has a point beyond which it will positively not go. Secondly, for most people, there is the limit of your own resources.

The Double-up Breaks Even in a Fair Game

Now you may ask, isn't the chance of a deadly losing streak so small you can ignore it? This is where fallacious reasoning comes in. During one sequence alone, the chance of a disastrous run may indeed be fairly small. But during a number of such sequences, the compounding effect can make the chance of a disaster unhealthily large. To convince you that this is true, however, may well require a numerical example.

In the first chapter, we made a point of the fact that comparison of results in a "fair" game is a very good yardstick for assessing an "unfair" game. Suppose for the moment we make roulette a fair game by removing the two green numbers. Play on red and black would then be equivalent to betting on heads and tails with a fair coin. Later on, we shall put the two green numbers back, and see what difference they make.

Suppose that you enter this game of heads and tails with a bankroll of 31 units. This number is the sum of 1, 2, 4, 8, and 16. Using the double-up system, the longest adverse run you could endure would be four straight losses followed by a win. You would be wiped out by five straight losses. The chance of five straight losses is $(1/2)^5$, or $1/32$. So, the chance that you *will not* have five straight losses, and hence the chance that you *will win* the sequence, is $31/32$, or 0.96875, or about 97 percent. Many people regard this as virtually a sure thing.

If winning a sequence is practically a sure thing, then nobody will be satisfied to win just one unit and quit for good! So the next question to answer is: "What is the chance of winning a number of sequences in a row, say, N of them?" This is simply the product of the chance of success on each try, or $(0.96875)^N$. Suppose we wish to know what chance we shall have to succeed in doubling our original bankroll. All we have to do is figure out how many sequences it takes to accomplish the doubling (that is, the value of N), and then compute the product given above. The number of sequences it takes to double depends on how we handle the winnings. If they are simply put in a stack and collected, then 31 sequences must be won. But if the winnings are piled back into the game, thereby increasing the bet sizes, then doubling of the original bank can be done with a minimum number of winning sequences.

There is a definite advantage, computationally, to assuming that you want to double your bank as fast as possible. Otherwise, you have to decide what to do with the excess win if the original 31 units are sacrificed in five straight losses. Suppose, for example, you have won ten units and set them aside, when suddenly you lose five times in a row. What do you do on the sixth bet? Do you bet your accumulated ten units, or do you start a new but shorter series, 1-2-4-3? Or do you handle it some other way? Whatever the decision, the various possible chains of events make the mathematical analysis a monumental job. For this reason, we shall assume that after each win, all bets are hiked by one part in 31. In this way, we maintain a constant 31-unit bank, but the units are getting steadily bigger. Then, if we lose five in a row, that's the end of it. There is no remainder to upset the analysis.

Each win boosts our holdings by $1/31$, or 3.23 percent. The situation is analogous to having money in a savings account at 3.23 percent interest compounded annually. The question then is: "How many years are needed for the account to double?" The banker would answer this question by solving the equation $(1.0323)^N = 2$. Actually, he would probably refer to a table that someone else had already worked out. But if he had to, he could recall his high school algebra and use logarithms or a slide rule. He would find easily that the closest integer that satisfies this equation is 22. Hence, it would take 22 years for the savings account to approximately double itself. And it would take 22 winning sequences for us to double our original bankroll by using the double-up system described.

Now we can return to the earlier question about the chance of doubling our bank by using this system. We have to evaluate (31/32) multiplied together 22 times, or as indicated before $(0.96875)^{22}$. By the same techniques that the banker uses with his interest tables, this is found to be 0.50, or 1/2. Surprise, surprise! Once again we find that in the "fair" game, there is a 50 percent chance of doubling our money. We see that nothing is gained by using the fancy double-up system. We can just as well risk our whole 31 units on one flip of the coin, for we shall have the same chance of success and will save a lot of time.

Stretching Out the Progression Has No Effect

But wait a minute, you may say. Can't we devise a double-up progression that gives us better than 97 percent safety on each sequence? Can't we make it closer to a sure thing? Let's split our bankroll into 1023 units. This means, of course, that for a given amount of money, our unit is considerably smaller than before. But now it will take a run of ten straight losses to wipe us out, since we can now place bets of 1, 2, 4, 8, 16, 32, 64, 128, 256, and 512. The chance of ten straight losses is $(1/2)^{10}$, or 1/1024. So, the chance of winning a sequence is 1023/1024, or 0.99902, or some 99.9 percent. This is definitely closer to a "sure thing" than the previous 97 percent, but the price we pay for this is that our bank now increases by only 1/1023 when we win a sequence. As a percent, this is 0.09775 percent, or just under one-tenth of a percent. Obviously, it is going to take a lot more wins to double our bankroll. Here the banker's equation becomes $(1.0009775)^N = 2$.

One can show that N is 710. Hence, it would take 710 wins to double our starting bank. Finally, we can compute the chance of winning 710 sequences and not getting clobbered in the attempt. On evaluating $(0.99902)^{710}$, we get 0.50.

Even though the chance of success on an individual sequence is closer to a sure thing, we have not improved our chances of doubling our bankroll one bit. We have merely stretched out the length of play. A general proof for any length of sequence is given in Appendix B.

Proof of the Double-up Fallacy in an Unfair Game

Indeed, it is the unfair game in which we are really interested. So let's put those two greens back on the wheel. The first effect, of course, is to increase the probability of loss on any one bet from 18/36 to 20/38.

Suppose we now examine what happens when we play our 31-unit double-up progression. On each bet, our probability of losing is 20/38, or 10/19. The chance of losing five times in a row is $(10/19)^5$, or 100,000/2,476,099. This ratio may be written as approximately 1:24.8, which is significantly greater than the 1:32 in the even game. As decimals, these numbers are 0.04039 versus 0.03125, which shows almost a 30 percent greater chance of losing five in a row on an actual wheel as contrasted with an even game! Subtracting from 1, we get 0.95961 as the chance of *not* hitting five losses in a row, which is the chance of winning a sequence. This number does not seem too much different from the previous 0.96875, but when it is raised to a high power, we shall see that there is a whale of a difference! As before, we need 22 wins in order to double our 31-unit bank. The chance that we shall win 22 sequences in a row, and not encounter any disastrous sequence containing five straight losses, is $(0.95961)^{22}$, or 0.404. This result is substantially lower than the 0.50 encountered previously. Instead of a 50 percent chance of doubling our bank, we have only a 40 percent chance!

Stretching Out the Progression Makes Matters Worse!

Now suppose we switch over to the 1023-unit progression, the one that monotonously returns one unit of profit unless we hit a run of ten losses in a row. Here the chance of losing ten straight is $(10/19)^{10}$, or about 1/613, as compared to the previous 1/1024; this is almost twice as great a chance of losing! The chance of winning the sequence is 0.99837, and the chance of winning 710 such sequences in order to double the bank is $(0.99837)^{710}$, or 0.314; we have dropped down to 31 percent.

This is a most instructive result! Thousands of system players have gone broke thinking they could *improve* their chances of an over-all profit by designing ever longer progressions. The preceding example shows that the *result is just the opposite*. Nor is it hard to give an explanation in very simple words. The longer the progression, the slower the rate at which profit is built up. So, in order to achieve a given monetary objective, you have to play for a much greater length of time. In so doing, you expose yourself to an even greater chance of a long losing run than you would in a shorter play of a moderate losing run. In the length of time necessary to double the 1023-unit bank, there is a greater chance of hitting a run of ten straight losses than there is the chance of hitting a run of five straight losses in the time necessary to double the 31-unit bank!

This same trend continues for other numerical examples given previously. In the cases that would require 15 and 20 straight losses, respectively, for the bank to be wiped out, the chances of doubling the initial bankroll are 22 percent and 14 percent, respectively. This information is compiled in Table 16-1.

Similar results can be figured for the use of the double-up progression against an even-money proposition at *craps*, say, on the pass

TABLE 16-1. CHANCE OF SUCCESS WHEN DOUBLE-UP
PROGRESSION IS USED

		"Fair" Game		Actual Roulette	
Number of Consecutive Losses That Are Ruinous	Number of Units in Bankroll	Chance of Doubling Initial Bankroll, Percent	Average Number of Plays to Double	Chance of Doubling Initial Bankroll, Percent	Average Number of Plays to Double
5	31	50	44	40.4	46
10	1,023	50	1,420	31.4	1,500
15	32,767	50	45,426	22.4	47,950
20	1,048,575	50	1,453,638	14.5	1,534,400

line. Since the house percentage is smaller in this case, namely, 1.414 percent, we should not expect the results to depart so drastically from those in the fair game. The chances of doubling the initial bank-roll turn out to be 47.2, 44.9, 42.5, and 40.0 percent. With a house percentage only about one-fourth as big as in roulette, there is only about one-fourth as big a difference from the fair game. But the fact that there *is* a difference still stands out clear as day! And for every game in which the house has an advantage, such a difference will be found.

Furthermore, for *every* type of proposition offered by the house, there will be a difference from what you would expect in the "fair game." On roulette, for example, a progression can be dreamed up for play on the dozens, the columns, the shared-number bets, and the single-number bets. But in principle, every one of these progressive schemes can be analyzed by methods similar to the one we have shown here for red and black. Invariably, the scheme will not be found to accomplish what the system player dreams that it would. When those two zeros are put on the wheel, the poor progression player is exposed to a *double-barreled* disadvantage: (1) The chance of long losing runs is increased over what it would be without the zeros. (2) It takes longer to win a given amount of money because, naturally, those extra zeros have to win occasionally. The combination of these *two* effects really puts the screws on the poor progression player. The chance of doubling his money is cut down severely from 50 percent.

Despite the reduced chance of winning by doubling, there is still a definite possibility of succeeding in doing so. With the 1023-unit progression, the chance is 31 percent, which is certainly a perceptible chance. Furthermore, anyone who succeeded in doubling his initial stake might very likely be tempted to try to do it again, and maybe again after that. So let's take a look at how these things compound. What we are asking is: "What is the chance of doubling our bank *three* times in a row without going broke?" (If we could, we should parlay our capital up to eight times as much as the bank we started with.) In the *fair* game, this would clearly be given by $0.5 \times 0.5 \times 0.5 = 0.125$, or 1/8. Thus, on the average, once every eight tries we double three times in a row, and the other seven times we go broke.

On the average, there will be no increase or decrease in our capital.

But let us now consider the *unfair* game. The chance of doubling our bank three times in a row with the 1023-unit progression would be given by $0.314 \times 0.314 \times 0.314 = 0.0310$, or about 1/32. Thus, on the average, once every 32 tries we double three times in a row, and the other 31 times we go broke. Things have really snowballed against us here. If we take 32 separate trips to the casino, each time with a separate bankroll, we shall have invested a total of 32 bankrolls, and wind up with eight bankrolls—for a net loss of 24 bankrolls. Wow! Is the deadly manner in which that house percentage grinds us down not painfully apparent?

With a progression, it is true that there is a large chance of winning a *small* fraction of our initial bank at the very beginning. But the chance of *multiplying* our bank (which is what all players are fundamentally interested in doing) is virtually *nil* when the odds are against us on each individual bet. Admittedly, there are always fluctuations, but these are superimposed on a *steadily losing* trend, a trend that slopes downward. This losing trend descends *so rapidly* that it is quite unlikely that a lucky fluctuation will overcome the house odds and put the player out in front. As more and more bets are wagered, the probability of occurrence of such a fluctuation tends very rapidly to zero.

It is not *necessary* to use the chance of doubling your bank as the criterion for comparison between the fair and unfair game, but it is extremely *convenient* because, intuitively, it is easy to grasp the idea that in the fair game you should have a 50:50 chance to double or go broke. This is the principal reason why doubling has been chosen for the numerical examples in this chapter. *Any other* arbitrary standard for comparison would serve just as well; for example, the chance of increasing your money by 20 or 50 percent. The mathematics would be just as simple.

Your Best Bet in an Unfair Game

From the results we have developed, it is apparent that the *shorter* the progression, the better the chance of doubling your bank. The shortest possible progression is a one-unit progression. This amounts to just a single bet. Technically, you could argue that this is no progression at all. The fact remains that if you want to double your bank on an American roulette wheel, there is *one and only one best bet.* You should take *all* the money that you intend to risk at roulette during your whole life and shove it all down on one spin of the wheel on one of the even-money propositions. Your chance of success is $18/38 = 0.474$, and that is the *maximum* chance of doubling your bank that you can ever attain on a perfect two-zero American wheel. *Any* system of play for doubling that exposes you to more than one spin of the wheel *inevitably* has *less* chance of success than 0.474; and the longer the play, the lower that chance drops down toward *zero.*

Progressions on the 2:1, 3:1, and so on up to the 35:1 (single number) payoffs call for a schedule of bets slightly more involved than a simple double-up progression. For one thing, if you win early in the sequence, you may unavoidably net more than a one-unit profit for a one-unit bet as a result of the noneven payoff. But it is often possible to devise a schedule of increasing bets such that if the sequence terminates after a number of bets have been made, the net profit is one unit or some small number of units. There are so many possible variations that it would be fruitless to try to give mathematical analyses for them. However, the basic conclusions as to the lack of validity of their use are similar to the double-up case. Indeed a mathematical proof is given in Appendix B of the fallacy of the double-up system or any other progression in which each successive bet exceeds the sum of all previous bets in the series.*

THE PYRAMID SYSTEM

So much for straight progressions. Another very common class of systems involves what you might call a combination of progression and regression. One of the most popular of these entails increasing

* There is an alternative mathematical approach known as the "theory of runs," which is treated in several probability texts. This enables you to calculate the probability of at least one run of any specified number of losses all in a row, during any specified larger number of total plays (notice that this approach deals with the total number of *plays*, rather than the total number of *sequences* as we have illustrated). The mathematics of this approach is more complex, however, and there are further subtle problems of interpreting the probability of more than one run as well as an incomplete run at the end of the assigned number of plays. For these reasons, the theory of runs is not treated here. But in all cases in which this approach has been worked out, the results agree with those given here.

bet size after a loss and decreasing bet size after a win. It is sometimes called the *D'Alembert* system, after the Frenchman who
allegedly invented it. Also it is dubbed the *pyramid* or *seesaw*.

The plan is exceedingly simple. Your first bet is one unit. If you
win, the sequence is ended, and you start a new one. If you lose,
you increase your bet by one unit, and after any subsequent loss, you
also increase by one unit. On the other hand, after every win, you decrease by one unit. The result of this system of play is that if the
number of wins in the sequence finally balances the number of losses,
you have returned to the point where the next bet will be one unit,
and hence you have terminated the sequence. At this point, you have
accumulated one unit of profit for each win in the sequence. This is
because, for each bet lost, there is a winning bet one unit bigger.
Figure 16-1 illustrates a typical chain.

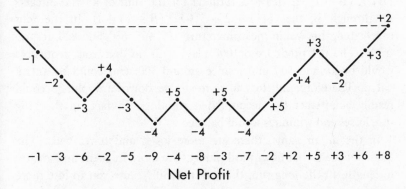

Net Profit

FIG. 16-1. Typical Chain of Bets in the Pyramid System

This is an extremely attractive system. In fact, in a game in which
the sequence of wins and losses is not purely random (as, for example, blackjack, played under certain circumstances, as discussed
earlier in the book), this system has certain merit. But, in the usual
unfair game, this system will produce only a loss in the long run.
The explanation is really quite simple.

First suppose that the seesaw is applied to a fair game, such as
heads or tails. In the chapter on the law of averages, we saw that
fluctuations could be expected of the order of a standard deviation.

Here, the standard deviation in 1000 plays is $\sqrt{1000}/2$, or about 15. That is to say, we should beware of 15 more (or 15 fewer) heads than the expected number of 500. This would mean a *difference* of 30 more heads than tails (or vice versa). Now, if you were betting on heads, and you got into a sequence in which there were 30 more tails than heads, you could wind up at the low point by quite a few hundred units in the hole. Furthermore, by the nature of the system, each sequence starts out from the highest point that has yet been reached in terms of excess number of heads over tails. This means that expected downward fluctuations will possibly be larger than the formula shows. So, let's say that you might very well get into a sequence where you would be down 25, 30, 35, or even 40 steps.

By inspection of a few series, it is easy to see that when you are down to a losing bet B, you have had to invest a total of $(B) \times (B + 1)/2$; this is a formula for the sum of all the integers up through B, that is, $1 + 2 + 3 + \cdots (B - 1) + B$. In the four cases cited, this would mean investing 325, 465, 630, and 820, respectively. The net profit from 1000 plays with *no* disastrous sequences would be around 500 units, since around 500 wins could be anticipated. Therefore, the loss in a moderate downward plunge could readily counteract the accumulated winnings. In fact, in the long run, losses and winnings would balance.

In the *unfair* game, there are more losses and fewer wins. The consequence is that downward plunges are more frequent and greater in length. In the long run, this will naturally cause you to lose more on the disastrous sequences than you will win on the successful sequences. As with the progressions, you will be defeated by the house limits and your own limited resources.

OSCAR'S SYSTEM

This is one of the most intriguing systems that I have ever run across. It was shown to me by a dice player who had used it consistently over a period of several years to win the price of many weekend trips to Las Vegas. To be sure, he was prepared to risk a considerable sum in backing up the play. Nonetheless I was amazed that in the long time he worked it, there was never a session of losses rough enough to discourage him from pulling each sequence through to a successful conclusion. He was very lucky indeed.

This system is designed so that in each sequence of plays, the player gains a net profit of one unit, and then starts over again. (In fact, the originator claims that it is the willingness to be content with a profit of *one* unit, where the greedy player might try for more, that is the saving feature of this system.) The first bet is one unit. Whenever a bet is lost, the next bet is the same size as the one just lost. Whenever a bet is won, the next bet is one unit larger—*unless* winning the next bet would produce for the sequence a profit exceeding one unit. If it would, the bet size is reduced to an amount that is just sufficient to produce a profit of one unit.

Some typical sequences will help to clarify the explanation:

Outcome:	L	W	L	W	W		L	L	L	L	L	W	W	W
Bet size:	1	1	1	1	1		1	1	1	1	1	1	2	3
Net gain:	−1	0	−1	0	+1		−1	−2	−3	−4	−5	−4	−2	+1

Outcome:		L	L	W	L	W	L	L	W	W	L	L	W	W
Bet size:		1	1	1	2	2	2	2	2	3	1	1	1	2
Net gain:		−1	−2	−1	−3	−1	−3	−5	−3	0	−1	−2	−1	+1

The middle sequence of five losses followed by three wins is a perfectly straightforward example. The other two sequences illustrate the special feature whereby the profit is held down to one unit. In the first sequence, for example, the second play is a win, and ordinarily the bet would be increased from the previous one unit up to two units. But the net gain at this point happens to be zero, and hence a one-unit win would suffice to yield a one-unit profit. Therefore, the bet level is held down to one unit. It turns out that this bet is actually lost in the sequence shown, and then the cycle of win-lose is repeated, and the final one-unit bet is won.

In the third sequence shown, this limitation on bet size occurs after both the fifth play and the ninth play. After the win on the fifth play, the bet is left at two units rather than being raised to three. After the win on the ninth play, the bet is dropped to one unit rather than being raised to four.

Whenever one of the reduced bets is lost, a new "chain" of bets is begun, which is not smoothly related to the preceding chain. This fact makes the exact mathematical analysis of this system quite complicated. I tried for some time to formulate a direct probability calculation of the chance that the player would reach the house limit for bet size in any one sequence. My efforts were fruitless along that particular line. But, fortunately, I was able to make some educated guesses based on the detailed records that the dice player showed me. (Unlike many system players, he was actually very "systematic," in that he had complete documentation on all the series he had played in the casino.) In addition, the whole scheme of play was later simulated with many thousands of sequences on a computer (described briefly in a subsequent discussion). The conclusion drawn from the projection of the player's results was this: The chance of reaching a house limit of $500, at increments of $1.00, is probably not less than 1 in 5000.

This appears to be a very small chance, but you must bear in mind that if you ever did reach the house limit, you would very likely be in the hole by at least $10,000 at that moment. Thus, a small probability of a gigantic loss must be balanced against a very large chance of a $1.00 win on each sequence. Each $1.00 win looks like almost a sure thing. As long as you don't hit a disastrous sequence, you can keep piling up enough dollars to pay for a lot of week-end trips to Las Vegas from Southern California, including airplane passage and deluxe hotel accommodations! But winning $100 to $150 per week end, monotonously on one trip after another, does not necessarily prove the validity of such a system. You have to get in there and play long enough to win an amount comparable to what you are willing to risk. In this case, the "long run" would be at least 5000 to 10,000 sequences.

Beware of Self-Hypnosis

Let us do a little computation, and see why a player should not let himself be hypnotized by a long string of successful week ends. We take 1/5000 as the chance of hitting the limit. We shall say also that the player would quit if he reached this point because he could then no longer adhere to his betting schedule. (The player *might* decide to continue on some other basis, such as a flat $500 bet, but he might continue to lose rather than succeed in pulling out of the hole. This change in method of bet-sizing would complicate the analysis. Since the player *must* set *some* prescribed quitting point, we shall take it to be the $500 bet limit.)

The chance that any one sequence will *not* reach the house limit, and hence the chance of the sequence terminating with the usual one-unit profit, is then 4999/5000. Now let's suppose, for the sake of simplicity of calculation, that the player sets a goal of $100 per week end (we choose 100 because it divides evenly into 5000). The chance of 100 successful sequences is then $(4999/5000)^{100}$, which is about equal to 49/50. In other words, the chance of a successful week end is about 98 percent.

Now we ask what outcome can be anticipated in 50 week ends. This may be figured by using the binomial distribution that we explained in the preceding chapter. Here we need the binomial expansion of $(49/50 + 1/50)^{50}$. When this is multiplied out, we have

$$\left(\frac{49}{50}\right)^{50} + \frac{50}{1}\left(\frac{49}{50}\right)^{49}\left(\frac{1}{50}\right)^1 + \frac{50(49)}{1(2)}\left(\frac{49}{50}\right)^{48}\left(\frac{1}{50}\right)^2$$

$$+ \frac{50(49)(48)}{1(2)(3)}\left(\frac{49}{50}\right)^{47}\left(\frac{1}{50}\right)^3 + \cdots$$

We find that these terms have the approximate values of $0.368 + 0.368 + 0.184 + 0.062 + 0.015 +$ smaller terms. The first term gives the chance of 50 successful week ends; the second term, the chance of 49 good week ends and 1 ruinous week end; the third, the chance of 48 good week ends and 2 ruinous week ends; etc.

The mathematician will note that we are actually approximating the binomial by a Poisson distribution and that the series can be expressed more simply as $0.368(1 + 1 + 1/2 + 1/6 + 1/24 +$ smaller terms). Let's tabulate the result:

Chance of 50 successful week ends and *no* ruinous week ends = 0.368
Chance of 49 successful week ends and 1 ruinous week end = 0.368
Chance of 48 successful week ends and 2 ruinous week ends = 0.184
Chance of 47 successful week ends and 3 ruinous week ends = 0.062
Chance of 46 successful week ends and 4 ruinous week ends = 0.015

0.997

(The sum would be exactly 1 if the smaller terms were not neglected.)

If a player were willing to back this play to the hilt, never scaring as bet size climbed, he would have nearly 40 percent chance of a seemingly endless chain of successes. He could go to Las Vegas one week end per month for four years, and monotonously drag down $100 in about 10 hours of play. In 50 such trips, he could rack up $5000 profit (before expenses).

But there is also a 37 percent chance that on one of those 50 week ends, he would run up against the house limit and be around $13,000 in the hole. Forced to quit on this one catastrophic sequence, the player would not have sufficient consolation from his 4999 successful sequences, which each yielded a $1.00 profit. He would still be loser by about $8000.

Nor is that all! There is a 18 percent chance of *two* catastrophic sequences, producing a net loss of $26,000 minus $4998, or about $21,000; also a 6 percent chance of *three* ruinous losses, for a net plunge of around $34,000; and so on.

The prospect is frightening to contemplate. Such a sweet little system! On the basis of several hundred, or even a few thousand sample sequences, it can look like a sure way to mint money, a dollar at a time. But push on out to tens of thousands of sequences, and the immutable law of large numbers reveals just how deadly this system can be. (Nor should the protesting proponent argue that he will never play that many sequences and therefore has nothing to worry about. The first ruinous loss may occur at any time. The fact that such losses average only once per 5000 sequences or so provides no assurance that lightning will not strike early for some hapless player!)

Computer Analysis

To give this system an acid test, some 280,000 sequences were run off on a computer.* Since the average sequence length entailed about six plays of the dice, this meant a simulation of almost *two million* decisions of the dice. Assuming an optimistic two decisions per minute, such a venture would require round-the-clock play for a

---

* This work was done by my gifted friend Julian Braun, who at the time was a computer programming supervisor with the Chrysler Missile Systems Division in Detroit.

whole month in a casino. On the IBM 709 computer, it took less than half an hour.

Decisions of the dice were accomplished by use of a random-number generator. (Note that the word "decision" of the dice is used here in preference to "roll" of the dice; as pointed out in the chapter on craps, the dice may have to be "rolled" several times before a decision is effected.) The concept of a random-number generator was described in some detail in Chapter 6 on blackjack. In simulating decisions of the dice, the following procedure was used. As each ten-digit random number was produced, it was classified as to whether it was less than or greater than 4929292929. If it was less, the event was considered a win for the player; if it was greater, the event was taken as a loss. Now there were 4929292929 possible numbers in the first group, and 50707070 in the second group. Accordingly, the probabilities for the event to be a win or a loss were 0.493 and 0.507, respectively, in conformance with known figures for the pass-line bet.

In addition to simulating the random decisions of the dice, the computer program was designed to do all the bookkeeping associated with this system. The bet size was appropriately incremented, and detailed information was compiled from the sequences. Cumulative totals were kept on such quantities as the sequence length, maximum bet size for the sequence, and total bank required for the sequence.

Of the 280,000 sequences simulated on the computer, 66 were disastrous; the maximum allowed bet level of $500 was reached, and the sequences had to be abandoned at an average loss of about $13,100. The frequency of occurrence of the disastrous sequences was 66/280,000, or about 1/4250. (Once in 4250 sequences is clearly more frequent than the once in 5000 that was assumed before. The latter was used for two reasons. It allowed some leeway for statistical fluctuation, and it was simpler to use the nice round fraction of 1/5000 in calculations which were patently approximate.) In either case, it is quite evident that a catastrophic loss is by no means an outlandishly impossible event.

The 66 fiascos yielded a deficit of about $864,000; on the other hand, the 279,934 successful sequences produced a gain of exactly that many dollars, which can be rounded to $280,000. The net loss, therefore, was $584,000. It is very instructive to note that the cumulative total amount wagered for all sequences was recorded as $40 million. Hence, the fraction extracted by the casino in this simulation of a month-long system play was $584,000/40,000,000 = 0.0146$, or 1.46 percent. This figure is remarkably close to the theoretical edge of 1.414 percent. The moral of the story is that the percentage extracted from the total amount bet in a long, complicated marathon is identical with the theoretical percentage as figured for a single decision of the dice—which is exactly as it should be! Indeed, were this not true, you could think up many a paradox.

Oscar's System on a Fair Game

A further dramatic verification of this principle was demonstrated by a subsequent simulation of the system as applied to a dead-even game. Here, the probabilities to win and to lose on each single decision were both 0.500, as in the flipping of a perfectly honest coin. In 500,000 simulated sequences (half a million!), 49 were disastrous. The frequency of occurrence was evidently much lower than at craps, being about 1/10,000. The average loss on these ravaging sequences was also lower, namely, about $10,600. The deficit came to about $521,000 on all sequences, while the successful sequences yielded just under $500,000. The net loss of $21,000 was virtually negligible when compared with the total $48,300,000 wagered. Percentagewise, the loss was 0.04 percent, which was entirely within reasonable agreement of the theoretical 0.00 percent for an even game.

The computer simulation put the coup de grace on this novel system. While it might be intellectually satisfying to be able to formulate the theoretical probabilities by direct mathematical analysis, it is no longer necessary. Indeed, I am not too optimistic about the prospects of such a solution. I tried to enlist some high-powered help by writing to distinguished probability experts at some of the large universities, but was unsuccessful. Any professional mathematician who would like to take up the challenge can find the exact problem statement posed in the *American Mathematical Monthly*, June–July, 1962, issue, pages 570–571. It might make a good Ph.D. thesis for a statistics student!

The main reason for going into the exposé of Oscar's system in so much detail is to show the reader at least one thorough analysis of an intricate betting system. It is essential to grasp the fact that although the probability of a single disastrous event may appear remotely small, the cumulative effect with many sequences leads to nearly certain disaster.

THE CANCELLATION SYSTEM

Another quite different class of system that has many devotees is the *cancellation* system. A magic series of numbers is written down and then used to determine bet sizes. As the sequence progresses, additional numbers are entered in the series, or numbers in the series are canceled out. When the entire series has been canceled, the sequence shows a certain number of units as profit.

A simple example is shown below, as applied to the sequence L-L-W-L-L-W-W-L-W. Note, incidentally, that a flat bet would lose on this sequence, since there are five losses and only four wins. Suppose the magic starting series is 1-2-3. The procedure is to start with a bet equal to the sum of first and last numbers, or in this case, $1 + 3$, or 4 units. If this bet is won, then the first and last numbers are crossed off in the series. Then the next bet is the sum of the first and last numbers in the remaining series. (If there is only one remaining number, as would be the case here, that one value is bet.) If a bet is lost, the amount lost is appended to the series, and the next bet is the sum of the first and last numbers in the now augmented series.

This procedure is continued until (the player hopes) the entire series has been canceled out. At this point, the sequence shows a profit equal to the sum of the original series, that is, $1 + 2 + 3$, or 6 units. All the features are illustrated in Table 16-2.

It is not necessary to rewrite the series after each bet, of course. The numbers may be written along in one line, and the cancellations made as you go.

As with the systems previously examined, this one has the apparent virtue of being able to show a profit in a sequence in which there are more losing bets than winning bets. Indeed, this fact is used by countless system players to warp their logic and convince themselves that

TABLE 16-2. PROCEDURE IN THE CANCELLATION SYSTEM

Magic Series	Result	Winning Bets	Losing Bets
1 2 3	L		1 + 3 = 4
1 2 3 4	L		1 + 4 = 5
1 2 3 4 5	W	1 + 5 = 6	
1 2 3 4 ~~5~~	L		2 + 4 = 6
1 2 3 4 ~~5~~ 6	L		2 + 6 = 8
1 2 3 4 ~~5~~ 6 8	W	2 + 8 = 10	
~~1~~ 2 3 4 ~~5~~ 6 ~~8~~	W	3 + 6 = 9	
~~1~~ ~~2~~ ~~3~~ 4 ~~5~~ ~~6~~ ~~8~~	L		4 = 4
~~1~~ ~~2~~ ~~3~~ 4 ~~5~~ ~~6~~ ~~8~~ 4	W	4 + 4 = 8	
~~1~~ ~~2~~ ~~3~~ ~~4~~ ~~5~~ ~~6~~ ~~8~~ ~~4~~		+33	−27

Net profit = +6

such a system can yield a long-run profit. (Alternatively, many system players admit that their system will lose in the long run, but they persuade themselves that the long run is so far away that they themselves could not possibly play that long.) The point is that although there are *many* sequences of more losing bets than winning bets that will show a profit, not *all* sequences will. The typical system player is inclined to underestimate the chance of hitting disastrous sequences.

Simulation of Roulette Play on a Computer

Instead of a direct mathematical analysis of the probabilities for the cancellation system, we once again have the benefit of a very extensive simulation on a computer. This was done on an IBM 704 by a curious programer who simulated winning colors on roulette by generating random numbers and using them to determine on each bet whether red, black, or green was the winner. (For example, a simple way in which this could be done, although not necessarily the method that was used exactly, would be as follows: Take an eight-digit number at random. If it lies between 00,000,001 and 18,000,000, you call *red* the winner. If it lies between 18,000,001 and 36,000,000, you call *black* the winner. And if it is between 36,000,001 and 38,000,-000, you say *green* wins. If it is any larger than 38,000,000, you reject it and take a new number.)

A computer program was written readily for applying the cancellation system to a long series of random bets as described. The computer was also programed to store in its memory the outcome of each sequence, including the largest bet made, and the largest amount invested in each sequence. The fantastic speed of the computer is indicated by the fact that in about 20 minutes it made close to 15,000 bets! This is 750 bets per minute, or better than 12 bets per second. On any normal, busy roulette wheel, it might take almost a week to rack up 15,000 bets, playing night and day, round the clock. *So, the computer simulated a week's play in 20 minutes!*

It turns out for this system that there are about nine bets per sequence, on the average. In this case, for example, there were a total of 1620 sequences. At $6.00 per successful sequence, the player would have won about $9700, or let's say $10,000 for a round number. It is interesting to compare this profit with the amount that the player would have to have risked. No less than six times he would have needed to risk amounts greater than $10,000—ranging in fact up to more than $50,000! Figures are given in Table 16-3.

TABLE 16-3. RISK REQUIRED FOR A PROFIT OF $10,000

Maximum Bet	Maximum Loss	Maximum Risk (max. bet + max. loss)
$16,992	$41,943	$58,935
9,843	40,886	50,739
4,843	25,044	29,887
3,632	20,384	24,116
3,879	9,430	13,309
2,368	8,134	10,502

The maximum bet values reflect the fact that the house limit has been temporarily suspended. Originally, this was done because it made the program for the computer easier. In the 1620 sequences, the house limit of $500 would have been exceeded some 15 times. It might seem unbelievable that such fantastic bet levels would be called for, but the bet sizes go up very rapidly in this cancellation system. If the reader doubts this, let him write down a moderate series in which losses dominate over wins in a significant ratio, say, 2:1. A sequence that goes L-L-W-L-L-W-L-L-W-, etc., for about 50 to 100 bets will do nicely. Such a sequence is not at all absurd. One of the sequences that the computer spewed out contained 104 bets, with 68 losses and 36 wins. Such sequences lead very quickly to gigantic bets. This, of course, is just the price that must be paid in using a scheme that returns such a generous six units for each successful sequence.

The fact that it was necessary to risk several times that much in a period of time that produced a yield of 10,000 units shows that this type of system is just as fallacious as the others we have investigated.

DUKE, A SYSTEM PLAYER TO TOP THEM ALL

It is characteristic of the system player that when his system finally takes its first terrific beating, he doesn't give up. Rather, he immediately starts to doctor up the system with all sorts of stop-losses and insurance bets intended to cure the defect that led to his downfall. He hangs on tenaciously to the basic principle of the system. After losing on many variations of the one theme, he eventually gives up on systems based on that principle and tries a new one.

It is also characteristic of the system player that the only system worthy of his consideration is the one he is currently working on. He fancies that he understands the fallacies of all the systems on which he has given up. Such an attitude should excite the distrust of any intelligent individual.

One of the most pathetic figures around the Nevada casinos is an elderly gentleman whom we shall call "Duke." Born of a wealthy East Coast family, he had traveled extensively, spoke several languages, and was a polished gentleman. Somewhere along the way, he got the bug for roulette. He played in casinos all over the world. We met Duke in the summer of 1948 when we first clocked that wheel at Harolds. Although in his sixties, he presented a trim, well-dressed figure. Around the casinos, Duke's principal distinction was his reputation for having played roulette for 22 years without ever winning. Somehow this seemed to qualify him as an expert in the game, and many people deferred to his advice. Generally, he was the nucleus of a little clique of system players. The financial arrangements seemed to vary, but usually Duke was contributing a sizable fraction of the pot. Often, one of the group was a young man, perhaps a player down on his luck, whom Duke hired at a pittance to help him take down information. They played various progressive betting schemes, usually embellished with some little flourish to make them appear unique. Actually, I could hardly avoid believing that he must have played these same systems before in his long career. Invariably they won for a while and then lost, whereupon Duke would go into excited arguments over how the stop-loss should be changed to prevent this.

One night Duke and his cohorts put on a truly funny show. The alliance included a retired engineer whom we nicknamed the "General," and a merchant marine sailor on leave. This group decided to play the seesaw system on the color red, and went at it as if they had finally found the secret way to beat roulette. Their system worked like a charm for the first night. The bets rocked up, but not *too far* up, and then down again. After several hours of play, their $500 bank showed about a $100 profit. They retired for the evening, all smiles and confidence. The next night they marched in, took their appointed seats, and prepared to duplicate this feat, but things didn't go so well. The bets went up, but they didn't come down. They began to talk more excitedly among each other, and one could detect a note of dissension. Finally, on one bet, as the General placed a pile of chips on red, the sailor placed his own chips on black. The General assumed that the sailor had made a mistake, and moved the sailor's chips over on red, too. Defiantly the sailor grabbed his chips and slammed them back down on black, and for the rest of the evening, the sailor proceeded to play the color opposite from the color chosen by the rest of the group.

The outcome of the evening's play was that *both sides went broke!* Evidently the runs on red and on black were long enough, and yet sufficiently balanced from one to the other, that the seesaw failed on *both* colors. This is remarkable for such a short duration of play as one evening.

CAN YOU DOUBT THIS AUTHORITY?

Throughout this whole chapter we have continually rephrased, reiterated, and re-emphasized a salient point: When the odds are against you in each single play in a game, there is *no system whatsoever* by which this game can be consistently beaten. The sceptic may ask how anyone can make sweeping general statements about the results of using *any* system? I base my uncompromising statements on the following facts:

1. This chapter reveals the extensive mathematical analysis of the double-up and other progressions that I have made, as well as penetrating analyses of other betting systems.

2. I have read a vast amount of literature on the subject of gambling, as the References list indicates. In *none* of this literature have I *read* a verifiable account of a successful betting system.

3. In a period exceeding ten years, I have spent an accumulated time of many months in the casinos of Reno and Las Vegas, and I have never even *heard* of a successful betting system, nor have I seen one in action.

4. I have personal knowledge of several individuals who have spent *years* of their lives experimenting with systems, and these persons have done nothing but lose huge amounts of money.

5. So many *million* people have devoted so much time over the years, both in this country and abroad, to devise successful betting systems, that it seems extremely unlikely that nobody would have stumbled onto *at least one* such system if any existed.

IF YOU THINK YOU HAVE A WINNING SYSTEM

If *you* are a sceptic, if *you* think you have a system, do yourself the following favor. *Play your system on paper for a length of time sufficient to double your bankroll several times.* Double it three times, say, so that you have eight times what you started with. Don't settle for winning 20 percent or 50 percent of your bankroll, or even doubling it just once. Double it three times. Give it the acid test. Get into the "long run" with it. My definition of the long run, for testing a system, is a length of time sufficient to double your investment three times. (Most system players who do make a trial run on paper make the mistake of too short a test!) For your test on paper, you might do well to use the random number table in Appendix F.

If you succeed in doubling three times without going broke, try to do it again, and if that succeeds too, write to me and I shall publish it in the next edition of this book as the rarest event of the twentieth century!

How to Size Your Bets

17

When the game is to your advantage, as with a biased roulette wheel or with blackjack (if properly played), it is still not a cinch to win. It is necessary to choose your bank-to-bet ratio wisely so that you can weather severe fluctuations and still win steadily in the long run. This problem, known as the *gambler's ruin problem*, was originally studied by European scholars, who sought to obtain exact probabilities for a player to be ruined (or to succeed) in a limited play at an unfair game.

THE GAMBLER'S RUIN PROBLEM

In the preceding chapter, we have in a sense already performed ruin calculations for certain progressions and other systems. "Direct" calculations were possible in these instances, leading to answers expressible as one (easily computed) number raised to one (easily computed) power. But for flat-bet play, a different approach is needed. For example, suppose that you are betting one unit per spin on the red at roulette, your objective being to double ten units of capital and then to quit. The *direct method* would entail writing down all the many possible paths by which you could get to a point ten units ahead without ever having been ten units in the hole along the way. Within just 100 plays, there could be *millions* of such paths (or maybe even *billions*—it would be quite a feat to figure out how many paths exist, let alone write them all down). In any event, there are so many that a direct enumeration is entirely out of the question. Fortunately, there is a clever way to bypass such an enormous computation.

The reasoning hinges on the fact that your chance of ruin *after* a play is related to the chance of ruin *before* that play. Suppose your capital at some point in an even-payoff game is a certain number of units. Following the next play, only two situations are possible. If you win, you are one unit richer. If you lose, you are one unit poorer. Thus, your capital after the next play is definitely linked to your capital before the next play. This implies that your chance of ruin after the next play is also linked to that before, since your chance of ruin depends on how much capital you have. In fact, we can say that the chance of ruin with your present capital is equal to the chance of a win times the chance of ruin with one unit more of capital, plus the chance of a loss times the chance of ruin with one unit less of capital. This is just an application of the combination of probabilities.

It can all be formulated in terms of simple algebraic equations. These can be understood by anyone who has modest proficiency at algebra. The details are given in Appendix C. The results are given with appropriate interpretation in the ensuing pages.

A RESULT EVERY PLAYER SHOULD KNOW

Consider now the familiar case wherein the player sets as his goal the doubling of his capital. In this case, the number of units that he wishes to win from his opponent is the same as the number of units that he starts with himself. Thus $b = a$ in the formula developed in Appendix C. (It does not matter in this calculation if his opponent is richer than a units. The player is trying to win only a units.) With b set equal to a in the expression, it can be factored and reduced to a simpler form:

$$r_{(a)} = \frac{1}{1 + (S)^a}$$

This is a *most important formula!* Here, $r_{(a)}$ is the *ruin probability* when the player attempts to double a bank of a units. S stands for the *success ratio*, that is, the ratio p/q, where p is the probability of winning on any single play, and q is the probability of losing on any single play. This formula applies to all games with an *even payoff*.

One significant fact is immediately apparent from the form of this equation as applied to the usual game in which S is less than 1, that is, p is less than q. The larger the value of a, the smaller the value of $(S)^a$. (As a number less than 1 is multiplied by itself numerous times in succession, the result gets successively smaller.) If a is large enough, then $(S)^a$ is utterly negligible when compared with 1, and $r_{(a)}$ is essentially equal to 1. That is to say that if you attempt to double a large number of units at flat bets, you are virtually certain of going broke.

Just how big is a "large" number of units? This depends on how much of an advantage the opponent (usually the casino) has against the player. To take a specific case, $S = (18/38)/(20/38)$ on the even-money bets at roulette. This simplifies to 18/20 or 9/10, or 0.9 as a decimal. Since powers of 9 are easily calculated, the reader may readily verify Table 17-1 for various values of a.

TABLE 17-1. CHANCE OF GOING BROKE TRYING TO DOUBLE YOUR MONEY WITH FLAT BETS ON THE EVEN-MONEY PROPOSITIONS AT ROULETTE

Units of capital, a	1	5	10	20	50	100
$(S)^a = (0.9)^a$	0.9	0.590	0.349	0.122	0.0052	0.000027
Chance of ruin, $r_{(a)}$	0.526	0.629	0.741	0.891	0.995	0.999

With one unit of capital, we see that the chance of ruin is 0.526, which is the usual 20/38 chance of loss on any single play. (With only one unit of capital, you will either double your bank or go broke immediately on one play.) As the number of units is increased, it is apparent that the house edge has more opportunity to work against you, and your chance of ruin swiftly increases. With 10 units, it is 74 percent; with 20 units, it is almost 90 percent. Beyond that point, you can take your choice as to what you want to regard as a *virtual certainty:* 50 units gives 99.5 percent and 100 units gives 99.9 percent!

The strength of a house advantage of 5 percent is displayed vividly in these figures. It is easy to see why practically nobody ever wins in the long run on the red and black at roulette. It would take a tremendous stroke of good luck!

The situation at craps is not quite so bad, but it is still pretty grim.

On the pass line, $p = 244/495$ and $q = 251/495$. Thus, $S = 244/251 = 0.972$ and using this, we compute Table 17-2.

TABLE 17-2. CHANCE OF GOING BROKE TRYING TO DOUBLE
YOUR MONEY WITH FLAT BETS ON THE EVEN-MONEY
PROPOSITIONS AT CRAPS

Units of capital, a	1	5	10	20	50	100	200
Chance of ruin, $r_{(a)}$	0.507	0.535	0.570	0.638	0.805	0.944	0.997

Whatever the number of units of capital, it is clearly apparent that the chance of doubling your money is notably better on the pass line at craps than on the red and black at roulette. But even the 1.4 percent house advantage at craps can grind you down quite fast.

In our examples here, we have chosen the convenient case of doubling your bank. In so doing, we were able to set b equal to a, and use the most simple form of the solution for the gambler's ruin equation. However, it is not *necessary* to choose the simple case of doubling. We could just as well go to the general formula of Appendix C and consider the general case of starting with a units and trying to win b units, where a and b are unequal. Whatever numerical instances we select, we find a certain similarity in the results. Just as it is harder to win 10 units starting with 10 (that is, to double 10) than it is to win 1 starting with 1, we find it is harder to win 50 units starting with 10 than to win 5 starting with 1. These latter chances may be computed by utilizing the general formula and inserting the combinations $a = 10$, $b = 50$, and $a = 1$, $b = 5$, respectively. The computation shows that the chance of ruin is 99.7 percent in trying to win 50 starting with 10, and is 87.5 percent in trying to win 5 starting with 1. As with doubling, the moral is clear. The more units you try to win, the longer it is going to take; and the longer you play, the more chance the house percentage has to work against you.

The Fair Game

It is most instructive to compare the preceding results with those for the fair game. Here we have $p = q$ $(= \frac{1}{2})$, or $S = 1$. The general formula in Appendix C becomes mathematically indeterminate in the special case $S = 1$, and must be replaced by $r_{(a)} = b/(a + b)$. A very striking conclusion pops out of this result if we merely note that the chance of *success* is $1 - r_{(a)} = a/(a + b)$. The ratio of the chance of success to the chance of ruin is a to b, or

$$\text{(Chance of success)}:\text{(chance of ruin)} = \text{(player bank)}: \\ \text{(opponent bank)}$$

Indeed, one might well guess this on intuitive grounds. If you flip pennies with a friend, and you start with 10¢ and he starts with 50¢, the odds are 5:1 that he will get you before you get him. Or your chance of ruin is $50/(10 + 50) = 50/60 = 5/6$, or 0.833 as a decimal. Note also that if you start with 1¢ and he starts with 5¢, the odds are still 5:1 that he will get you, and the chance of ruin is still 5/6.

This is in definite contrast with the prediction for the unfair game. On the even-money bets at roulette, for example, we saw that if you start with 1 unit and try to win 5 more, your chance of ruin is 0.875; but if you start with 10 units and try to win 50 more, your chance of ruin is 0.997! In the fair game, it is only the *ratio* of your capital to your opponent's that counts; but in the unfair game, it is not only the ratio, but much more important, the actual amounts of capital also. In any case, the chance of ruin is always greater than the corresponding chance in the fair game. Here we see that both 0.875 and 0.997 are worse chances of going broke than 0.833.

If you choose to attempt to *double* your money at the fair game on flat bets, then $b = a$ and $r_{(a)}$ reduces to 1/2. Your chance of doubling your money is 50 percent, regardless of whether you try to use 1 unit to get 1 more, 10 units to get 10 more, or 100 units to get 100 more.

HOW MUCH RISK DOES A CASINO TAKE?

All discussions so far have concerned what one player can expect to happen in his valiant but almost futile attempt to enlarge his capital. Or better, what a large group of players can expect, on the average. But still there is always the fanciful possibility of a fantastic streak of good luck. Hence, it is interesting to ask what sort of risk the house is taking that a lucky player will break the house. After all, the house takes on just about all comers, and in comparison with its own large but finite resources, the house is bucking an effectively infinitely rich public.

About the worst situation the house could get into would be in bucking a coalition of players, all of whom were making house-limit bets on the same proposition. Suppose the house limit per player were $200, as it is in many casinos, and that 5 players were betting together on the pass line at craps. Then the total bet would be $1000, which we may regard as one unit. If the house bankroll were $1 million, the house would possess 1000 such units. (We need not concern ourselves with how many units the players possess. If they were rich Texas oil men, they might indeed possess many thousands of such units and be richer than the syndicate that owned the casino! On the other hand, if the players were not that rich, we could assume that, over the years, there would be a number of such coalitions whose combined resources would exceed that of the casino.)

It is simple to compute the house's chance of ruin under the above assumptions. In our original statement of the ruin problem, the house must be identified with the player, and the Texas oil men with the opponent. Here we have $p = 0.507$ and $q = 0.493$ instead of the usual opposite values. The value of a is 1000 and b is infinite. Since a and b are not equal, we use the general formula given in Appendix C. In this formula, certain terms drop out by virtue of the fact that b is infinite. Thus $(1/S)^b$ is zero, and the formula simplifies to

$$r_{(a)} = \left(\frac{1}{S}\right)^a = \left(\frac{0.493}{0.507}\right)^a = (0.972)^a$$

For $a = 1000$, this chance of ruin is 0.0000000000005! The house certainly is not taking much of a chance. Starting with its 1000 units, the house will get steadily richer, and richer, and richer—if the bank is allowed to accumulate. Of course a large fraction of a casino's haul must be spent on operating expenses, but there must be plenty of profit from the successful casinos, judging from the eagerness with which people are willing to invest in new ones! As long as a casino keeps enough capital on hand and sticks to its practice of limiting bets, there is nothing for the casino to worry about. The risk is even further reduced by the fact that when a number of players are in a game, their bets often tend to cancel each other; on these bets, the house has a sure thing. At roulette, for example, if one player has $1.00 on red, and another player has $1.00 on black, the house either draws or wins. If either red or black wins, one bet pays the other; but if the green wins, the house rakes in both bets. Accordingly, the house takes a risk only on the noncanceling bets.

BET SIZING WHEN YOU HAVE THE ADVANTAGE

We have now reached the best part, that of deciding how to size your bets when the game is to your advantage! As implied at the beginning of the chapter, there are rather few games in the casino where this can occur. There are three principal possibilities: play on a biased roulette wheel, correct play at blackjack, and play in the poker or poker-type games where the house runs the bank. But our remarks will *also* apply to numerous games *outside* the casino! Many people play all sorts of card games for stakes ranging from peanuts to important money. Any successful card player who knows that he has an edge in his game should have a realistic appraisal of his chance of going broke as a result of fluctuations. The same goes for a successful handicapper at the horse races or at other sporting events. Of course many players set up their own operating criteria on the basis of experience. But it is much better to have some scientific basis for bank-to-bet ratio, since it is easy to be overly optimistic when you have an edge, and to wind up with a truly realistic outlook only after a number of brutally unhappy experiences. Undue optimism is the bane of many a gambler. Even when you have the edge, Lady Luck can be very fickle, and it pays to be scientific wherever possible.

There are two easy ways to approach the situation where the player has the advantage. Neither of these involves any new mathematical concepts. One approach is to say simply that the player is in effect trading places with the house, so that whatever figures previously applied to the house now apply to the player, and vice versa. The other approach is to go ahead and do computations similar to those done before, but with values of p and q reflecting the fact that the game is to the player's advantage. (In our original formulation of the gambler's ruin problem, we made no assumptions as to whether p

was less than or greater than q, so those results were perfectly general.)

Both viewpoints give the same answer. Indeed they must, for they are merely different ways of expressing the same thing. The equivalence of the two methods is also apparent from inspection of the formulas, because of a certain symmetry which they possess.

Figure 17-1 presents a convenient graphical summary of results, both for the case where the player has the edge and for the case where the house has the edge. Curves are drawn for various simple values of $p - q$, expressed in percent; those given are 1/2, 1, 2, 4, and 10 percent. (If $p - q$ is positive, then the player has the edge; if it is negative, the house has the edge.) For intermediate values of $p - q$, you can easily interpolate between the given curves. In fact, two familiar and important cases are sketched in with dotted curves. These are craps (pass line) and roulette, for which results were cited in Tables 17-1 and 17-2. The curves bring out dramatically what a crushing advantage the house possesses. It is clearly evident, for example, that the chance of doubling 50 units at roulette is virtually nil. It is interesting to note that the horizontal line of symmetry corresponds to the special case of the fair game ($p - q = 0$, or $p = q$). In this case, whatever the number of units you attempt to double, the chance of success is always 50 percent.

The way to use these curves to determine a proper bank-to-bet ratio when a game is to your advantage is very simple. Suppose, for example, you have a 1 percent edge ($p = 0.505$ and $q = 0.495$, so that $p - q = 0.010$, or 1 percent. Go to the curve labeled +1 percent. For whatever chance of success you wish to stipulate, the corresponding bank-to-bet ratio may be read from the scale at the bottom. For instance, if you wish to set your chance of success at 80 percent, you locate the intersection of the +1 percent curve and the horizontal 80 percent success line, and drop down to the bottom of the graph; there you read 70 units. If you do not consider 80 percent chance of success close enough to a sure thing for you, then you should glide further up the +1 percent curve. The highest point plotted in the figure is at the right border, at 88 percent; the corresponding bank-to-bet ratio, as read at the bottom, is 100. Personally, I should consider

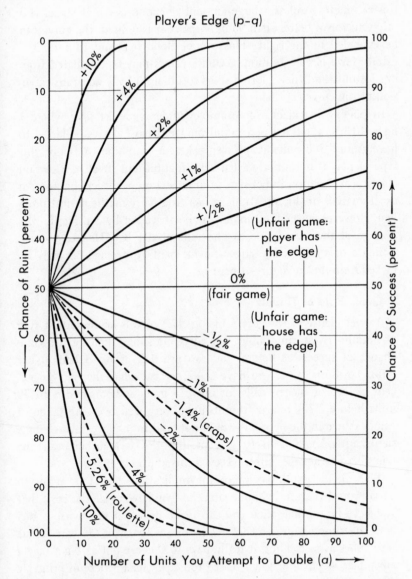

Player's Edge (p−q)

FIG. 17-1. Chances of Success and of Ruin in Attempting to Double
Your Bank on Flat-Bet Play in an Even-Payoff Game

this satisfactory unless a large amount of money were at stake. If a safety factor of better than 90 or 95 percent is desired, the curve can be extended to the right. This can be done freehand to a limited extent; for a large extension, accurate values may be calculated from our formula and then plotted so as to obtain a truly accurate extension of the curve.

In playing blackjack, for example, under circumstances where I figured I had about a 1 percent advantage, I have always preferred to have around 100 units at my disposal, as a minimum. Actually, this type of play is not strictly a flat-bet situation, but involves a certain amount of variation in bet size, as discussed in an earlier chapter. An exact analysis of this situation, in fact, is a hairy mathematical problem. However, a rough estimate may be arrived at by considering the average of the varied bets as one unit of flat bet. Hence, a quick estimate of a reasonably safe ratio for bank to average bet may be picked from the curve for +1 percent.

A Quick Rule of Thumb

A brief glance at the curves in Fig. 17-1 reveals an important rule of thumb. If you can double your edge in a game, then for the same chance of success as before, you can use half as big a bank-to-bet ratio. To illustrate: If you have a +2 percent edge, then an 80 percent chance of success calls for only 35 units as compared with 70 units before. This rule of thumb holds very well over the range of values shown in the figure. It would not hold for a player's percentage significantly larger than 10 percent, but this is a rather academic point because a player rarely has even this much edge.

The rule of thumb has important implications if you are trying to parlay your bankroll. If in one situation you have twice the edge that you have in another, then you can make bets that are twice as big, with the same margin of safety. This means that you can win dollars *four* times as fast. Thus, it really pays to squeeze out as big a player advantage as possible. On a biased roulette wheel, where in principle you can win on a number that averages better than 1/36, a number that yields 1/32 is vastly better than one that yields 1/34, and a 1/30 number is an utter dream!

The Case of Uneven Payoff

A question that may occur to the reader at this point is whether the curves we have just developed can be used for bets that are not even-money propositions. A case in point is betting on a single number at roulette where the payoff is 35:1. It turns out that a very simple rule of thumb may be employed, but before stating it, perhaps we had better see why the question arises in the first place.

In an even-money proposition, when you win a play, your bank increases by one unit; and when you lose a play, your bank decreases by one unit. But in the single-number proposition at roulette, when you win a play, your bank increases by 35 units; while when you lose, your bank decreases by one unit only. There is an unbalanced situation. Of course you win much less frequently than you lose, so there is a compensation for the high-win payoff.

Now the ruin problem may be formulated by use of the same simple line of reasoning we used at the beginning of the chapter. But in this case, if your bank contains x units prior to a play, it will contain either $x + 35$ or $x - 1$ units after the play. This is in contrast to the even-money game in which your bank contains either $x + 1$ or $x - 1$ units after the play. This leads us to another difference equation:

$$r_{(x)} = p \cdot r_{(x+35)} + q \cdot r_{(x-1)}$$

Furthermore, in this case, p will be a number around $1/38$ and q will be around $37/38$, whereas before p and q were about $1/2$.

This difference equation is not quite so easy to solve as the one in Appendix C. In the even-money case, the possible values that your bank can have after a play (namely, $x + 1$ and $x - 1$) differ by only two units. The resulting difference equation is what the mathematician calls a *second-order* linear difference equation. But in the single-number case, the possible values of the bank after a play (namely, $x + 35$ and $x - 1$) differ by 36 units. Therefore, the resulting difference equation is what the mathematician calls a *linear difference equation* of order 36. First- and second-order equations are generally a lot easier to solve than are higher-order equations, and 36 is a pretty high order. However, things aren't really so bad as they could be, for a lot of terms are missing from the difference equation. In fact, terms all the way from $x + 1$ to $x + 34$ are absent, and the upshot of the matter is that certain potent methods of approximation may be used to get a result. Uspensky's book has the original and most thorough coverage of this.

If we get back to the roulette problem, it turns out that the approximate solution mentioned above is identical with the value obtained from our even-money curves by using the proper trick. For a given player's edge and for a given chance of success, the bank-to-bet ratio as obtained from the curves for the even-money game should simply be *multiplied by 35* to get the proper bank-to-bet ratio for single-number play. This trick yields a correct result, except for very low values of bank-to-bet ratio, which would hardly be of interest because of the large risk involved. And the trick perhaps agrees with what intuition would tell us to do.

We must make it quite clear how the player's edge should be computed. First of all, this expression simply means the player's expected net profit, on the average, with a one-unit bet. On an even-money proposition, there is probability p to win 1 unit, and probability q to lose 1 unit. Therefore, the expected net profit is $1 \cdot p - 1 \cdot q$, or simply $p - q$. On the single-number proposition at roulette, there is probability p to win 35 units and probability q to lose 1 unit. Hence, the expected net profit is $35 \cdot p - 1 \cdot q$ or, dropping the multiplication dots, $35p - q$.

Suppose a number is averaging (over an extended sample) one hit in every 34 plays. Then $p = 1/34$ and $q = 33/34$. The expected net profit is $35 \cdot 1/34 - 1 \cdot 33/34$, or $35/34 - 33/34 = 2/34 = 1/17 = 0.0588$, which as a percentage is $+5.88$ percent. To find the proper bank-to-bet ratio to use for some arbitrary chance of success (say, 90 percent), we simply proceed as follows: Between the given curves for $+4$ percent and $+10$ percent edge, we mentally interpolate a curve for $+5.88$ percent (say about $+6$ percent). On the horizontal 90 percent success line, such an interpolated curve would cross at about the vertical line, which is numbered 20 at the bottom. Therefore, we should use a bank-to-bet ratio of about $35 \cdot 20 = 700$. That is to say, with 700 betting units, there would be a 90 percent chance of doubling your bank on a number that is averaging 1/34. You will recall from the chapter on roulette that this is roughly the bank-to-bet ratio that we used in playing on that biased wheel which Harold eventually changed. We had number 3 tagged for about a 1/34 number, and we used 800 betting units to start. Later, we chose a more conservative bank-to-bet ratio of 2500 because of the larger stake involved. Unfortunately, Harold then broke up our game.

ONLY A LARGE BANK-TO-BET RATIO IS SAFE

It is a striking (and alas, regrettable) fact that such a large bank-to-bet ratio must be employed in playing single numbers at roulette. Consider, for example, the case of a +1 percent advantage on a single number. Before we figured that in an *even-money* game, you would need about 100 units to assure 90 percent chance of doubling your money with a +1 percent advantage. According to our new rule of thumb, you would need $35 \cdot 100$, or 3500, units for the same chance of success on a single number. That is a depressing number of units. Averaging 0.01 unit of profit per play, it would take $3500/0.01 = 350,000$ plays to double your bank. Wow! Playing around the clock, you would need three or four months to do it.

Unless you are really loaded, playing on such a small percentage is utterly prohibitive. A realistic rock-bottom figure for single-number operation is around +5 percent, and you really should be looking for something closer to +10 or even +20 percent. The latter figure corresponds to a number that is averaging about 1/30 (thus, $35p - q$ is $35/30 - 29/30 = 6/30 = 1/5$, or 20 percent). Such numbers have existed. The Rover Boys found one at the Pioneer Club in Las Vegas, and we found two on a single-zero wheel at the Nevada Club in Reno. But it's tougher than prospecting for gold!

A PARLAY IS REALLY ROUGH

The bank-to-bet ratios quoted so far have not conveyed the whole story. We have talked always in terms of doubling your bank, *once*. But if you wish to pull off a parlay, this means doubling your bank several times. The chances of ruin at each step of doubling must now be compounded, to give an over-all chance of ruin. This, of course, leads to an even larger bank-to-bet ratio. A little calculation will show that if you wish to double your bank five or six times and retain a 90 percent chance of success for the entire operation, then for each step of doubling, it is necessary to have between 98 and 99 percent chance of success. This calls for about twice the bank-to-bet ratio that a single step at 90 percent would call for. So, even with a good, juicy advantage of 10 to 20 percent on a number, it may be advisable to have 500, 1000, or even 2000 betting units available, depending on the degree of confidence you have in your estimate of your advantage.

BANK-TO-BET RATIO WHEN BET SIZE VARIES

The question of proper bank-to-bet ratio in a game where your bet sizes may vary over a considerable range is a mighty tough one. In the classic illustration of poker, there will be small pots and big ones, all in the same game. Unless the big pots are really few and far between, it is smart to play safe and act as if the large bets are the standard bet size for your whole operation. It is very bad policy ever to gamble with "scared money." This means betting such a large fraction of your available bank on any one play that it affects your judgment. If you have to chicken-out on a good hand because of normal fluctuations in your bankroll, then you may as well not be playing at all. You are a sucker in the full sense of the word, and can look forward only to a career of huge losses. There are numerous men who have made a business out of gambling in the armed forces. While many of them are good players without question, one of their principal secrets of success is to have plenty of bankroll available when the tide is running against them. Their greater resources eventually just sweep the small fry right out of the game, and they have almost as much a sure thing as if the bettors with lesser resources simply handed over their cash at the start of the game!

Of course we are talking here about games in which your own skill is as good as or better than the skill of your opponents. We are assuming you have the sense to stay in your own class. If you insist on feeding your ego by getting into games with the Nick the Greeks and the Killer Crawfords, so you can boast to your friends about it, then your fate is a foregone conclusion. Your lost bankroll will merely be the price of your brief flight with the gods.

In games where bet sizes or payoffs vary greatly from one play to the next, it must be said that experience can be a good guide for bet sizing. One obvious reason for this is that, granted you *do* play the game to your advantage, it takes a considerable amount of play before you have an accurate idea of what your advantage is. To determine this, you need a reasonable record of your total investment and the net profit that it has produced. In the process of accumulating this information, you will get a good introduction into the fluctuations which you can expect in your bankroll.

Nonetheless, some knowledge of what theory predicts in the simpler cases of fixed-payoff ratio, and a more precisely known advantage, can provide a stabilizing influence. Besides, most people who play the sophisticated games also play the simpler ones, at least occasionally. So they will naturally want to know what the score is in the simpler games.

FINAL REMARKS

This concludes our treatment of the problem of bet sizing. The applications of the material in this chapter are universal, wherever one man will take a wager from another. For this reason, this chapter is of vast importance to all gamblers. We have tried to keep it reasonably simple and yet include enough detail so that you are convinced that we know what we are talking about. We strongly urge you to *read this chapter over again* from time to time. Review the *principles* and *examples*, and try to digest fully the significance of the curves in Fig. 17-1.* The smart gambler does not have to know a whale of a lot. But this stuff is surely a part of what he does need to know. Not the difference equations and formulas, but the *ideas* and the *results!*

* See also Appendix G, "Optimal Betting," which contains additional important information on bet sizing.

The Future of Gambling in the Electronic Age

18

What will happen on the gambling scene in coming years? I predict three areas of change. (1) There will be a stepped-up "player offense" utilizing computers and other electronic devices. (2) There will be a corresponding "house defense" in the same direction. (3) The games themselves will become more electronically oriented.

THE STEPPED-UP OFFENSE

We have already witnessed the effect of the availability of high speed computers on blackjack. It forced at least one (temporary) change in the playing rules. (See page 159.) It is a testimony to the inertia and skepticism of the casino operators that the reaction did not take place until 1964 even though the proper basic strategy for flat bet play was published by Baldwin in 1957. Devices for implementing the count on the 10's ratio will undoubtedly shower the market, unless the casinos make further changes in the game, or declare such counters illegal and then actually prosecute or otherwise intimidate their users.

Such a counting aid, designed to assist the player who lacks the requisite memory and mental agility, cannot properly be called a computer. Whether mechanical or electrical, its function is too simple. It merely needs to count down in two registers in response to push-button input, and also to display the ratio of the numbers in the two registers. Operating with this aid concealed in his hand, the player must then make use of a memorized table (such as Table 7-4) to effect the proper strategy decision for the particular hand.

To dispense with memorizing a decision table, the player would need a considerably more sophisticated device, capable of all the mental operations one goes through in using the table. The prospect of fabricating this with a sufficient degree of miniaturization is still some ways off into the future. What the casino player of the future would *really* like to have is access to a computer that would permit each and every hand to be played optimally. (Even the 10-count tables only permit a play which is best "on the average" for a given ratio value.) Possibly the *most efficient* computer scheme would be one in which, for any hand dealt, it would complete the hand around 1000 times with simulated random draw, according to each of the two available alternatives. Fast, present-day computers could play the 2000 hands in 1 to 5 seconds. The sample size of 1000 would be large enough so that usually the correct recommendation would be given to the player, except in very close cases where it wouldn't matter very much.

In the current state of the art, such a computer would have to be deployed at a remote location, such as a hotel room, and a secret radio link would be needed for communication purposes.

The extension of such techniques for card memory and decision-making to other card games is obvious, assuming the participants allow such electronic devices.

ROULETTE PREDICTION

One of my forecasts is an increase in the use of computer analysis of the human factors which control the outcome of gambling games. Specifically, in roulette there will be attempts to "psychoanalyze" the dealer's characteristics in spinning the ball and the wheel. Today when computers can predict complicated orbits and can guide a defensive missile to intercept an attacking missile, it would appear to be child's play to predict where a roulette ball will land on the next spin. Provided one can assume reasonably consistent operation of the wheel, the mechanical situation is elementary. All you need is the "initial conditions" at the instant the ball is spun, and some empirical data on the slowing down of the ball.

Of course the problem is complicated by the presence of the eight small diamond-shaped deflectors located on the sloping bowl, but only a fraction of the time does the ball hit a deflector. The sometimes helter-skelter bounce of the ball as it falls into the wheel is also a complicating factor. These two considerations make a 100 percent successful prediction utterly out of the question. But you don't *need* anywhere near 100 percent accuracy. You must merely overcome the house's 5 percent margin, and the rest is gravy. If the predictor could rule out half of the wheel, the advantage would be so enormous that you could start with $100 and win the whole club virtually overnight. With half the wheel excluded, you would win 1/19 of the time on your number. At payoff odds of 35:1, you would have almost 100 percent profit.

There are two distinct possible playing conditions that you might have to contend with: (1) the bet may be placed up to a few seconds after the ball is spun, and (2) the bet must be placed prior to the spinning of the ball.

The first of these would be more advantageous. Variations in the speed with which the dealer propels the ball wouldn't matter. On each throw you would clock the first spin or two, inject this information into your computer, get the prediction back in a second or so, and then place the bet. The accuracy of the clocking would depend on whether it would have to be performed visually (mighty rugged on the eyes), or whether some instrumentation could be used. (One fanciful suggestion has been to find a casino where there are hotel rooms available for rent directly above. Then drill a small hole in the ceiling above the wheel, and use a telescope and stroboscope to determine the required speeds. The computer itself could be located either in the hotel room or in the pocket of the player at the table. In either case, the setup would entail a radio link between the participants.) A more realistic operation might involve sensors, operating on any of several simple physical principles, concealed on a confederate standing near the wheel.

If the dealer required the bet to be placed prior to the spin of the ball, it would be much harder to make a good prediction. But on the other hand, they would be much less likely to suspect you of being able to do it. You would have to "take data" on each dealer, and find out each dealer's average speed of spin. Some dealers might display so much natural variation that it would be hopeless to try to win against them. On the other hand, a slow roller might be very susceptible to good prediction.

With some slow spinners the ball takes only 3 or 4 revolutions before it drops in the slot. This is in marked contrast to some dealers, who put every ounce of available energy into propelling the ball.

Unfortunately I never have recorded dealers on a regular basis. Perhaps a golden chance was missed, for with all the thousands of trials we logged, it would have been a cinch to later analyze the record for individual dealer trends. Thus our failure to follow a classic principle of statistics: The best time to design an experiment is *before* you do it! Now that my student days are gone forever and I am too busy to sit by a roulette wheel around the clock, I would excitedly welcome the opportunity to get my hands on some data of this sort.

If the bet had to be placed before the spin of the ball, it would of course take very little effort on the dealer's part to break up a prediction operation. The bettor might have to pretend to be a happy-go-lucky inebriate, strewing chips all over the board, but somehow managing to concentrate the bigger bets in the sector which the computer specified. By this stratagem, the phenomenal rate of winning which the scientific prediction might produce could be passed off for a while as blind luck. (In this regard, the alert "sector" player observes that he does not necessarily have to play a sequence of individual numbers, in an obvious chain. Some of the lower payoff bets may fill the bill. Although the 1:1 wagers like red-black, odd-even, and high-low are uniformly distributed around a double-zero wheel, the same is not true of all of the 2:1 wagers. In particular, there is a very strong grouping of 10 of the 12 numbers in the "second column" on a sector comprising less than half of the wheel. There are other pronounced groupings on the "third column" and the "second dozen." These facts are readily apparent by inspection of the roulette layout in Fig. 1-1.)

Make no mistake. Despite its nominal 5 percent house advantage, roulette will come under increasing attack by the analysts. Predictive theory, fortified by physical traits like those laid bare in Chapter 3, will make some stunning victories.

THE HOUSE DEFENSE

The casinos will make use of more and more electronic devices and computer analyses to protect themselves. Closed circuit television is an accepted technique for surveillance of the gaming tables. Video cameras are readily installed above the tables, and wired to a central console. The boss can sit in his easy chair and flip the channel selector to view the action at all locations.

As indicated in Chapter 10, an electronic system is available and has been installed at one of the Las Vegas casinos for monitoring the take on the slot machines. It is only a matter of time before the use of such "data-logging" systems is expanded to other games, to speed up the accounting and to check on the honesty of house employees.

Harrah's Club, of Reno and Lake Tahoe, has engaged the services of the Control Data Corporation computing center at Palo Alto, California, for independent blackjack analyses. Harrah's whole operation is a marvel of business efficiency. Anyone who wonders how he overtook Harolds Club in volume of business should read "The New Gambling King and the Social Scientists" in the January 1962 issue of *Harper's Magazine*. His colonization of Lake Tahoe was a master stroke. With this he has been able to tap a vast new market of players from Northern California, whose inhibitions previously prevented their going to Reno. Now they can rationalize "a trip to the mountains" for their health, and send home postcards with California postmarks to their morally repressed friends, while patronizing the casinos just over the state line.

In addition to attracting these middleclass families in their automobiles, Harrah has proselytized another segment of the population, namely those low-income and retired folk whose means limit them to bus transportation. He obtained an accurate assessment of this market by paying the Stanford Research Institute to do a study; it appeared in 1957 under the innocuous title of "An Investigation of Factors Influencing Bus Scheduling." The motivation researchers readily convinced him that he could haul these people free from their hometowns, and still make a profit by the time they walked away from his gambling tables. So he launched into a giant advertising campaign, and his free bus trips are now a way of life for countless thousands within a radius of several hundred miles. (The effect which all this activity has on the welfare case load and other civic problems in these communities is of little concern to the gambling czars.)

It is quite likely that Harrah's competitors will take heed to the success of his methods, and we shall see increased use of sociological and psychiatric research to lure new customers into the casinos. Electronic data processing will be the key to such statistical studies.

Returning to the scene of the action, the casino operators will be increasingly vigilant about concealed aids on the players and about radio communication devices. While it is doubtful that casinos will ever reach the point of being built inside an electrically "shielded" room, to prevent radio transmission to the outside, they will nonetheless make more use of consultants who can keep them abreast of what is feasible in this regard. Even the gamblers have learned respect for the electron.

INTRODUCTION OF ELECTRONIC GAMES

As players become more sophisticated they will demand more sophisticated games. Probably electronic games will begin as variants on existing games, as perhaps an electronic slot machine. The one factor that will sell these games will be speed. The turn-around time on the action will be virtually nil. In fact, it will probably be necessary to build in some delay, so as to satisfy the player's psychological need for suspense.

A man in Reno claims to have invented an automatic blackjack-playing machine. The player just pushes a button, and the card values are displayed on a register. What a cure for players who mark the cards! Electronic roulette would be even easier to build.*

Of course there will be great opposition in some quarters. Many players will distrust electronic devices as too easy to rig, so much care will be needed in the technique for randomization. The "pseudo-random number generation" method of Chapter 6 is very attractive for this purpose. It is true that such a sequence of apparently random digits is actually fully determined in advance, and someone armed with the formula would be able to predict the next immediate num-

---

* As this book goes to press, such a machine has made its appearance in the casinos of the Reno–Lake Tahoe area. Coin-operated, it has place for up to four players. After the "deal," the player has about a dozen seconds to make a decision such as to stand or draw, or he gets passed up. Some of the customary options are not offered. Since each card is effectively drawn from a fresh deck, the player is bucking a game with an "infinite deck," and thereby faces a house percentage of around ½ percent, plus an additional loss due to the less favorable options. Machine blackjack is distinctly a poorer bet than the regular game on the tables, unless blackjack is paid better than 1½:1.

ber in the chain. However, the chain could be set going continuously at a rate of 1000 digits per second, and interrogated when needed by the player; with only manual timing of this intermittent read-out from the chain, no human would be able to select particular digits. As an alternative, one could utilize the same principles that underlie various types of noise generators that are common in the analog computer field. These depend upon some physical phenomenon which is known to be random in nature, such as the emission of charged particles from a radioactive source, or the arrival of cosmic rays.

Automated methods of simulating randomness are commonplace in the computing and control fields of today. Indeed, they are far more reliable than the time-worn procedures of shuffling cards and shaking dice. Yet before traditional gambling methods bow under the winds of electronic change, powerful human forces must be reckoned with. Dealers have a vested interest in the status quo, and any alterations which might deplete their ranks can be expected to meet with opposition. But more important than this issue is whether the player will accept a machine as his adversary rather than a man. The popularity of slot machines tends to support it, but this is not a proof. Automation in the factory is one thing, where the machine takes over thankless "work"; but people flock to casinos for "play," and many have a psychological need for someone to beat!

CONCLUSION

Some readers will scoff at my "science-fiction" view of the near-term future of gambling. The fact remains that we live in a dynamic world. On the one hand, gambling is a hallmark of an affluent society, and we can expect a steadily increasing volume of play. On the other hand, technological change sweeps over us at an ever-rising rate, producing changes in a decade that we would not have expected for a lifetime. With this, our population becomes better versed in mathematics, the widespread understanding of which is the principal enemy of organized gambling. Education in practical probability and statistics is a far more potent foe to gambling than all the moral pronouncements and preachings. I foresee a race between the effects of affluence and education!

How to Calculate the Odds on a Ten-Spot Keno Ticket

The game of keno is described at the beginning of Chapter 12. We shall show here the proper method for calculating the chance of picking any particular number of winners in the ten-number selection. We begin with a clear statement of the problem. We have a total of $n = 80$ objects. There are $s = 20$ objects of type 1 (winners) and $n - s = 60$ objects of type 2 (nonwinners). From these 80 objects, $r = 10$ objects are selected at random. We seek the probability that x of these are of type 1 (winners), and $r - x = 10 - x$ are of type 2 (nonwinners).

To obtain this probability, we must combine three separate factors:

1. The number of ways to choose x winners from among a total of s winners; that is, the number of combinations of s things taken x at a time.

2. The number of ways to choose $r - x$ nonwinners from among a total of $n - s$ nonwinners; that is, the number of combinations of $n - s$ things taken $r - x$ at a time.

3. The number of ways to choose r numbers at random from among n; that is, the number of combinations of n things taken r at a time.

The probability will be the product of (1) and (2) divided by (3). Using the standard notation for combinations, we write this as

$$\frac{\binom{s}{x}\binom{n-s}{r-x}}{\binom{n}{r}} = \frac{\binom{20}{x}\binom{60}{10-x}}{\binom{80}{10}}$$

Expressions of the form $\binom{n}{r}$ stand for the number of combinations of n things taken r at a time. (Note that there is *no line* between the two quantities in the parentheses!) As an example:

$$\binom{80}{10} = \frac{80!}{10!\,(80-10)!} = \frac{80!}{10!\,70!}$$

The exclamation point means *factorial*. Thus,

$$10! = 10 \times 9 \times 8 \times 7 \times 6 \times 5 \times 4 \times 3 \times 2 \times 1$$

At this point, we should draw attention to an alternate, and equally logical, derivation that leads to the same result. In our previous statement of the problem, we treated the draw as if it were predetermined, and considered the player's selections as taken at random. Now it is just as logical to treat the player's selections as predetermined, and to consider the draw as taken at random. (In fact, chronologically, this is the way the game is played.) This new point of view leads to the following restatement of the problem:

We have a total of $n = 80$ objects. There are $r = 10$ objects of type A (picked by the player to win), and $n - r = 70$ objects of type B (not picked by the player to win). From these 80 objects, $s = 20$ objects are selected at random (actual winning numbers drawn by the operator). We seek the probability that x of these are of type A and that $s - x = 20 - x$ are of type B. By identical reasoning as before, this gives probability

$$\frac{\binom{r}{x}\binom{n-r}{s-x}}{\binom{n}{s}} = \frac{\binom{10}{x}\binom{70}{20-x}}{\binom{80}{20}}$$

This expression looks different from the one first given for probability, but they may be readily shown to be equivalent by expanding each one in terms of the factorials. Indeed, both expressions must have the same value, inasmuch as they both give the probability of the same event. On expanding either one of these formulas, and collecting terms into a compact form, we get

$$\frac{20! \ 60! \ 10! \ 70!}{x! \ (20-x)! \ (10-x)! \ (50+x)! \ 80!}$$

For a "compact form," this looks like a beast! However, using proper tools, and canceling wherever possible, we can lick it.

The most interesting case to evaluate of course is $x = 10$, which is the case of hitting all 10 winners, for a 25,000:1 payoff! Substituting this value, and making use of the fact that $0! = 1$ (we need not worry here about this apparently peculiar value for zero factorial), we have

$$\frac{20! \ 60! \ 10! \ 70!}{10! \ 10! \ 0! \ 60! \ 80!} = \frac{20! \ 70!}{10! \ 80!} =$$

$$\frac{20 \times 19 \times 18 \times 17 \times 16 \times 15 \times 14 \times 13 \times 12 \times 11}{80 \times 79 \times 78 \times 77 \times 76 \times 75 \times 74 \times 73 \times 72 \times 71}$$

There are several ways to evaluate this goodie. An exact computation can be done in a straightforward manner by using logarithms. (Most handbooks that have ordinary log tables also have logs for the factorials.) Or a slide rule can be used to grind out the successive products and quotients. Or a trick may be employed to obtain an approximate value. For example, the product of the ten descending numbers in the numerator is roughly equal to the tenth power of the mean. The mean between 20 and 11 is 15.5; applying the same reasoning to the denominator, we get 75.5 for a mean. Thus, the big, hairy ratio given above is approximately

$$\frac{(15.5)^{10}}{(75.5)^{10}} = \left(\frac{15.5}{75.5}\right)^{10} \text{ or about } \left(\frac{1}{5}\right)^{10} = \frac{1}{(5)^{10}} = \frac{1}{(5^5)^2}$$

$$= \frac{1}{(3125)^2} \text{ or } \frac{1}{9,000,000}$$

Ouch! There is only one chance in 9 million to hit the big jackpot at keno. Did you really think the chance was *that* small?

The preceding rough approximation procedure is the sort of thing I went through in making my estimate of the keno odds on the side while playing roulette at Harolds Club. It is indicative of the fact that with a little ingenuity you can make reasonable estimates, without need for a slide rule, log tables, or an IBM computer.

There is no point listing the full expressions for all 10 values of x. They are all quite similar in form. If they are evaluated by using the logarithms of the factorials, each one entails the same amount of work. If they are written out as ratios of two long chains of products, as shown previously, some may involve more work than others; this is due simply to variations in the number of terms that cancel.

If only approximate values are wanted, you can find *one* of them as we have done, and then obtain the next one (in this case, x = 9) by merely setting up the ratio between the next one and the preceding one. The point is, in the beastly expression on page 282, five of the nine factors are fixed, regardless of the value of x, whereas the remaining four factors either grow or diminish by one multiplier as the value of x changes by 1. So, it is easy to set up the *ratios* of the expressions for successive values of x. In numerical evaluations, cancellation is a wonderful thing!

Actual values of the probabilities for all values of x from 10 to 0 are given in the middle column of Table 12-1.

Proof of the Fallacy of a Progression in an Unfair Game

This is the first time that a mathematical proof of the fallacy of a progression has ever appeared in print, to my knowledge. Since it is so simple, the novelty of it is all the more amazing. Anyone who is at all proficient with high school algebra can follow each step and understand it readily.

In Chapter 16 we emphasized that if the player has negative expectation on each individual play, there is no conceivable way to arrange a long-run betting scheme to overcome this in a series of plays. The so-called *progression* is a scheme that has been tried countless times and has inevitably led to failure. We shall define a progression here as a scheme in which the successive bet levels are such that the current bet exceeds the sum of all previous bets in the series; thus, a win cancels all previous losses in the series and produces a profit. The popular *double-up* or *Martingale*, as applied to the even payoff propositions, is a special case of the progression.

The proof is given here for the case of even payoff, but may be readily generalized to the case of uneven payoff. Let

b_k = bet value at the kth level.

p_k = probability that series terminates with a win at the kth level, having been preceded by $k - 1$ losses in a row.

$n - 1$ = greatest number of losses in a row that can be sustained (that is, the nth play *must* be a win if preceded by $n - 1$ losses; otherwise, all playing capital is lost).

By direct probability principles, the player's expectation (ε) in such a series may be written down as follows:

$$\begin{aligned}
\varepsilon = &+ p_1 b_1 + p_2 (b_2 - b_1) + p_3 (b_3 - b_2 - b_1) + \cdots \\
&+ p_n (b_n - b_{n-1} - \cdots - b_1) \\
&+ (1 - p_1 - p_2 - \cdots \\
&- p_n)(-b_n - b_{n-1} - \cdots - b_1)
\end{aligned}$$

The successive terms on the first line of this expression represent products of the probability that the series will terminate with a win at each successive level times the net profit at that level. The term on the third line gives the product of the probability that the series ends in failure at the nth level times the net loss.

For purposes of producing a more compact form from which conclusions may be drawn, we now perform some algebraic manipulations. The first step is to regroup the terms in the preceding expression:

$$\varepsilon = 2p_1b_1 + (2p_2 + p_1)b_2 + (2p_3 + p_2 + p_1)b_3 + \cdots$$
$$+ (2p_n + p_{n-1} + \cdots + p_2 + p_1)b_n$$
$$- (b_1 + b_2 + \cdots + b_{n-1} + b_n)$$

We can now get rid of the subscripts on the p_k upon noting that $p_k = (1-p)^{k-1}p$, where p is the probability of a win on any individual play and $1 - p$ is the probability of a loss. Thus, the probability that the *series* will terminate in a win at the kth level is the product of the probability of $k - 1$ losses in a row times the probability of a win on the kth trial. Substituting this expression for each p_k, we get

$$\varepsilon = [2p]b_1 + [2p(1-p) + p]b_2 + [2p(1-p)^2 + p(1-p) + p]b_3 + \cdots$$
$$+ [2p(1-p)^{n-1} + p(1-p)^{n-2} + \cdots + p(1-p)^2 + p(1-p)^1$$
$$+ p(1-p)^0]b_n - (b_1 + b_2 + \cdots b_{n-1} + b_n)$$

In general, the common quantity p may be factored out so that the kth term may be rewritten as

$$p[(1-p)^{k-1} + (1-p)^{k-1} + (1-p)^{k-2} + \cdots + (1-p)^2$$
$$+ (1-p)^1 + (1-p)^0]b_k$$

Excluding the first term in the brackets, we recognize that the other terms constitute a geometric series. Using the formula for the sum of such a series, the entire kth term may be written more compactly as

$$p\left[(1-p)^{k-1} + \frac{(1-p)^k - 1}{(1-p) - 1}\right]b_k$$

or $p\left[(1-p)^{k-1} + \dfrac{1 - (1-p)^k}{p}\right]b_k$ or $[(2p-1)(1-p)^{k-1} + 1]b_k$

We are now in a position to write a very compact form for the complete expression for player expectation with this progression:

$$\varepsilon = \sum_{k=1}^{k=n} [(2p-1)(1-p)^{k-1} + 1]b_k - \sum_{k=1}^{k=n} b_k$$

$$\varepsilon = \sum_{k=1}^{k=n} (2p-1)(1-p)^{k-1}b_k + \sum_{k=1}^{k=n} b_k - \sum_{k=1}^{k=n} b_k$$

The last two summations cancel, and the fixed quantity $(2p - 1)$ may be factored out of the first summation, finally giving

$$\varepsilon = (2p - 1) \sum_{k=1}^{k=n} (1 - p)^{k-1} b_k$$

Since $(1 - p)$ and any power thereof is a positive quantity, and since the bet value b_k is also a positive quantity, the summation is clearly a positive quantity. Thus, the sign of ε depends strictly on the sign of $(2p - 1)$. In an even-payoff proposition in an unfair game, p is less than $\frac{1}{2}$ and $(2p - 1)$ is a negative quantity. Thus, we have proved dramatically that the player's expectation is negative *for any progression* as defined in this Appendix!

Some mathematicians might claim that the final expression as given above could be written down directly. It simply says that the expectation is the product of the basic house edge $(p - q)$, or $(2p - 1)$, times each bet size b_k times the probability $(1 - p)^{k-1}$ that this particular bet size will occur in the series. For those to whom this logical appeal to intuition is not obvious, this detailed proof stands as sure evidence that such reasoning is indeed correct.

It should also be noted that in the fair game, $p = \frac{1}{2}$ and $(2p - 1)$ is zero, and hence $\varepsilon = 0$. In the fair game, the progression is neither better nor worse than any other betting scheme.

Development of the "Gambler's Ruin" Formula

The gambler's ruin problem was introduced in Chapter 17. Continuing with the line of reasoning presented there, we may readily write down and then solve the gambler's ruin equation. First, we shall take up the even-payoff game, in which you either win or lose one unit at each play. As done in previous chapters, we let the chance of a win on a single play be designated by p; also, let the chance of a loss be q, where naturally $p + q = 1$. Then let the chance of ruin when your bank is x be given by $r_{(x)}$. Then

$$r_{(x)} = p \cdot r_{(x+1)} + q \cdot r_{(x-1)}$$

This merely says with symbols what we have already said with words. On the left side, we have the chance of ruin when the bank is x units. The first term on the right is the product of the chance of a win times the chance of ruin when the bank is $x + 1$ units. Similarly, the second term on the right is the product of the chance of a loss times the chance of ruin when the bank is $x - 1$ units.

For a specific case, betting on red at roulette, we have $p = 18/38$ and $q = 20/38$. The equation becomes

$$r_{(x)} = \left(\frac{18}{38}\right) \cdot r_{(x+1)} + \left(\frac{20}{38}\right) \cdot r_{(x-1)}$$

or, simplifying,

$$38r_{(x)} = 18r_{(x+1)} + 20r_{(x-1)}$$

We thus obtain a simple equation relating the chances of going broke with amounts $x - 1$, x, and $x + 1$, respectively. These latter three numbers incidentally, must be integers because our bank is counted in integral units. This type of equation, in which the variable x can take on only integer values, is called a *difference equation* or an equation in *finite differences* because, for each successive value assigned to x, the value of $r_{(x)}$ changes in a finite step or difference.

In a gambling game, your bank changes *in finite steps*. Therefore, it is reasonable that the equation which describes the status of your bank is a difference equation. This is in contrast to a *differential equation* which, for example, may be used to describe the motion of a moving body such as an automobile, an airplane, or a missile. In such cases, since the motion is smooth or *continuous*, *all* possible values of the distance variable x will satisfy the equation. The only limitation in verifying that the equation does actually predict the motion it is intended to predict is the accuracy with which x can be *measured*.

We shall not actually work with the difference equation itself, but shall assume that its solution (or answer) may be shown to have the following simple form:

$$r_{(x)} = A + B \cdot \left(\frac{q}{p}\right)^x = A + B \cdot \left(\frac{1}{S}\right)^x$$

For simplicity, we replace the ratio p/q by a single symbol S. The numbers A and B depend on the initial capital of the player and his opponent. Suppose, for example, that the player starts with a units of capital, and his opponent with b units. When we ask the chance of the player's being ruined, we are asking for the chance that the player will lose his a units rather than win his opponent's b units. (We are presuming that the participants plan to play until one of them wins all capital of the other.) Now, if the player's capital gets reduced to zero, his chance of ruin is 1, since he has been cleaned out and can no longer continue to bet. On the other hand, if the player accumulates a total of $a + b$ units, he has cleaned out his opponent, and his chance of ruin is zero. These two facts may be stated mathematically as follows:

$$r_{(0)} = A + B \cdot \left(\frac{1}{S}\right)^0 = A + B = 1$$

$$r_{(a+b)} = A + B \cdot \left(\frac{1}{S}\right)^{a+b} = 0$$

Thus, we have two equations with which the values of A and B can be solved. With the resulting values of A and B inserted, and with x set equal to a, the solution to the difference equation becomes

$$r_{(a)} = \frac{1 - (S)^b}{1 - (S)^{a+b}} \quad \text{or} \quad \frac{1 - \left(\frac{1}{S}\right)^b}{(S)^a - \left(\frac{1}{S}\right)^b} \quad \textit{General Formula}$$

By canceling T on both sides of the equal sign and factoring the constant $(1 - t)$ out of the summation, we have

$$(1 - t) \sum \frac{1}{R_i} = 1$$

This is readily solved for t, giving

$$t = \frac{\sum (1/R_i) - 1}{\sum (1/R_i)}$$

We note now that the tote board usually quotes "odds-to-one." This quantity, call it Q_i, is related to R_i by $Q_i = R_i - 1$, or conversely, $R_i = Q_i + 1$. Thus, the final expression for the take is

$$t = \frac{\sum \dfrac{1}{Q_i + 1} - 1}{\sum \dfrac{1}{Q_i + 1}}$$

A simple numerical example illustrates how to use this formula. Suppose there are four horses in the race $(N = 4)$, and the tote board gives these odds: $Q_1 = 1{:}1$; $Q_2 = 1\frac{2}{3}{:}1$; $Q_3 = 3{:}1$; $Q_4 = 7{:}1$. Thus,

$$\frac{1}{Q_1 + 1} = \frac{1}{1 + 1} = \frac{1}{2} \qquad \frac{1}{Q_3 + 1} = \frac{1}{3 + 1} = \frac{1}{4}$$

$$\frac{1}{Q_2 + 1} = \frac{1}{\frac{5}{3} + 1} = \frac{3}{8} \qquad \frac{1}{Q_4 + 1} = \frac{1}{7 + 1} = \frac{1}{8}$$

Putting all fractions over a common denominator of 8 and inserting,

$$t = \frac{\frac{4}{8} + \frac{3}{8} + \frac{2}{8} + \frac{1}{8} - 1}{\frac{4}{8} + \frac{3}{8} + \frac{2}{8} + \frac{1}{8}} = \frac{\frac{10}{8} - 1}{\frac{10}{8}} = \frac{\frac{2}{8}}{\frac{10}{8}} = \frac{2}{10} = 0.2$$

or 20 percent. In this illustration, the take is 20 percent, which goes for operating expenses, taxes, and profits. In terms of the dollars bet on individual horses, it might correspond to the following situation:

$$A_1 = 40,000; \quad A_2 = 30,000; \quad A_3 = 20,000; \quad A_4 = 10,000$$
$$\text{Gross pool } T = \sum A_i = A_1 + A_2 + A_3 + A_4 = 100,000$$

With $t = 0.2$, the net pool $P = (1 - 0.2)T = 0.8T = 80,000$. Thus, $R_1 = 80,000/40,000$; $R_2 = 80,000/30,000$; $R_3 = 80,000/20,000$; $R_4 = 80,000/10,000$. Or $R_1 = 2{:}1$; $R_2 = 2\frac{2}{3}{:}1$; $R_3 = 4{:}1$; $R_4 = 8{:}1$. Recalling that $Q_i = R_i - 1$, we see that the Q values are indeed those quoted at the beginning of the example.

Handy fractions have been used to simplify this illustration. In general, decimal calculations would be needed. The take usually ranges from 10 to 20 percent; in Mexico, it may be higher. Caveat emptor!

Roulette Tabulations

DATA FROM A MODERATELY BIASED DOUBLE-ZERO ROULETTE WHEEL AT HAROLDS CLUB, RENO

Approximately *80,000* consecutive trials, recorded for each number as a *deviation* from a nominal 100 wins in 3800 trials. (Such grouping actually represents 10 periods of 380 trials each, as illustrated by the typical data sheet on page 21.)

Roulette numbers, in cyclic order around the wheel ———————→

Period Numbers	00	1	13	36	24	3	15	34	22	5	17	32
1– 10	7	−13	−10	9	−18	−5	−4	13	−2	1	−5	12
11– 20	8	−6	14	5	−4	−23	−11	5	6	−14	16	12
21– 30	−7	7	3	12	11	−4	−7	−11	−22	31	−6	0
31– 40	1	7	8	3	1	−20	−6	−1	−3	11	−5	−8
41– 50	18	−4	−2	14	−21	−6	−4	−8	7	5	1	−4
51– 60	−17	−4	0	19	9	−3	−9	−12	5	0	7	13
61– 70	1	−7	−6	6	13	−7	−3	1	−2	2	−17	−4
71– 80	7	11	−5	6	3	−2	11	−2	−8	−6	−13	−19
81– 90	1	2	−16	14	12	8	2	−4	−4	3	12	16
91–100	1	−1	20	4	−10	2	3	7	−19	−6	−12	11
101–110	14	−7	−4	3	0	−12	−3	11	13	6	8	15
111–120	−2	17	−13	13	12	2	10	7	9	12	−7	10
121–130	12	5	9	−12	17	−11	−11	−12	−16	17	−3	10
131–140	12	15	6	5	12	4	−14	5	1	4	−5	−3
141–150	−10	7	−1	−14	11	−3	9	−1	6	1	−2	−11
151–160	15	−7	−5	10	13	−15	−6	10	2	17	7	−15
161–170	−11	−23	−8	10	14	18	−7	3	−10	6	−7	2
171–180	−15	−23	8	1	−1	−4	−19	0	22	−9	−5	2
181–190	−9	5	5	10	−4	−9	6	10	−2	−2	−6	7
191–200	7	1	−15	3	4	−3	1	−5	10	26	−8	0
201–210	−6	0	22	0	18	1	−3	−3	6	−6	−6	−13
Total Deviation												
+	27		10	121	92			13		99		33
−		18				92	65		1		56	

DATA FROM A MODERATELY BIASED DOUBLE-ZERO ROULETTE WHEEL (*Cont.*)

Roulette numbers, in cyclic order around the wheel ⟶

Period Numbers	20	7	11	30	26	9	28	0	2	14	35	23	4
1– 10	6	−9	−3	−14	−6	9	−11	−3	−3	20	37	3	−21
11– 20	0	1	−1	−5	7	−7	−17	−17	−1	−2	−1	5	−5
21– 30	−15	−36	−3	−7	−20	−16	1	−7	0	−4	10	11	7
31– 40	4	−1	3	−18	−26	0	−4	5	−14	6	8	−6	11
41– 50	−23	−10	−12	−3	23	−1	−6	−8	2	14	−4	0	−8
51– 60	−8	3	8	−14	−11	14	−10	11	−11	9	2	−9	−2
61– 70	1	−8	−23	9	−12	16	−4	−10	16	16	0	3	−14
71– 80	13	−15	0	27	5	−2	10	4	−12	−8	−6	−17	−13
81– 90	−10	−7	−14	−8	−7	−27	1	8	−1	6	1	−9	−1
91–100	−14	0	−7	8	−9	7	0	0	−17	−5	−12	−10	6
101–110	−19	−11	−14	7	−19	−10	−10	−2	−3	−3	18	−1	9
111–120	−14	14	−24	−6	−19	−6	3	−14	0	0	−6	−4	−4
121–130	−19	−1	−11	−15	2	10	−12	−8	7	7	−6	−1	11
131–140	−25	−5	−10	4	2	−2	−6	−11	−9	−8	7	−11	−3
141–150	−8	5	−26	−14	−18	−13	0	9	−11	6	3	−6	−11
151–160	−20	−12	−9	−7	−11	−13	−8	16	−21	0	5	3	1
161–170	3	−6	11	1	−8	−6	−17	−4	−9	7	−8	−14	−7
171–180	−4	−1	−18	−4	−16	−3	−3	14	8	−6	12	17	−9
181–190	−9	3	19	0	18	−7	−11	−7	−14	8	6	−9	−5
191–200	−8	−14	5	−8	2	16	8	−20	2	0	−18	−2	9
201–210	−19	9	3	18	7	−6	15	−10	−10	5	2	−2	−4
Total Deviation +										68	50		
−	188[a]	101	126	49	116	47	81	54	101			59	53

[a] Worst number, 20, averaged out to $\dfrac{+2100 - 188}{79,800} = \dfrac{1912}{79,800} = \dfrac{1}{41.7}$.

DATA FROM A MODERATELY BIASED DOUBLE-ZERO ROULETTE WHEEL (*Cont.*)

Roulette numbers, in cyclic order around the wheel ⟶

Period Numbers	16	33	21	6	18	31	19	8	12	29	25	10	27
1– 10	2	−14	−1	−11	−2	12	26	11	−3	−10	15	−8	−7
11– 20	8	−2	15	−6	−1	9	6	4	−4	−2	−4	−3	15
21– 30	9	17	2	16	21	26	3	−6	−17	25	−5	−14	−5
31– 40	−3	11	0	−19	5	−9	30	−4	−8	−7	−4	35	17
41– 50	5	1	3	11	6	2	28	10	−11	0	−1	−4	−10
51– 60	10	4	5	8	−4	8	8	−13	0	−12	−6	−16	18
61– 70	−8	−9	5	2	14	−6	14	−4	13	−20	2	14	16
71– 80	20	5	−17	0	18	0	−7	−1	15	−14	2	6	4
81– 90	−1	−1	7	3	2	−8	13	−20	−5	19	4	−1	10
91–100	9	−2	−2	3	−5	17	−1	16	4	−22	5	15	16
101–110	−16	−2	−1	7	−19	4	7	−4	8	11	17	6	−4
111–120	−3	5	7	5	4	2	3	27	−31	4	2	−13	−2
121–130	−11	4	6	10	−12	21	−8	1	11	1	−2	0	10
131–140	8	11	4	8	−8	8	−4	9	−4	3	15	−8	−7
141–150	−4	0	−3	17	10	6	12	7	27	−3	8	20	−5
151–160	−11	11	18	3	22	−1	9	−7	0	−6	10	5	−3
161–170	7	3	3	−14	14	8	6	10	−10	−9	38	7	7
171–180	9	4	13	−3	19	2	11	−1	8	−8	−9	1	10
181–190	−12	7	−10	12	−4	−5	10	−1	0	−5	13	−6	−2
191–200	−13	−6	19	11	7	1	17	−4	1	−13	−10	−4	1
201–210	−14	−5	23	−10	4	−5	1	6	16	0	−2	−11	−21

Total Deviation

	16	33	21	6	18	31	19	8	12	29	25	10	27
+		42	96	53	91	92	184[a]	36	10		88	21	58
−	9									68			

[a] Best number, 19, averaged out to $\dfrac{+2100+184}{79,800} = \dfrac{2284}{79,800} = \dfrac{1}{34.9}$.

DATA FROM A STRONGLY BIASED DOUBLE-ZERO ROULETTE WHEEL
AT HAROLDS CLUB, RENO

Roulette Numbers			4 Days Sampling	Averages	13 (More) Days Sampling	Averages
00			291	1/40.4	997	1/37.0
1			294	40.0	940	39.0
	13		318	37.0	943	39.1
		36	281	41.9	970	38.0
	24		271	43.4 worst	893	41.3 worst
3			385	30.6 best	1053	35.0 best
	15		314	37.5	950	38.8
		34	315	37.4	1020	36.1
	22		344	34.2	998	36.9
5			297	39.6	935	39.4
	17		326		1000	
		32	327		975	
	20		286		941	
7			296		896	
	11		308		970	
		30	312		1024	
	26		316	37.2	980	37.6
9			289	40.7	1009	36.5
		28	285	41.3	920	40.0
0			299	39.4	890	41.4
2			275	42.8	896	41.1
	14		291	40.4	988	37.3
		35	295	39.9	1020	36.1
	23		300	39.2	996	37.0
4			324	36.3	932	39.5
	16		306		998	
		33	332		972	
	21		344	34.2	1007	36.6
6			325		956	
	18		348	33.8	1044	35.3
		31	337	34.9	969	38.0
	19		316		1014	
8			276	42.6	990	37.2
	12		290		934	
		29	282		908	
	25		284		945	
10			330	35.7	990	37.2
		27	357	33.0	979	37.6
			11,766		36,842	

NOTES:
1. Total sample size 48,608.
2. Worst number was *next to* the best number, but the second worst number was *diametrically opposite* to the best number.
3. The best numbers were red and the worst ones were black.

DATA FROM A VERY STRONGLY BIASED SINGLE-ZERO ROULETTE WHEEL AT THE NEVADA CLUB, RENO

Actual Cumulative Totals (read directly from registers over the wheel):

Roulette Numbers	At First Discovery	About 30 Hours Later	Averages for Dominant Numbers	(Registers Re-set) Read 1 Week Later	Averages for Dominant Numbers
0	813	925	1/31.8	417	1/31.5
32	663	744		313	
15	700	786		380	
19	704	806		378	
4	679	764		347	
21	640	740		280	
2	825	929	1/31.6	385	1/34.1
25	684	775		385	
17	726	815		360	
34	754	839	1/35.0	392	1/33.5
6	663	761		346	
27	678	756		341	
13	647	721		330	
36	679	744		346	
11	666	765		357	
30	715	775		387	
8	736	842	1/34.9	419	1/31.3
23	649	720		307	
10	592	682	(1/43.1) worst	318	(1/41.3)
5	699	773		358	
24	695	788		334	
16	722	810		386	
33	866	971	1/30.3 best	426	1/30.8
1	712	799		361	
20	719	814		364	
14	706	773		287	
31	685	772		330	
9	671	771		310	
22	737	823		366	
18	753	841	1/35.0	367	1/35.8
29	732	827		372	
7	725	800		343	
28	641	724		348	
12	656	740		356	
35	744	842		330	
3	695	793		346	
26	742	851	1/34.5	357	1/36.8
	26,113	29,401		13,129	

NOTE amazing fact that each number generally continues its trend in the second *independent sample!!* Both samples are quite large (29,000 and 13,000). "Hot" numbers stay hot, and "cold" ones stay cold!

Table of Pairs of Random Digits

The reader is cautioned against using the same sequence in the table on the following pages for every test he may conduct. Erroneous conclusions might be drawn because a particular scheme might be found that would "work" on one special sequence. It is advisable to start different tests at different arbitrary points in the table, and to proceed in different directions, such as from bottom to top, on alternate rows, on diagonal rows, etc.

If necessary, this table may be readily extended by the same method that was used to make it, as explained on pages 84–86. The method amounts to multiplying a given random 10-digit number by 101, dividing the product by 10000000001, and treating the 10-digit remainder as a new random number, etc. The table is made from the leading two digits of these 10-digit numbers.

(The wording of the above paragraph expresses the procedure for the random number generation in the most proper language. In the description of the method as given on page 84, it is possible, although not very likely, to produce a *negative* number. This would occur if the current 12-digit sum contained zeros in the digits 3 through 10, and if the 2-digit left excess were a number larger than the 2-digit right-hand end. A disruption in an otherwise smooth sequence of numbers would then occur, but this could be avoided simply by adding 10000000001 to the negative number, and using this positive sum.

The wording of page 84 was selected because the author believed that the explanation given there would appear to most readers to be simpler. Presumably anyone alert enough to notice the possible "bug" would also be sharp enough to figure out a cure!)

Optimal Betting

Calculations on page 272 for the roulette parlay were presented in terms of a succession of doublings, the bet size remaining *fixed* during each stage. Now, a doubling represents a 100% increase in capital, which is a substantial step. You could alternately elect to proceed in smaller steps, say 50% or 10%. The applicable ruin probabilities could be found using the appropriate a and b values as discussed on page 288. But intuition suggests that it might be optimal to vary bet size in some smooth and continuous manner, "optimal" meaning that you will make money faster with no greater risk of going broke.

It can be shown (see reference by Kelly) that indeed there is such a betting method, provided that no minimum or maximum limits on bet size are imposed. If you have a fixed expectation ε on each play in an *even* payoff game, you should always bet a fraction ε of your current capital. (Thus with a 3% advantage, you bet 3% of your capital.) This particular fraction will actually cause your capital to grow at the fastest rate consistent with exactly zero chance of ever going completely broke!

If you bet a smaller fraction, your capital will still increase indefinitely, with zero chance of your ever going broke in a fluctuation, but the rate will be slower. If you bet a larger fraction, up to a value 2ε (approximately), the same thing applies. But if the fraction wagered ranges from 2ε up to 1, then even though you may enjoy a temporary faster winning rate, eventually fluctuations will occur that will steadily drive your capital toward zero. (Note that by betting an *amount which varies* according to current capital, it is *in principle* impossible to go *completely* broke. This is in contrast to a finite chance of going broke when a *fixed amount* is wagered, until an initial capital is doubled, say, as in the example of page 272.)

Proof of this optimal principle is short and instructive. Let there be W wins and L losses during N trials, where $W + L = N$. If you bet a fixed fraction f of your current capital, then an initial capital C_0 will be built up to $C_N = C_0 (1 + f)^W (1 - f)^L$. The *average* ratio R by which the capital will be multiplied at each step is the limit (as N becomes indefinitely large) of the Nth root of $\dfrac{C_N}{C_0}$. Thus

$$R = \underset{N \to \infty}{\text{Limit}} \sqrt[N]{\frac{C_N}{C_0}} = \underset{N \to \infty}{\text{Limit}} \left[(1+f)^{\frac{W}{N}} \ (1-f)^{\frac{L}{N}} \right]$$

$$\text{or } R = (1+f)^p (1-f)^q \qquad \text{where of course } p + q = 1.$$

The ratio R as a function of the fraction f is shown in the graph.

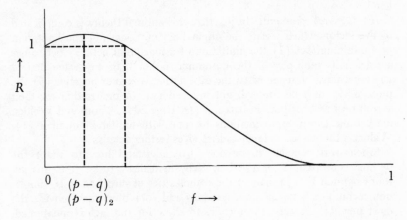

For your capital to grow, R must be larger than 1. This occurs for a range of values of f from 0 (uninteresting case!) up to approximately $2\varepsilon = 2(p - q)$; the latter value applies provided that ε is a small quantity (you should be so lucky as to find a game with ε *big* for the player)! Using the standard calculus technique, the value of f giving a maximum for R is found by differentiating R with respect to f, and equating to zero. This leads to the condition $f = p - q$, which verifies the statement above that the optimal f is equal to the player expectation on each single play (valid only for $p - q$ positive)! Some interesting conclusions follow.

(a) *Application to betting on a single number at roulette:* The method is easily generalized for a game where the payoff is uneven. For roulette, the factors in the original expression should be $(1 + 35f)$ and $(1 - f)$, and the proper fraction to bet turns out to be $(35p - q)/35$ $= \varepsilon/35$. (Note the similarity between this relationship and the "trick" used on page 270.)

(b) *Application to blackjack:* The method can also be generalized for a game like variable-bet blackjack, where the probabilities change as cards are dealt out of the deck. Using the subscript i to denote the various different probability situations, the cumulative capital would be

$$C_N = C_0 \, \pi_i \, (1 + f_i)^{W_i} \, (1 - f_i)^{L_i} \text{ where } \Sigma_i \, (W_i + L_l) = N$$

(The symbol π_i denotes a *product* of all terms of the type shown, for each of the possible values of the subscript i. Σ denotes a summation.) Again R may be optimized, using partial derivatives, and the result is $f_i = \varepsilon_i$. This says that the appropriate fraction to bet is the expectation value existing *on each particular hand*, prior to the deal of cards on that hand.

(c) *General comments:* In practice, this optimal theory is complicated by five factors which violate the original assumptions: (1) the limitation of a minimum bet (2) the limitation of a maximum bet (3) bet values are generally multiples of the minimum, rather than any value desired (4) a bet must be made when the expectation is zero or negative (5) the probabilities may be coupled, not independent. In preparation for their assault on the "side bet" in baccarat (see page 208), Thorp and Walden made some clever approximations to cope with limitation number (1). Walden's thesis (see References list) gives further details.

Much work remains to be done to understand how to adapt the optimal concept first suggested by Kelly in realistic cases. It is this author's opinion that in view of the complexities of direct analysis, simulation techniques using random numbers and computers may provide the most practical answers. Meanwhile, to allow for the factors mentioned, one can bet *somewhat less* than the indicated theoretical fraction.

TABLE OF PAIRS OF RANDOM DIGITS

28	80	17	44	11	82	56	51	54	18		71	65	20	73	59	37	27	87	41	19
16	79	10	89	50	66	70	46	36	91		05	46	07	70	14	13	85	85	39	25
37	79	89	31	66	17	89	80	48	48		10	52	99	33	44	23	05	72	19	12
75	49	06	61	61	04	97	42	79	23		58	43	63	59	95	05	49	49	27	14
49	45	42	02	98	59	28	18	09	48		92	79	05	19	74	32	86	56	66	73
52	10	44	92	59	61	21	20	05	29		94	23	43	79	24	44	56	84	82	03
53	95	08	20	07	33	61	44	01	11		84	91	27	07	52	09	57	79	58	20
43	54	37	98	49	62	18	65	23	31		90	39	93	17	99	54	88	03	83	87
95	57	96	74	99	35	40	73	17	81		65	18	67	97	72	67	50	15	85	38
73	55	07	51	67	22	13	57	46	72		10	03	03	23	70	30	64	07	42	33
74	92	28	23	81	97	67	56	73	94		63	22	56	22	50	83	54	28	80	46
31	76	01	56	70	25	75	48	86	80		38	15	60	33	22	05	33	72	69	25
74	26	25	02	52	58	65	56	45	28		25	13	69	26	41	72	65	78	65	26
58	70	09	55	95	67	85	35	17	47		94	94	09	16	57	45	66	75	76	69
50	27	60	79	14	43	65	42	16	98		21	80	82	37	52	17	17	57	20	17
60	11	99	10	78	16	12	21	63	40		20	22	02	82	11	47	34	96	58	34
61	25	59	42	57	39	39	74	77	46		99	38	74	51	96	22	91	35	09	92
13	93	41	19	44	79	38	41	01	75		83	78	93	50	77	29	08	69	69	93
86	56	76	52	24	82	08	04	31	93		49	07	17	43	66	38	70	20	45	40
95	68	63	52	36	46	79	31	43	68		23	10	84	09	94	63	49	06	04	27
10	59	70	32	95	62	29	16	30	76		88	03	44	89	94	07	64	44	78	60
44	45	72	76	93	97	59	68	64	36		31	90	84	44	29	90	83	82	33	29
59	84	36	06	12	45	80	42	98	46		68	53	51	73	52	65	86	32	89	61
82	20	97	74	88	76	47	88	88	53		25	34	17	19	48	48	58	04	74	71
93	72	72	12	91	91	11	93	04	53		94	16	51	67	18	46	67	20	99	33

19	78	85	42	42	45	09	98	39	83	59	59	49	20	11	45	73	23	78	67
58	10	19	54	86	32	42	84	84	46	15	35	68	07	29	82	48	73	65	59
59	09	78	28	55	32	95	68	33	74	47	80	08	38	74	72	56	12	49	26
40	89	46	69	76	05	22	78	37	02	06	97	50	37	21	49	56	15	97	49
34	18	48	41	28	23	03	59	57	04	28	74	43	36	45	34	53	03	97	10
64	82	93	71	19	11	06	54	28	01	34	72	86	48	27	53	51	48	27	00
25	16	29	43	56	59	23	65	09	27	83	05	23	59	99	09	32	63	90	94
02	52	93	32	38	41	80	07	58	13	55	90	40	83	41	25	41	54	03	58
38	89	13	70	16	67	08	82	15	06	52	47	92	87	16	03	57	83	93	93
90	07	56	43	71	57	17	16	16	16	83	41	51	98	72	82	20	07	93	87
39	92	32	99	99	62	54	41	89	68	83	26	28	75	36	80	52	43	14	60
95	51	11	68	67	04	82	91	47	20	28	60	80	80	64	13	29	55	93	40
37	88	98	56	89	28	21	28	73	50	93	59	95	69	15	42	74	56	79	73
96	85	68	06	20	96	96	91	54	42	95	42	09	63	69	97	79	95	16	31
67	82	10	11	43	93	93	14	52	84	79	97	85	14	04	36	60	08	79	34
77	48	16	02	41	09	70	63	95	03	44	24	31	45	34	05	84	84	58	63
65	20	22	05	72	34	89	97	80	42	41	94	85	81	87	10	61	67	94	58
20	19	74	20	47	80	61	69	07	50	64	50	66	29	57	10	35	04	81	67
93	19	38	32	99	64	60	84	73	94	90	09	27	72	29	48	41	45	58	06
19	23	85	42	98	02	28	87	86	26	06	90	19	26	12	31	10	20	57	26
34	33	33	73	97	17	81	37	60	59	54	96	32	41	77	12	41	49	71	14
14	02	94	42	23	22	26	35	18	85	70	00	65	93	70	66	35	49	08	64
03	36	16	39	86	15	26	45	84	55	55	39	74	59	61	66	39	43	88	66
64	30	48	29	35	25	17	40	10	89	61	14	02	29	65	80	33	66	76	53
42	69	61	63	94	97	76	28	85	17	35	17	74	71	03	66	35	90	46	46

References

Books

ANONYMOUS. *How to Win at Blackjack*. Blackjack Research Corporation, Box 575, Los Angeles 53, Calif., 1958.

BALDWIN, ROGER, et al. *Playing Blackjack to Win: A New Strategy for the Game of 21*. New York: M. Barrows & Co., 1957.

BEST, KATHARINE, HILLYER, KATHARINE. *Las Vegas: Playtown U.S.A.* New York: David McKay Co., 1955.

BLANCHE, ERNEST. *You Can't Win: Facts and Fallacies about Gambling*. Washington, D.C.: Public Affairs Press, 1949.

BOLL, MARCEL. *La Chance et les Jeux de Hasard*. Paris: Librairie Larousse, 1936.

——. *La Roulette*. Monaco: Le Triboulet, 1944.

——. *Le Baccara, Chemin de Fer—Banque*. Monaco: Le Triboulet, 1944.

CRAWFORD, JOHN R. *How to Be a Consistent Winner in the Most Popular Card Games*. Garden City, N.Y.: Doubleday & Co., 1961.

CULBERTSON, ELY, MOREHEAD, ALBERT, MOTT-SMITH, GEOFFREY. *Culbertson's Card Games Complete, with Official Rules*. New York: The Greystone Press, 1952.

DAVIS, CLYDE BRION. *Something for Nothing*. Philadelphia: J. B. Lippincott Co., 1956.

DOWST, ROBERT S. *Win, Place and Show*. New York: Pocket Books, Inc., 1948.

FELLER, WILLIAM. *An Introduction to Probability Theory and Its Applications*, I. New York: John Wiley & Sons, Inc., 1957.

GOODMAN, MIKE. *How to Win at Cards, Dice, Races and Roulette*. Los Angeles, Calif.: Holloway House Publishing Co., 1963.

HEINRICH, RUDOLPH. *Roulette, Trente-et-Quarante, Baccarat*. Vienna, Austria: Verlag Adalbert Pechan, 1954.

HERALD, GEORGE W., RADIN, EDWARD D. *The Big Wheel*. New York: William Morrow & Co., 1963.

HOEL, PAUL G. *Introduction to Mathematical Statistics*. New York: John Wiley & Sons, 1947.

JACOBY, OSWALD. *How to Figure the Odds*. Garden City, N.Y.: Doubleday & Co., 1954.

———. *Oswald Jacoby on Gambling*. Garden City, N.Y.: Doubleday & Co., 1963.

KENDALL, MAURICE. *The Advanced Theory of Statistics*, I. London: Griffin and Co., 1943.

KINGSTON, CHARLES. *The Romance of Monte Carlo*. London: John Lane, The Bodley Head, Ltd., 1925.

LEVINSON, HORACE C. *The Science of Chance: From Probability to Statistics*. New York: Rinehart & Co., 1950.

LEWIS, OSCAR. *Sagebrush Casinos: The Story of Legal Gambling in Nevada*. New York: Doubleday & Co., Inc., 1953.

LONDON, JACK. *Smoke Bellew*. New York: World Publishers, 1912.

MacDOUGALL, MICHAEL. *MacDougall on Dice and Cards*. New York: Coward-McCann, Inc., 1944.

PEARSON, KARL. *Tables of Incomplete Gamma Functions*. London: Biometrika Office, University College, 1934.

———. "The Chances of Death and Other Studies in Evolution," chap. 2, *The Scientific Aspect of Monte Carlo Roulette*. London: Edward Arnold, 1897.

PRICE, AL. *Secrets of Gambling*. Chicago, Ill.: Cuneo Press, 1956.

RADNER, SIDNEY H. *Roulette and Other Casino Games*. New York: Wehman Brothers, 1958.

REID, ED, DEMARIS, OVID. *The Green Felt Jungle*. New York: Trident Press, 1963.

RIDDLE, MAJOR A., HYAMS, JOE. *The Weekend Gambler's Handbook*. New York: Random House, 1963.

ROXBURY, L. E. *Your Chances at Roulette*. Warwick, Va.: High-Iron Publishers, 1959.

SCARNE, JOHN, RAWSON, CLAYTON. *Scarne on Dice*. Harrisburg, Pa.: Military Service Publishing Co., 1945.

SCARNE, JOHN. *Scarne's Complete Guide to Gambling*. New York: Simon and Schuster, Inc., 1961.

SMITH, HAROLD S. *I Want to Quit Winners*. Englewood Cliffs, N.J.: Prentice-Hall, 1961.

SZABO, ALOIS. *The Pitfalls of Gambling and How to Avoid Them*. Paris: D'Auge-Tribune, 1954.

THORP, EDWARD O. *Beat the Dealer: A Winning Strategy for the Game of 21*. New York: Blaisdell Publishing Co., 1962.

Uspensky, J. V. *Introduction to Mathematical Probability.* New York: McGraw-Hill Book Co., 1937.

Weaver, Warren. *Lady Luck: The Theory of Probability.* Garden City, N.Y.: Doubleday & Co., Inc., 1963.

Williams, John D. *The Compleat Strategyst.* New York: McGraw-Hill Book Co., Inc., 1954.

Woon, Basil. *Gambling in Nevada.* Reno, Nev.: Bonanza Publishing Co., 1953.

Articles in Popular Magazines, Newspapers, and Technical Journals

"Argentina Bank Breakers," *Time* (Feb. 12, 1951).

Baldwin, Roger, et al. "The Optimum Strategy in Blackjack," *Journal of the American Statistical Association* (Sept., 1956).

Beebe, Lucius. "Nevada: Heir to the Wild West," *Holiday* (Feb., 1956).

Beltrand, Eugene. "You Can Beat the Roulette Wheel," *Epic* (Dec., 1958).

Brown, T. K., III. "Odds Man Out," *Playboy* (May, 1960).

Camellan, Eli. "Why You Lose When You Gamble," *Monsieur* (Sept., 1960).

"The Chinese Lotteries," *San Francisco Chronicle* (Aug. 13, 1951).

De Beaumont, P. S. "Monte Carlo, Gambler's Paradise," *Modern Man* (Nov., 1952).

"Clamp on '21' Ends in Vegas," Las Vegas Review Journal (June 21, 1964).

Donovan, Richard. "How to Run a Gambling Casino," *Colliers* (Jan. 31, 1953).

Donovan, Richard, Greenspun, Hank. "Nick the Greek—Fabulous King of the Gamblers," *Colliers* (April 2, 1954).

Dubins, Lester, Savage, Leonard. "Optimal Gambling Systems," *National Academy of Sciences, Proceedings*, XLVI 1960).

"Eight Days to Win," *Time* (Jan. 13, 1958).

Fairfield, William. "Las Vegas: The Sucker and the Almost-Even Break," *Reporter* (June 9, 1953).

"Fearless Man: Ian Fleming," *Glamour* (Jan., 1963).

Finney, Jack. "5 Against the House," *Good Housekeeping* (June–Sept., 1953).

Fox, Philip. "A Primer for Chumps," *Saturday Evening Post* (Nov. 21, 1959).

Guild, Leo. "I Investigated 17,000 Gambling Systems," *Stag* (July, 1950).

HOWARD, TONI. "Dirty Work at Monte Carlo," *Saturday Evening Post* (Nov. 21, 1959).

"How to Win $6,500 at Roulette," *Life Magazine* (Nov., 1947).

I.B.M. *Reference Manual on Random Number Generation and Testing* (1959).

JAMES, T. F. "Gambling Boom in America," *Cosmopolitan* (July, 1958).

JONES, KEVIN. "They Paid Me to Win," *Stag* (April, 1957).

KELLY, J. L. "A New Interpretation of Information Rate," *Bell System Technical Journal*, XXXV (1956).

KEMENY, JOHN, SNELL, LAURIE. "Game—Theoretic Solution of Baccarat," *American Mathematical Monthly* (Aug.–Sept., 1957).

KOBLER, JOHN. "The Gamblers of Monaco," *Cosmopolitan* (March, 1956).

"Las Vegas: Gambling Take Creates New Force in U.S.; Millions in Untaxed 'Black Money' Give Obscure Figures Power that Extends from Underworld to Government," *New York Times*, western edition (Nov. 18, 1963).

LOUIS, F. ROBERT. "Basics of 21," *Las Vegas Playground* (Jan., 1964).

MACDOUGALL, MICHAEL. "Why Nevada's Gamblers Toe the Mark," *Look Magazine* (Oct. 28, 1958).

MASCOTT, TRINA. "I Was a Gambling House Dealer," *Saturday Evening Post* (May 13, 1950).

MONROE, KEITH. "William Harrah: The New Gambling King, and the Social Scientists," *Harper's* (Jan., 1962).

MOREHEAD, AL. "How to Win $100 a Week Gambling," *Esquire* (Feb., 1957).

O'FAOLAIN, SEAN. "The Coarse and Lovely Illusions of Las Vegas," *Holiday* (Sept., 1956).

O'NEIL, PAUL. "The Professor Who Breaks the Bank," *Life* (March 27, 1964).

PARKER, LANCE. "How You Can Win at Blackjack," *Man's Conquest* (Aug., 1961).

PLAIN, CARL. "Computer Monitors Slot Machine Play," *San Diego Union* (March 1, 1964).

"Playboy on the Town in Las Vegas," *Playboy* (March, 1960).

POLAND, JEFF. "How to Beat the Blackjack Odds," *Climax* (Sept., 1961).

SCHERMAN, DAVID. "It's Bye! Bye! Blackjack," *Sports Illustrated* (Jan. 13, 1964).

SEVIER, F. A. C. "Using Brains to Beat the Table," *Nugget* (July, 1957).

SHARNIK, JOHN. "How to Live Off the Wheel," *True* (Aug., 1952).

SHEINWOLD, ALFRED. "It's in the Cards: Blackjack—Counting the Cards," *Argosy* (Aug., 1961).

———. "Las Vegas on a Shoestring," *Argosy* (Jan., 1959).

SINGER, KURT. "G-Girls of Las Vegas," *All Man* (July, 1962).

TAUSSKY, OLGA, TODD, JOHN. "Generation and Testing of Pseudo-Random Numbers," *National Bureau of Standards*, Report No. 3370, published in the proceedings of the 1956 Symposium on Monte Carlo Methods (June, 1954).

THORP, EDWARD. "A Favorable Strategy for Twenty-One," *National Academy of Science, Proceedings*, XLVII (1961).

———. "A Prof Beats the Gamblers," *Atlantic Monthly* (June, 1962).

"Three Youths Win $33,100 on a Roulette Wheel," *Oakland Post Enquirer* (May 19, 1948).

TINKER, FRANK A. "You Can Beat the Slot Machines," *Argosy* (Dec., 1961).

"Vegas Casinos Cry Uncle, Change Rules," *Los Angeles Times* (April 2, 1964).

WALDEN, WILLIAM. "A Winning Bet in Nevada Baccarat." Unpublished Ph.D. thesis, New Mexico State University.

WECHSBERG, JOSEPH. "Blackjack Pete," *Colliers* (July 25, 1953).

———. "Rouge, Impair, et Manque," *New Yorker* (July 9, 1949).

"The Weird World of Gambling," *Look Magazine* (March 12, 1963).

Index

Aberdeen Proving Ground (Md.), 92–93

Absolute deviation, 228, 230

Actual deviation, 228

Aids for card counting, mechanical, 274

American double-zero roulette wheel, 1–2

American Mathematical Monthly, 209, 252

American Mathematical Society, 98

American single-zero roulette wheel, 8

"Anchor man," 150

Antiprogression gambling systems, 7

Antipyramid gambling system, 7

"Any craps," 181–182

Argentina, biased-wheel roulette, 38–39

Argosy magazine, 172

Atlantic Monthly, 166

Atlas missile, 93

Atomic Energy Commission, Los Alamos Laboratory, 90–92

Automatic blackjack machine, 279

Averages. *See* Law of averages

Baccarat, viii, 198–209
  banker's percentage, 203–205
  card counting, 207–208
  continental, 208–209
  difference between European and American games, 208–209
  difference from blackjack, 207–208
  difference from chemin de fer, 198, 200, 205–206
  house percentage, 205–206
  mixed strategy, 209
  object of the game, 199–203
  with options, 209
  rules of play (table), 200
  side bets, 206–207, 208

Baccarat (*Continued*)
  symmetrical game, 200, 201, 203–205, 207
  "twin" to chemin de fer, 198

"Back peek," by blackjack dealer, 153

Balance, of roulette wheels, 27–28

Baldwin group, 92–93, 98, 170

Baldwin method, 165–166

Baldwin, Roger, 56, 92–93, 94, 95, 96, 159, 161, 162, 168, 171

Balls, on roulette wheels, 10, 27

Bamford, Robert, 96–98

Bamford's black box, 96–98

"Banco," 198

Bank-to-bet ratio, ix, 101, 155, 158, 259–273; *see also* Bet sizing
  need for large bankroll, 101, 155
  when bet size varies, 272–273

Banker's percentage, in baccarat, 203–205

Bankroll needed by player. *See* Bank-to-bet ratio

Barring of players, by casinos, 142–143, 220

Beat the Dealer, viii, 56, 98, 116, 121, 126, 150, 163, 165–166

Bernstein, Joe, 102–103

Bet sizing, vii, ix, 114, 122, 123–124, 134–135, 259–273
  craps, 261–262
  in a fair game, 262–263
  formula for even-money payoff games, 260–261, 263
  parlay, 271–272
  roulette, 261, 263, 266, 270–271
  uneven payoff games, 269–271
  in an unfair game, 263
  at variable-bet blackjack, 114, 122, 123–124, 134–135, 268